D0209411

HONOR THY LABEL

DR. BRONNER'S UNCONVENTIONAL
JOURNEY TO A CLEAN, GREEN, AND
ETHICAL SUPPLY CHAIN

GERO LESON

Foreword by David Bronner

PORTFOLIO / PENGUIN

PORTFOLIO / PENGUIN
An imprint of Penguin Random House LLC
penguinrandomhouse.com

Most Portfolio books are available at a discount when purchased in quantity for sales promotions or corporate use. Special editions, which include personalized covers, excerpts, and corporate imprints, can be created when purchased in large quantities. For more information, please call (212) 572-2232 or e-mail specialmarkets@penguinrandomhouse.com. Your local bookstore can also assist with discounted bulk purchases using the Penguin Random House corporate Business-to-Business program. For assistance in locating a participating retailer, e-mail B2B@penguinrandomhouse.com.

Photo credits: photo by Gero Leson pgs 2, 18, 34, 82, 100, and 276; photo courtesy of Dr. Bronner's pg 48; graph courtesy of Dr. Bronner's pg 53; photo by Christel Dillbohner pgs 62, 132; photo by Dana Geffner pg 158; photo by Dickson Wenyonu, courtesy of Serendipalm pg 163; photo by Lani Ready pg 192; graphic courtesy of Ecotop pg 206; photo by Steve Jeter, courtesy of Dr. Bronner's pg 222; photo by Les Szabo pg 252.

Insert photo credits: photo by David Corvey, courtesy of Dr. Bronner's pg 1 (top); photo by Michael Carus pg 1 (center); photo courtesy of Dr. Bronner's pgs 1 (bottom), 2 (top); photo by Katie Schuler, courtesy of Dr. Bronner's pgs 2 (bottom), 3 (top); photo by Steve Jeter, courtesy of Dr. Bronner's pgs 3 (bottom), 7 (bottom), 8 (top); photo by Gero Leson pgs 4, 5 (top); photo by Nancy Metcalf, courtesy of Dr. Bronner's pg 5 (bottom); photo by Marc Doradzillo, courtesy of Rapunzel pgs 6 (top, bottom), 7 (top); photo by Christel Dillbohner pg 8 (bottom).

ISBN 9780593087411 (hardcover)
ISBN 9780593087428 (ebook)

Printed in the United States of America
1   3   5   7   9   10   8   6   4   2

BOOK DESIGN BY TANYA MAIBORODA

To Christel and David who, at critical junctures,
gave serendipity a helping hand

Contents

Part 1
WORK HARD! PROSPER!

Foreword

'VE BEEN PRESIDENT AND NOW CEO — cosmic engagement officer — at Dr. Bronner's since 1998, the year my father, Jim, passed.

A year before that, we lost my granddad Emanuel Bronner—Dr. Bronner himself. I stepped into my role because I was inspired to leverage our family business as an engine for social change, the way Emanuel did with the "All-One" message of his Moral ABC.

Emanuel's life's work was the development of that Moral ABC— what he called his script of inspirational messages that adorns our signature products—because he believed that human beings must realize our unity across religious and ethnic divides, or perish.

All of us who have roles in the leadership of Dr. Bronner's today— including me; my brother and president, Mike Bronner; Mom and CFO, Trudy Bronner; and brother-in-law and COO, Michael Milam; along with our rock star senior management team—believe that what you do, and how you act, is more important than what you say.

As stewards of this beautiful company, founded by my grand-father in 1948 and sustained and improved by my dad, mom, and uncle Ralph through the late '80s and '90s, we continue to build on their legacy by applying the values reflected on our label in all our spheres of influence. Our commitment to embody these values drives us to model progressive business practices, source the most ethical and ecological ingredients, and fight for a more just and ecological world. It's how we Honor Our Label.

One of the first big initiatives to model our "All-One" values was to make sure our major supply chains were clean, green, and ethical. While what we do in our soap factory headquarters in Vista, California, is important as far as ecological manufacturing processes and great wages and benefits for our staff, we have ten times more impact in terms of the people and land involved that are farming and processing our major raw materials. In 2003, we began buying our major agricultural ingredients—coconut, palm, olive, and mint oils—from certified organic sources. But we soon recognized it wasn't enough. If we wanted fair supply chains, we were going to have to build them ourselves—which is exactly what we decided to do.

Gero Leson, our ace among aces, details this journey in the pages that follow, revealing why our supply chains matter and the remarkable story and people involved in each of them. He explains why we've gone to such great lengths to ensure accountability, transparency, and fairness that benefit not only the farmers and workers directly involved, but also their families and communities.

I actually met Gero years before we began our fair trade and regenerative journey—when Dr. Bronner's was embroiled in a battle with the DEA to keep industrial hemp products on store shelves. At the time, we had many activists on board with our mission to destigmatize a plant that had a myriad of practical uses, located at the nexus of drug policy reform and sustainable agriculture. But in order to make a solid case in court, we needed more than activist passion; we also needed disciplined legal minds and real scientists.

With his doctorate in environmental science and engineering and master's in physics, Gero was well qualified to design an experiment that proved that consuming hemp food products would not lead to positive drug tests, a crucial part of our ultimately successful defense of hemp foods and the defeat of the Drug Enforcement Administration's case.

Of course, Gero was more than just a scientist—he had his own countercultural background that would serve him well when he officially joined Dr. Bronner's to help us build our own fair trade, organic, and regenerative supply chains.

As you'll soon discover, Gero has not only a deeply curious scientific mind, but also a real talent for building meaningful relationships with hardworking and committed allies—from his old friends who were inspired to travel with him to Sri Lanka and build our coconut mill, to the certifiers he's worked with to build practical fair trade agricultural standards, to the NGOs who understand our mission and provided invaluable funding to our fair trade projects in their early days before they became profitable.

The work of Gero and his "Special Ops" team informed and led to the launch of a new standard that goes beyond fair trade and organic, called Regenerative Organic Certification (ROC).* ROC is the gold standard for ethical agricultural production, encompassing high-bar standards for fairness for farmers and workers, soil health and ecological land management, and pasture-based animal welfare. By adopting regenerative organic practices on farms around the world, we can create long-term solutions to some of the biggest dilemmas of our time, including mitigating the climate crisis, ending the factory farming of animals, and healing fractured rural economies.

It's fitting for Gero to take you inside our very unconventional company because he has also played a pivotal role in helping our family connect with our ancestral roots in Germany and establishing a presence for Dr. Bronner's there and elsewhere in Europe. My family was devastated by the Holocaust, and that traumatic experience was what drove Emanuel's mission to unite all human beings in "All-One" respect and love—understanding that we are all children of the same transcendent source that refracts through different cultures and faith traditions. Gero's work in helping us connect to and understand our family history has been incredibly healing as well as powerfully grounding, and I hope you find the experiences he shares in these pages as moving and important as we do.

---

* www.regenorganic.org

I realize that as you read about our journey, you may be tempted to think what we do is too difficult to replicate. It is true that our size, our relatively small product ingredient list, and the fact that we are a private company makes it easier to do things our way. But we weren't the first: we were inspired by long-standing, pioneering fair trade companies like Equal Exchange and Guayaki, who also go to market in partnership with their farmers and suppliers instead of trying to exploit the lowest price possible, enabling their supply chain partners to be responsible custodians of their land and communities. Others can and are choosing to follow a similar path, and ethical consumers are rewarding them with their business. It's possible for businesses and entrepreneurs to leverage the same kinds of grants that have made it possible for us to be pioneers in regenerative organic agriculture and dynamic agroforestry.

Our take is that everyone can choose to consume and produce products in a way that regenerates communities and ecosystems rather than degenerating them. In fact, our planet depends on it. Conventional capitalism—with its brutal devotion to profit above all—has wreaked havoc on the natural world and created incredible wealth disparity and kept millions locked in poverty. It's on all of us to turn this tide—to regenerate our planet and create true social justice and rewarding livelihoods for all. For those of us in business, we have the responsibility to remake the market and create alternatives to a status quo of corporate greed that benefits few and robs so many of the joys of life and the beauty of Earth.

I'm immensely grateful to Gero for his friendship, brilliant mind, and dedication to help our company achieve clean, green, ethical—and profitable—supply chains, and in turn for inspiring many other companies to do the same. Gero and his team's work, along with our incredible local partners, have helped literally thousands of farmers, workers, and their families regenerate and improve the health and vibrancy of their farming communities and ecosystems.

As you read the pages that follow, I am confident you will share my gratitude to Gero, for mapping this journey, and for outlining a blueprint for ethical sourcing specifically and progressive business generally. He leads a life that inspires all of us who want to live with more purpose and integrity, who want to do better in a world that so desperately needs each of us to make individual choices that honor our values to the benefit of the collective good. Because we truly are "All-One"!

As Gero's story reveals, many of the actions you take today—a bicycle trip with a friend, a journey to help victims of natural disaster, or activism on behalf of a plant shrouded in controversy and mystery—can be seeds that may blossom in very unexpected and incredible ways tomorrow.

Sometimes that action is just asking the question "What can I do to help?"

If that's a question you've ever asked, then I feel confident you will find some answers in this book. Bam!

—David Bronner, October 2020

Glossary of Acronyms and Commonly Used Terms

CBD Cannabidiol, one of more than 100 cannabinoids, chemicals produced by the cannabis plant

CH₄ Methane, a greenhouse gas

CO₂ Carbon dioxide, by-product of all combustion processes and essential plant nutrient. The most important greenhouse gas and contributor to global climate change.

CPO Crude palm oil, the red oil expelled from the flesh of palm fruits

DAF Dynamic agroforestry, the concept of highly diverse and stratified designed utility forests

DEA (US Federal) Drug Enforcement Administration

FFB Fresh (palm) fruit bunch, the ultimate source of palm and palm kernel oil

FTO Fair Trade and Organic

GHG Greenhouse gas

MFE Magic Foam Experience

MT Metric ton (or tonne) = 1,000 kg = 2,200 pounds. Not to be confused with "short ton" used in the US = 2,000 pounds or 0.91 MT.

NGO Nongovernment(al) organization, an organization that operates independently of any government. These are usually nonprofit organizations with a charitable mission.

NOP National Organic Program of the USDA (US Department of Agriculture)

PKO Palm kernel oil, the oil expelled from the white kernel of the palm nut or seed

RBD Refined, bleached, and deodorized

SME Small and medium-sized enterprises, in the US companies with typically less than 500 employees

THC (Delta-9)-Tetrahydrocannabinol, the key psychoactive cannabinoid produced by the cannabis plant

VCO Virgin Coconut Oil

COMMONLY USED TERMS

Castile soap Originally referring to soaps made in the Spanish Castile area from olive oil, now synonymous for soaps made exclusively from plant oils, such as Dr. Bronner's liquid and bar soaps.

Carbon negative—climate positive Any process that results in a negative balance of emissions of greenhouse gases, i.e., removes more GHG from the atmosphere than it adds.

Geographic and climate zones Most of Dr. Bronner's supply projects are in the tropics, the area surrounding the equator and located between 23° northern and southern latitudes. The subtropics are located between 23° and 35° northern and southern latitudes and host, e.g., Pavitramenthe and Canaan Palestine. Temperate zones are between 35° and 66° and include most of the US and Europe.

Raw foods Foods that have not been heated above approx. 118° F (48° C), i.e., not cooked, pasteurized, and sterilized. Due to their process conditions, even our unrefined coconut and palm oils are not raw foods; Canaan's unrefined olive oil is.

UNITS OF MEASURE

Weight

1 metric ton (MT) = 1,000 kilogram (kg) = 2,200 pounds = 1.1 short tons (US)

Length

1 kilometer (km) = 1,000 meters = 0.63 miles = 3,280 feet

(Agricultural) Area

1 acre = 0.4 hectare (ha), 1 ha = 2.5 acres

Introduction

A S A TEENAGER IN 1960s GERMANY, I had it all figured out. There were still too many former Nazis in industry and politics. Capitalists were raking in profits created by underpaid workers alienated from the product of their sweat. The few entrepreneurs I knew owned retail stores and small businesses, and they sure weren't capitalists. As for the politicians: they were on industry's payroll. No wonder they didn't crack down on increasingly obvious environmental pollution—such as that found in the Rhine River, a stinking sewer.

As my hair grew longer, I read thought-provoking philosophical literature with friends, explored altered states of mind, and traveled by car as far as Turkey and Iran. Things became even clearer to me. The imperialist North—notably, the United States—was robbing developing countries of their resources and keeping their authoritarian regimes in power. Meanwhile, the Americans and the Soviets were pointing their nuclear missiles at each other, and Germany was in the middle.

Nothing short of a global revolution would change this unfair, destructive, and joyless structure, I concluded. Since I was fourteen I had worked summer jobs in department stores and a paper mill, later for my dad's publishing firm. I liked the work and the freedom the extra cash bought—but I couldn't see myself working for industry. I liked the communist enthusiasm of fellow university students, for systems where the people owned the means of production. Yet their dogmatism and closed-mindedness kept me from joining. I saw potential in the emerging Green Party, but could they truly make Germany greener and fairer? They started to have an impact in the early eighties; but alas, politics was slow, and majority ruled. I realized that widespread social change would require commitment from other quarters.

When my wife, Christel Dillbohner, and I left for Los Angeles in 1986, there were few progressive firms in Germany that had meaningful jobs for a young physicist. As part of my dissertation at UCLA, I began working as an environmental consultant for US industry, from foundries making golf club heads to integrated oil and gas companies. We had no "green" clients. Environmental control was driven by regulation, and one had to comply. None of the companies I worked with seemed abusive, but when it came to their predominantly Hispanic workforce, making a profit sure took priority over providing full-coverage health care and above-minimum wages.

At the same time, my perspective on the private sector changed as I came to enjoy my work for industry and had to adjust some of my stereotypes about capitalism. Yet I couldn't see myself as environmental consultant for life. The work was mostly about damage control and end-of-pipe treatment; my ideals of fairness and ecological sustainability, which I'd held on to, played little role—except in the choice of marketing and PR language.

I found more meaning in work with the hemp movement, built on the promise that responsible small firms could build a new economy using versatile ecological agricultural raw materials, fairly produced and traded. Yet no economy can operate on a single agricultural ingredient; markets were lukewarm on hemp, and some of the hemp entrepreneurs had unsavory manners.

One in particular did not. I first crossed paths with the magic world of Dr. Bronner's in 1999. As I met the officers of this family company and became involved in its global operations, my perspective changed again. I learned that corporations can play a serious role in stabilizing the health of the planet and ensuring more equitable sharing of wealth—if they put their minds (and money) to doing so.

Dr. Bronner's soaps had long been a mainstay in health food stores thanks to their simple formula, natural ingredients, the company's activist roots, and founder Emanuel Bronner's determination to use a soap to unite and bring peace to the world. His family built on that legacy by asking themselves where the agricultural raw materials for their soaps came from, and whether their production benefited farmers, workers, and communities along the way. Then and now, the main raw materials are coconut, palm and palm kernel oils, and olive and mint oils, with another ten minor yet significant ingredients accounting for the balance—sugar, alcohol, a few more essential oils, and jojoba oil.

The Bronners' vision was a transparent and beneficial supply chain—which naturally began with shifting all major and several minor raw materials to organic and fair trade sources. That shift is the story covered in this book—mostly. Because in 2005 the Bronners asked me to coordinate that shift, even if it required building our own vertically integrated projects with farmers, production, staff, and their communities in the tropics. Of course, I was very interested—and my life would never be the same.

Since 2005, I've traveled more than half the time, met and worked with people from all over the planet, and helped set up several commercial projects—from smallholder farms to processing in the village, all the way to Dr. Bronner's and other customers. They've become sizable companies with teams that keep to the principles of Dr. Bronner's in their respective local setting and are fueled by demand for their excellent products, not charity. Our growing Special Operations team has had its share of adventures: elating, depressing, and mostly invigorating.

But the motivation that has powered me on this long road trip since 2005 is similar to what inspired the anti-capitalist German teenager. Imagine getting older and wiser and realizing you have a say in a company that tackles persistent global problems you felt strongly about when you were sixteen—social justice, environmental stewardship, international development, and drug policy reform. And does so in a strategic, constructive, undogmatic, effective, and enjoyable way. Such a career and the accompanying joy would have been difficult to imagine back in Cologne.

This book will introduce you to a company that works in a way very unlike what we've come to expect of business. To tell its story, I'm going to take you to the places where our organic and fair raw materials are now sourced and processed: Sri Lanka, Ghana, India, Samoa, Palestine, and Latin America. I will tell stories of farming, partnerships, and the challenges our Special Operations team had to overcome when building complex production systems and teams. If you are curious about the social and ecological problems with palm oil and cocoa—even with petroleum—you will find colorful accounts. If you are interested in what the excitement about the hemp plant is all about or wondered how soap might play a role in cleaning the planet, please keep reading. And if you wonder how an essential business navigated a family of likeminded companies worldwide through the COVID-19 pandemic that exposed weaknesses in global supply chains everywhere, you'll read about that, too.

In addition to the more involved stories of our main ingredients, we'll also take detours into the stories of some of our minor ingredients as well as into the ideas and practices of the four members of Dr. Bronner's executive team.

As the sentences for this book entered my head, they were often accompanied by pictures: people, settings, and atmospheres. Wouldn't it be nice to show at least some of the images to the readers, giving them an impression of the actors who played key roles in this story and its backdrop in the rural Global South? I included only a small subset of some twenty thousand photos that were taken during the last twenty years of the *Honor Thy Label* story. They introduce people who appear frequently in this book and some of the main scenes. You will find a larger collection of images on the book's website.

I hope you will enjoy the expedition.

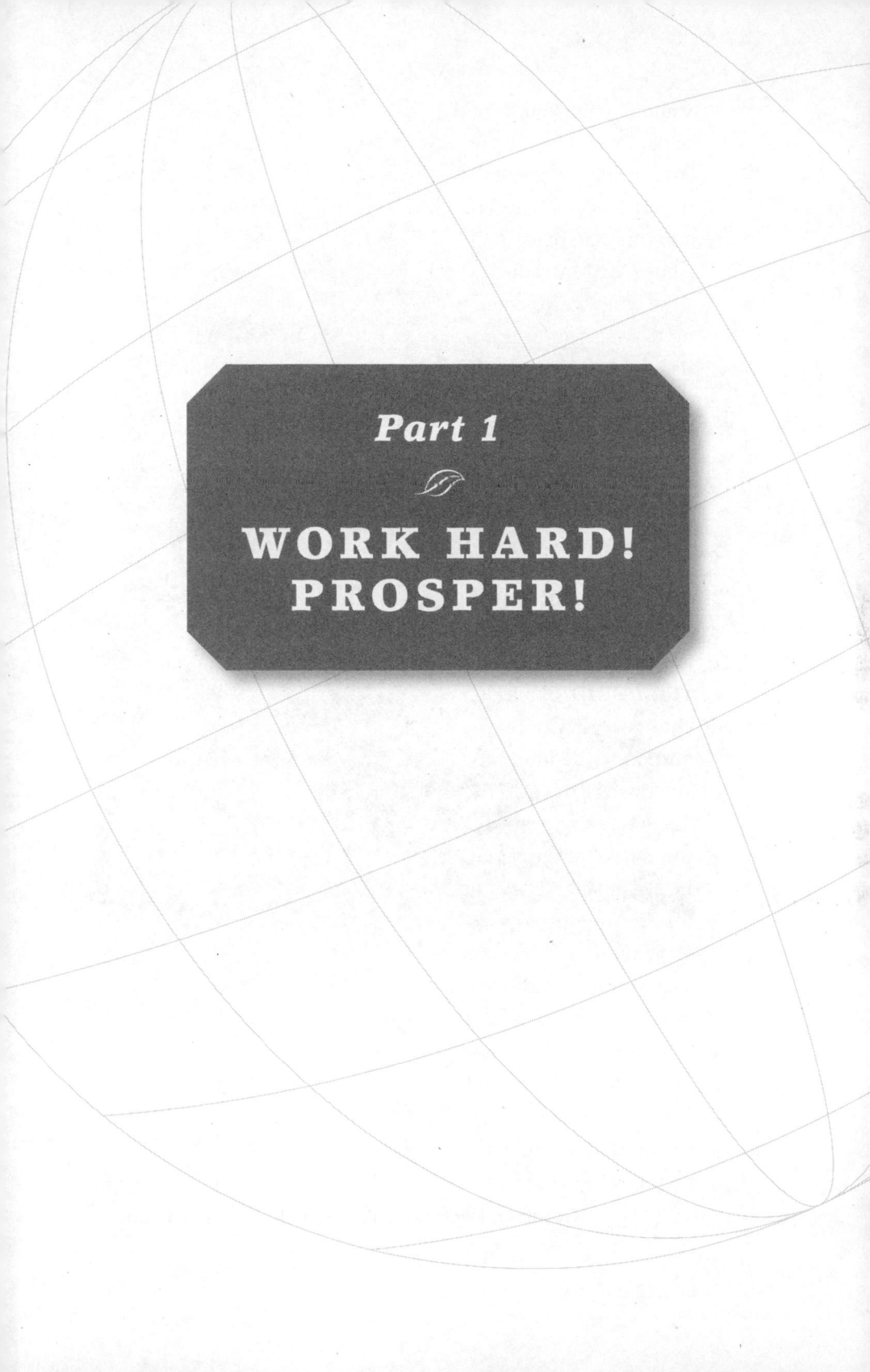

Part 1

WORK HARD!
PROSPER!

Gordon reflecting on tsunami damage in Sri Lanka

CHAPTER 1

What Do You Do When Disaster Strikes?

Sri Lanka, April 2005

A T FIRST SIGHT, THE PLACE did not look like the scene of a disaster; but then you look closer.

The train cars had been lifted back onto the repaired tracks, but the broken glass and crushed metal were evidence of what had occurred just four months earlier when a massive tsunami wave struck the *Queen of the Sea* passenger train, flooding its cars and knocking it off its tracks. More than 1,700 people had been killed, by far the deadliest rail disaster in history anywhere, and only one instance of the utter devastation that hit the island nation of Sri Lanka and many other places around the Indian Ocean on December 26, 2004.

The tracks had been repaired swiftly, since the train service from Colombo to Galle was one of the country's main arteries—but the wave had also struck and flooded the lower-lying village next to the tracks. There, many buildings had been completely destroyed, residents had died, and most trees, too, had been killed by saltwater. The coconut trees, which naturally tolerate salt, had survived.

A few miles up the coast near Moratuwa were the ruins of a

shantytown paralleling the train tracks. Two years earlier Christel and I had taken the train along this stretch that had been home to thousands. Now, only a couple of the houses and huts remained, some of them eerily intact. A small Buddhist temple had survived, almost untouched. Yet most of the buildings had been swept clear off their foundations.

While some activist aid organizations had donated simple wooden sheds and tents for temporary shelter, and a few villagers had started rebuilding their simple cement-block houses, one crucial thing was largely missing: international aid to help rebuild lives and livelihoods of the victims.

To be sure, there had been a huge inflow of donations—governmental and private—to the disaster areas around the Indian Ocean, notably Indonesia and Sri Lanka. But actually getting that money funneled, often through inefficient and conflicted governments, to all the places that needed it to help people rebuild their livelihood was a different story.

It was April 2005 when I visited these scenes of the disaster with my good friends Bernd Frank, a German serial entrepreneur whom I had met in 1996 through my consulting work in the hemp industry, and Gordon de Silva, a Sri Lankan businessman with decades of experience in the coconut fiber industry. The three of us were touring Sri Lanka's west and south coasts to witness the destruction caused by the tsunami, and to assess the work of our impromptu relief project, SecondAid, which we'd launched while Christel and I were at home in Berkeley. Soon after the tsunami struck, we'd jumped into action and began raising funds with the help of friends and family in Germany and the United States.

Among the donors were good friends and allies in the US hemp industry, including John Roulac, founder of Nutiva, and David Bronner, president of Dr. Bronner's. David had long been interested in my work in Sri Lanka, and the previous year he'd jokingly asked whether there was any fair trade coconut oil in Sri Lanka. At the time, the answer was no, but as I'll share in the pages to come, our collaboration would change that.

What brought me to Sri Lanka in the first place?

I had fallen in love with the country in 2001 after the US Agency for International Development (USAID) had hired me to consult on coconut fiber. Inspired by the work of Harvard Business School competitiveness guru Michael Porter, USAID had brought together major Sri Lankan industries—ceramics, rubber, tea, tourism—with the aim to build "industry clusters" and improve their global competitiveness through collaboration.

The "Coir Cluster" (referring to the common term for coconut fiber) was one such cluster. It included members of the Sri Lankan coir industry: processors, exporters, and two technical research organizations. I was brought on as a technical consultant because I had firsthand expertise in the production, uses, and research of other natural fibers, such as hemp and flax.

While some of the other consultants preferred the cool restaurants and spectacular sights, I met the locals and spent time in the field. After all, I was one of a team of consultants founded by Frank Riccio, a veteran of the natural fiber industry who had taught me much about doing business with a human perspective. I immediately found a friend in Gordon de Silva, a Sri Lankan in his late fifties who managed the coir export division of a large industrial conglomerate. I liked his international perspective, his often corrosive humor, and his focus on results. Whereas many other cluster members loved lamenting, Gordon wanted to get things done—and he knew how to go about it.

On that first visit, I enjoyed observing Sri Lanka and tried to understand it. Since my first trips to the Mediterranean and Middle East in the 1970s, I'd been drawn to places that were, to my eye, culturally traditional yet in a state of transformation. Places like Turkey, Iran, and Greece made me curious: What's driving this place? How do people make a living? So as I began visiting fiber mills, processing plants, and farms in Sri Lanka, I also began to wonder whether development work shouldn't help maintain local traditions and lifestyles while improving efficiencies. In most Western development work, this was obviously an afterthought.

After my initial assignment ended in early 2002, USAID asked me back for several follow-up assignments with the Coir Cluster and to brainstorm new product ideas. Bernd Frank loved foreign travel as I did and had also become friends with Gordon; once when he was visiting me, we went sailing with six local fishermen in the beach town of Negombo. As we took off in their dug-out traditional catamaran with its heavy fabric sails, we tried to wrap our heads around the logistics and economics of their operation. How do things run on this boat? Who makes the money—and how? During our two-hour trip we asked the crew of six many questions.

As it turned out, none of them owned shares in the boat—they were all hired labor; the owner made the money. Bernd and I both had leftist leanings but also liked small businesses—including our own—as long as they were run responsibly. The fishermen seemed eager to improve their livelihood, and we thought it best not to donate but to help this crew finance their own boat. At $1,500 a boat, that seemed very doable.

It was our first personal experiment combining business and development in Sri Lanka. And like all other projects I later embarked upon in the tropics, it soon became more complicated than we thought.

To start, the crew members came from different social strata and had different ideas about running a business. It was simplistic to think we could just finance these six men a boat to share—they didn't really *want* to share, at least not all of them. We swapped letters with the group's leader, and, on December 26, 2004, while we still argued, the tsunami struck.

Immediately thereafter, Christel (who had accompanied me to Sri Lanka twice), Bernd, Gordon, and I began talking. Our gut reaction was both a question and a call to action. *"So, what can we do to help?"*

IMPACT UNDER THE RADAR

Reports of widespread destruction of fishing boats suggested we fund a few boats. Yet at a price tag of $4,000 for a motorized fishing boat, we'd be able to support only a handful of people. We correctly expected that Sri Lanka would soon be inundated with fishing boats financed by larger aid organizations. Thus, we decided to stay small, under the radar, and focus on "impact for money." We knew that among the hardest hit were the small businesses on the coast that were the heart of the economy, as they provided nontourism employment to many in the area. Our theme became to directly support businesses that had lost their means of production to the waves and required small investments of between $100 and $200 to get back on their feet.

We programmatically called our project "SecondAid." Unlike government and international agencies, such as the Red Cross, who provided shelter and basic food supplies, we wanted to help victims rebuild their lives themselves, with just a little bit of help.

Our simple, almost naive, idea? If you want to support communities, you'll be most effective if you directly support their livelihood. Provide them with the tools they lost. SecondAid was an excellent, albeit small, first experience with rebuilding small businesses—creating jobs and opportunities along the way. It also served as the foundation for our later commercial work with smallholder farmers and villagers, setting up farming and processing projects for Dr. Bronner's. (More about that later.)

But how would we find trustworthy partners on the ground? Gordon would know. His style reflected both his coir marketing trips to the West and his local knowledge. When I first watched Gordon interact with potential partners, I was a little taken aback by how suspicious he seemed. I've always been a skeptic, yet quick to trust—maybe too quick. But I came to respect his manner of scrutinizing every potential partnership. He showed me that we would need to be deeply involved with the process. Investing isn't just about giving people money and hoping for the best.

"There are two churches on the coast that have already surveyed the losses suffered by locals," he told me on the phone in mid-January. He believed they'd be reliable partners when it came to gauging and addressing needs in their communities. For Gordon, that was strong approval. He was a devout Catholic, the church in Tangalle was Methodist, and the majority of victims were Buddhist. But Gordon didn't care. What mattered was finding a partner he could trust to spend our money wisely.

Our third location of operation was the shantytown along the railroad tracks near Moratuwa, just south of Colombo. Most houses had been washed away and their inhabitants evacuated to a hastily set up camp in a nearby school. Gordon's daughter Sonali was studying for her MBA; with her husband, Shuhail, and one of her classes, Sonali initiated a relief project to help the overwhelmed camp manager with administration. Yet they had no funds to help camp dwellers rebuild their businesses.

Without much debate we swiftly agreed on a simple concept: have local partners assess critical losses of equipment for some thirty to fifty families in each location. What was needed? Fishing nets and knives, woodworking tools, sewing machines, and bicycles. Gordon and Sonali began looking for good deals on the items needed, often shopping with local project coordinators or beneficiaries, and monitored the distribution of the goods. We gave no cash.

During our visit in April 2005, Bernd and I were impressed with how well this simple relief concept worked. Along with Gordon, we helped distribute the hand-selected items at churches and the camp. A humbling experience and reminder of how simple items so many of us take for granted can have a large impact on the lives of people without means.

By the end of 2005, SecondAid had helped a hundred families, with typically around $180 per family, to resume their businesses. Very modest amounts; no money spent on fundraising, administration, or travel; lean and mean. Gordon's occasional follow-up visits to the projects found that many beneficiaries stayed "in business," too. Our direct tactics to support small businesses had apparently worked.

How had we done it? With motivated and trustworthy partners, we had first identified victims' needs, bought needed materials, and then made sure of their proper and fair distribution. We had avoided the bureaucracy of the central government but cooperated with local government project managers, who appreciated our support in the face of very slow distribution of other funds.

The experience of this modest project illustrated that when disaster strikes—or anytime, really—and you want to achieve results swiftly and effectively, it's best to recruit allies and build your own structures. Keep things simple, avoid bureaucracy, and make sure all involved are strongly motivated by a common purpose. That approach had worked well under difficult conditions with SecondAid, a charitable project by design. It would soon turn out to be just as effective an approach for business by Dr. Bronner's.

SecondAid also would soon change the course of Christel's and my life. The project had emerged out of spontaneous response: our desire to do something meaningful and effective for tsunami victims. Its success made me wonder whether I should turn SecondAid into a permanent organization. But doing what?

I loved the purpose and diversity of issues I had worked on the years prior, often with Christel, my wife and life companion since 1975. A visual artist also born in Cologne, Christel draws much of her inspiration from natural environments. We both enjoyed the freedom, stimulation, and meaning that our self-employment gave us. We supported each other on our respective projects, often traveled together, and believed that we had the right livelihoods. Yet I had learned that, as a consultant, I would mostly be operating at a distance from "the real action" and never quite see the impact of my work.

So when David Bronner, one of SecondAid's key donors, called me just after my fiftieth birthday in July 2005 and said, "Come on, Gero, SecondAid did great work in Sri Lanka; you have an effective team on the ground. How about building an organic and fair trade coconut oil mill for Dr. Bronner's there?" I was intrigued, accepted the offer, and over the next year became a full-time Bronnerite.

When David had previously asked me about Sri Lankan fair trade coconut oil in 2004, I'd met a few producers of organic tea and spices, some of them from fair trade tea plantations. I had visited the production of coconut flakes and milk for food. Yet there was no serious production of virgin coconut oil (VCO), let alone fair trade.

My experience in Sri Lanka combined with David's dream of his own coconut oil production ultimately spawned the hands-on development of the world's first organic and fair trade supply chain for a manufacturing company. David knew I had no experience setting up vertically integrated farming and processing projects. Conversely, I knew that Dr. Bronner's had never set up a foreign company before. Thus, as I sometimes joke, both parties were perfectly qualified for such a project.

Where did this trust and confidence originate that we could do such a thing? I actually knew David from an earlier rather successful collaboration on a crop quite different from coconuts: industrial hemp. He and I first spoke by phone in 1999 when I was preparing a scientific study on behalf of several hemp food companies in the United States and Canada, to assess whether eating such foods—hemp seed oil, shelled seeds, protein powder—could possibly cause a positive urine test for marijuana. At the time, the writing was on the wall: the US Drug Enforcement Administration (DEA) would soon propose federal rules aimed at eliminating the use of hemp seeds and oil from all food items. Dr. Bronner's had cofunded our study, and David showed keen interest in the outcome.

Back in 1999, I had wondered why the head of a *soap company* was so interested in hemp food products. Hemp oil was a minor ingredient of Dr. Bronner's iconic soaps—and not even in the original recipe. Couldn't Dr. Bronner's have just avoided trouble by removing the ingredient or just ignoring the DEA, since their proposed ruling would not affect soap makers? But as I would discover over the years, David was generally more interested in running toward meaningful action than away from it, even if it promised no obvious short-term benefit to his family's company.

To understand his willingness to later head a court battle against the DEA, a powerful and unpleasant adversary, one must appreciate the company's history—especially, the vision and activism of David's grandfather Emanuel Bronner, who founded Dr. Bronner's in 1948.

UNITING "SPACESHIP EARTH"

Emanuel Bronner was born in 1908 into the third generation of an increasingly successful Jewish German family of soap makers in the town of Heilbronn. Emanuel learned the trade but struggled with his dominating father and loathed the noisy and hateful anti-Semitism of the Nazis, who emerged as political force in the 1920s.

He emigrated to the United States in 1929, resettled in Milwaukee, and stayed "in the business," working for and with several soap companies. Around that time, he also became an activist and cofounded, with several likeminded people, the Brotherhood of Man—an organization with loosely defined plans for promoting a world where all humans lived together peacefully, regardless of nationality, ethnicity, or faith.

The following decade of personal tragedy—especially the murder of his parents during the Holocaust and death of his wife, Paula (the mother of his children Jim, Ralph, and Ellen)—made him even more activist. After time in a mental asylum, he escaped to Los Angeles and started a soap business to spread his message, using his family's old recipe for liquid soap and adding lots of peppermint oil to it. Initially a sole proprietorship, Emanuel incorporated in 1973 under the name All-One-God-Faith Inc. with Dr. Bronner's Magic Soaps added as the DBA name later on.

In the era of the Vietnam War, the civil rights movement, Rachel Carson's *Silent Spring*, and growing awareness of humanity's destruction of the natural world, the counterculture of the 1960s embraced both Emanuel's natural, biodegradable soap and the message on its label; Emanuel saw the product and its label as a vehicle to get his message of universal peace, self-sufficiency, and cooperation to the masses. His ultimate goal was to help save "Spaceship Earth," as he called it, through "constructive capitalism," in which companies used their profits to benefit people and planet. His operational philosophy was fairness to his small staff, the use of natural ingredients, the rejection of modern chemistry in cleaning products, and his label as a platform for his vision.

He was not a very savvy business leader, however, and it took the work of his sons Ralph and Jim and Jim's wife, Trudy, to rescue the company from bankruptcy. In the 1990s, they turned it into the exemplary employer and generous supporter of local and global philanthropy it is now. In parallel, Jim and Trudy continued to run Bronner Chemical, Jim's consulting firm, which focused on firefighting foam and Snofoam—fake snow for Hollywood.

Dr. Bronner's, the name the company and its followers increasingly used as its range of products expanded beyond soap, offered a motivating and respectful working environment, employee compensation, and health benefits uncommon for small, family enterprises. They supported local charities, such as the Boys and Girls Club of Greater San Diego. In part, Jim engaged in youth programs to make up for his father's abdication of parental responsibilities while focusing on his mission to unite Spaceship Earth.

Emanuel died in March 1997 knowing that his family would continue his vision. But Jim was diagnosed with lung cancer shortly after and died in June 1998. With Trudy and Ralph, he had laid the foundation for the charitable social venture engine that Dr. Bronner's would soon become. Shortly after Jim's passing, David and Trudy institutionalized elements of the vision set forth by Emanuel and Jim. They implemented a 5-to-1 cap on executive compensation over the lowest-paid, fully vested warehouse position, thus ensuring that the company would generate money to spend on philanthropy and activism. They also agreed that owners would not receive dividends for personal purposes.

The causes Dr. Bronner's has actively engaged in and supported since Jim's and Trudy's sons David and Mike joined in 1997 and 2000, respectively, have become more diverse, radical, and modern than their grandfather's and parents'—advocating for the re-legalization of hemp farming in the United States being just one example.

All family members will confirm that David carries a high dose of Emanuel's DNA and follows the most in his grandfather's footsteps. Yet while Trudy, Mike, and David have rather different personal styles and priorities for saving Spaceship Earth, they have jointly steered the development of an expansive, coherent, and effective "giving program."

All self-respecting companies give to philanthropy; Dr. Bronner's just gives a lot and it funds more than conventional charities. Between 2014 and 2019, Dr. Bronner's has contributed some $49 million to charitable and activist causes. This corresponds to 7.6 percent of our total global revenue over this period, or some 45 percent of our profit before charity and taxes. For comparison, other progressive companies are proud of contributing 1 percent of their revenues to causes; more radical ones may contribute 2 percent. It's safe to say that we put our money where our mouth is.

What are we doing with it?

A listing of what David would call the company's "core causes" include animal advocacy; community betterment, including a focus on youth and child services in Greater San Diego; criminal justice and drug policy reform; fair pay and fair trade; and regenerative organic agriculture. Take fair pay, where we have successfully supported ballot initiatives in several states aimed at raising the minimum wage—accompanied by in-store education through the labels on our bestselling quart soaps boldly declaring "FAIR PAY TODAY." Or take drug policy reform, which includes our support of scientific trials to demonstrate the efficacy of psychedelic-assisted therapy in the treatment of depression and trauma. Under the banner of criminal justice reform, Dr. Bronner's funds organizations dedicated to addressing the myriad problems of mass incarceration, offering resources and opportunities to formerly incarcerated people reentering society.

The company's animal advocacy work was sparked by David's multiple-decade personal commitment to live with a respect for all animal life and, consequently, to a vegan lifestyle. The program specifically supports organizations that address the exploitation and cruel treatment of billions of animals on factory farms, as well as groups working to protect marine wildlife.

Dr. Bronner's swift engagement in the groundswell of protest and public discourse that followed the police murder of George Floyd is a great example of how we respond to the influence of social movements but are also inclined toward self-reflection and improvement. Internally, we ramped up our efforts to promote diversity, equity, and inclusion with a new antiracism task force led by black employees. Publicly, the company pledged to support the Movement for Black Lives (M4BL), a decentralized influential network of activist groups, with a total of $1 million over the next ten years.

These numbers show that our activism extends far beyond paying lip service to a popular movement, as is rather common in industry. We're interested in impact. We do lose customers who don't support our causes, and they let us know via social media, as happened after our commitment to Movement for Black Lives. Not too many—and it's a free country after all. Most customers appreciate that we're for real, and I'm certain that our credibility is one large contributor to our consistent growth.

Besides hemp, one of the first activist fights David and Mike led the company into was education and lobbying around the support of organic standards for food and personal care items and the labeling of genetically engineered foods (GMOs). In recent years, our advocacy work in these areas has evolved into support for regenerative organic agriculture, a concept that I'll write quite a bit more about in the pages to come. The sums spent on this charitable and activist work do not include Dr. Bronner's purchase of more expensive "ecological and fair raw materials," from the projects set up and supported by my Special Operations team or our partners. That money is part of our COGS—or cost of goods sold—of producing our soaps.

For David and Mike, the opportunity to run the family company came with a responsibility of stewardship for the legacy they inherited. Emanuel Bronner saw his soap as a vehicle for the world peace plan he exposed on his label. They see the business act as an engine to grow and support movements, campaigns, and organizations advancing social change.

As I'll share in the next chapter, what better way to explore that concept than engaging with a controversial crop: industrial hemp.

Trudy Bronner on taking care of a company

Trudy Bronner was no stranger to the family business when she and David took over after Jim's death. Since Emanuel let go of the reins of the business in 1993, the retired schoolteacher worked for years with her husband—first at Bronner Chemical and then at Dr. Bronner's—commuting two hours from their home in Glendale to the Escondido plant before eventually moving south.

Trudy describes those years of working with her husband as her best years.

"We were working side by side," she said. "At the end of the day we were just as tired as each other, just as exhausted, just as frustrated, or just as happy."

Dr. Bronner's move since 2003 into organic and fair trade was, in many ways, a natural evolution of the work Jim and Trudy had long been doing, not only in the business itself but also with the local community—just on a more global scale. From their first days at the helm of the company, the Bronners have been focused not only on managing a successful business but on engaging with their community. So when David first brought up the idea of going organic and fair trade, it resonated with Trudy.

"It just absolutely made sense," Trudy told me about the decision. "You know you make an organic soap that doesn't have pesticides sprayed on its raw materials. But then you hear about farmers not being able to earn a living and slave labor in factories overseas. . . . It just made sense to go fair trade. But how to do it? And who should come on the scene to help manage?"

The transition to organic and fair trade sources was a big jump and an expensive one—especially because the company did not yet have relationships with bankers at the time. And so Trudy began to develop those much-needed relationships with financial institutions. But how?

"Personal integrity," she said. "I serve on the board of the Boys and Girls Club with the principals at Pacific Western Bank and got to know them. Michael (that is, Mike Bronner) knows them through his volunteer work. You just find people who seem to share your values."

The secret formula is a fine balance between the integrity and shared values Trudy talks about—and the willingness to fight for causes that matter. Of course, there is always lots of discussion about where to focus—what's important to the core of the business, and what's a "distraction."

"This company was never mine," Trudy explains. "I still feel that I'm just its steward, and there are times I feel like we really got to fight for that."

What does stewardship mean to Trudy?

"It's a family company . . . the business is a vehicle to take care of our All-One family and to make sure to give back to those who give into it."

Christel in German hemp trial field

CHAPTER 2

Hemp and Hysteria

San Francisco, April 2002

WALKING UP THE STEPS TO THE federal court building in San Francisco in 2002, it was hard not to notice the number of homeless people sitting on the stairs. Two decades before the city would combine a homeless population of 7,500 with the nation's largest income gap between top and bottom, the distance between the haves and have-nots was already on full display.

I entered the courtroom with Christel and several friends and allies from the hemp industry, including David Bronner; his adviser on activism and public relations, Adam Eidinger; and John Roulac, a hemp activist, serial entrepreneur, and founder of Nutiva, a fast-growing natural food company involved in hemp. And there was our legal team, Joe Sandler and Patrick Goggin, all grinning confidentially and convinced of the strength of the arguments they were about to make.

The courtroom was filled with even more hemp activists and spectators, who had done their best to blend in. I knew most but it took a few seconds to recognize some who had traded their casual clothing for jackets and ties.

What had brought this motley crew into the halls of justice this day?

Months earlier, the DEA had passed a set of rules that would in effect outlaw the sale of foods containing hemp seeds and their derivatives in the United States. They had also begun putting pressure on retailers of such products. At the core of the debate was that hemp and marijuana are in essence of the same plant species, *Cannabis sativa*. Defined in operative terms, marijuana contains, in its flowers and leaves, sufficiently high concentrations of THC, or tetrahydrocannabinol, the dominant psychoactive ingredient in any cannabis, to give you a high. "Industrial hemp," on the other hand, includes varieties bred for a low THC content such that smoking its flowers will have no such impact. Note that the flowers of drug cannabis typically contain 15 percent THC, compared with less than 0.3 percent in industrial hemp, and you know why.

Non-psychoactive hemp had been grown for seeds and fibers across Europe and North America into the 1950s under increasing regulatory oversight but then vanished, largely due to a lack of markets and the labor-intensive harvesting and processing. While many European countries had learned by the late 1990s to differentiate between high- and low-THC varieties, the US DEA, responsible for regulating marijuana, was not willing to acknowledge that difference and continued to claim that any cannabis is marijuana and was eager to ban the production of retail products related to cannabis seeds.

Most members of the fledgling industry despaired. Some suggested that hemp food companies should simply claim that their products had "non-detectable" levels of THC and hope for the best.

Not David Bronner. He persuaded the Hemp Industries Association (HIA), the trade association of North American hemp companies, to sue the DEA and keep industrial hemp products on the shelves. Because HIA was a California organization, the case would be heard by the 9th Circuit District Court in San Francisco— expected to be more open to reason than other federal courts. It helped that David put together the legal team, and Dr. Bronner's paid for most of the cost.

The trial would not only change the course of my life, it would further establish Dr. Bronner's as an effective activist organization committed to saving the planet—against all odds.

HEMP—A MOST CONTROVERSIAL PLANT

I'm writing this in 2020, a time when more and more US states and foreign countries, including Canada, have legalized or decriminalized both medical and recreational cannabis. Products containing CBD, short for cannabidiol, a major non-psychoactive but pharmaceutical ingredient, are advertised everywhere. Today, a scandal surrounding the non-psychoactive industrial hemp used in clothing, technical, and food products would seem a quaint memory from a different time. However, the same fascination and many of the same misperceptions around the plant still flourish today.[1]

Personally, I have been looking at the plant through multiple lenses: as a cannabis and hemp user who appreciates its many benefits, a scientist who has evaluated its nutritional attributes, a businessperson whose company utilizes hemp seed oil in its soaps, an environmental activist who is optimistic about regenerative agriculture and agroforestry practices. And always, with a curious scientific mind.

Of course, I didn't know anything about the origins of the plant or the difference between industrial hemp (hanf in German) and medicinal cannabis when a fellow high school student passed me a hashish joint in 1969 at fourteen—or when, in 1976, another friend brought seeds home from a trip to Amsterdam and explained that these would produce marijuana plants. It was a hot summer in Cologne, and the plants almost grew into small trees in our garden. The harvest produced sufficient flowers and leaves to keep us supplied for three years.

In 1986, when Christel and I moved to Venice for my doctorate program in environmental science and engineering at UCLA, Ronald Reagan was in his second term and the War on Drugs was ramping up. At the time, Venice was in transition. Still a mix of low-income housing and modest family homes, but the last affordable beach town in LA, it became a frontier of gentrification. As far as I could smell, cannabis was smoked very discreetly. There was a large community of homeless people, and patrol cars were ubiquitous. And there were the skaters, body builders, performing musicians, and chainsaw jugglers—blending in with tourists from all over the world, eager to drink in some of the Venice spirit.

I must have first heard of the "miracle of hemp" in 1991. On the boardwalk, young hemp activists set up tables on weekends, selling hemp seeds and preaching the miraculous benefits of the plant. They struck me as excited and dogmatic with an almost religious zeal for their idea, and our brief chats implied that legalizing smokable high-THC cannabis had a higher priority for them than farming hemp for fiber. I was all for activists demanding the legalization of "recreational" cannabis—I found the impact of the War on Drugs, with its stifling of a rational public discourse and its escalating prisoner populations, nauseating. Yet I also found the arguments of the promoters of industrial hemp a bit contrived. I remember thinking, "Where's the science and the facts?"

DISCOVERING JACK HERER

The tables on the Venice boardwalk prominently featured a book by one Jack Herer. Titled *The Emperor Wears No Clothes*, the book by the pro-cannabis activist was first published in 1985. Most early hemp and marijuana enthusiasts in the United States have heard of Herer—or at least of the marijuana strain named after him. He became known as the "Emperor of Hemp" thanks to his untiring activism and his book—an account of how a conspiracy of federal bureaucrats and US industry magnates, such as Hearst and DuPont, had since the 1930s sabotaged the revival of hemp as the world's preeminent natural resource.

A key piece of Herer's evidence was the article "Billion Dollar Crop," published in the February 1938 issue of *Popular Mechanics*[2]—a magazine committed to explaining "the way the world works" in plain language. The article featured a recent mechanical advance in separating the bast fiber and hurds of the hemp stalks, thus replacing manual labor and allowing cost-competitive domestic production of thousands of everyday items that could be grown on American farms: "fish nets, bow strings, canvas, strong rope, overalls, damask tablecloths, fine linen garments, towels, bed linen." Hemp bast fiber and hurds were also expected to become a key feedstock for the production of all grades of paper. This diversity of potential products—most of which are conceivable and technically feasible—inspired Herer and the vision of a hemp-based economy.

Alas, the *Popular Mechanics* article that inspired Herer did *not* consider in detail the fast-changing industrial landscape where synthetic fibers, such as nylon, were about to explode in popularity—nor did it consider the production of pulp and paper from wood using the recently improved Kraft process. In an increasingly modern economy, it mattered less what a raw material can do in theory than whether it can do it competitively and on a large scale.

His book had a great and lasting impact on the rediscovery of hemp (though Herer used a great deal of imagination to connect dots). Whatever shortcomings Herer's account had, it became the inspiration for a global movement, and the story he told had fundamental truth to it—notably, that versatile plants can contribute to our world's supply of raw materials in a sustainable way.

And despite my skepticism on the boardwalk, it was Herer's book that eventually got me into hemp, as well.

THE YELLOW BOOK

In the summer of 1993, my friend Michael Carus told me about a publishing project that would ultimately take me into industrial hemp and into working with Dr. Bronner's. Michael had been my closest friend during our years as physics students at the University of Cologne. We had traveled together to Greece and Holland and spent many nights arguing over the meaning of quantum physics. Before I left Cologne for California, we had collaborated on environmental research projects for KATALYSE, an independent environmental research institute, including one to measure and assess contamination of food and soil samples by radioactive fallout from the 1986 disaster at Chernobyl.

When I visited Michael in Cologne that summer, he explained that he'd just been recruited to augment a German translation of Jack Herer's book with a scientific assessment of the modern agronomic and economic potential of industrial hemp. Quite a challenge for a crop with a poor track record in Western countries since the 1940s—but Michael was up for it. The "yellow book," also known as "the German Hemp Bible," was an instant success, was translated into ten languages, and became a pillar of the modern hemp movement in Germany and beyond.[3] The enthusiastic reception of the yellow book prompted Michael and his NOVA Institute in mid-1994 to organize a real scientific hemp conference, and he asked me to help prepare and manage it. It would cover agronomy, breeding, processing, markets, legal issues—at a time when hemp was still not legal to grow in the EU, except for France.

In March 1995, the first BIORESOURCE HEMP became the "mother of all hemp conferences," with an eclectic gathering of some three hundred people involved in hemp: Eastern European hemp breeders, German academics developing novel processes and products for hemp fiber, and American hemp activists and entrepreneurs. Many were potheads, others were dry, somewhat boring researchers. I loved the group's diversity, chaired several conference sessions, and helped communicate between the worlds. When we threw the second BIORESOURCE HEMP conference in 1997, I remember sitting one night in a dark bar with a few American friends and the actor Woody Harrelson, a known hemp advocate, all somewhat hazed and talking awesome nonsense. What fun! Afterward, I was pretty certain that hemp would help change the world in one way or another and decided to spend at least some of my future on it. A wise decision!

TROUBLE WITH THE DEA

In spite of all that enthusiasm, there was a serious obstacle to anyone in the United States wanting to explore the potential of industrial hemp. Because the Controlled Substances Act of 1970 had in effect banned hemp farming, the fledgling US hemp industry had to rely entirely on imported hemp products from fibers and seed products.

Such hemp companies primarily offered hemp apparel: pants, shirts, baseball hats. They sourced it, as did their EU counterparts, in Romania and Hungary, where labor-intensive and inefficient hemp industries had survived the fall of the Iron Curtain. Inconsistent quality and reliability of the supplies soon made most hemp brands shift to China—the country had significant hemp acreage, more efficient technology for processing hemp into spinnable fiber, cheap labor, and also produced hemp seeds, traditionally for bird feed, now also for food.

By the mid-1990s, such "hemp foods" became available in small stores and by mail order in North America. It was not just hype or loyalty to the plant that drove demand. Analysis of hemp seed oil found a unique and nutritious fatty acid spectrum, including two omega-3 fatty acids that could help balance the dominance of omega-6 fatty acids in the typical North American diet. And quality hemp seed products just tasted good!

Seeing an opportunity for Canadian oil seed growers, the Canadian federal government legalized commercial hemp farming in 1998 under tight regulations by Health Canada, including the mandated use of low-THC varieties. Since then, the vast majority of hemp foods in the United States has come from Canada's prairie provinces, Manitoba, Saskatchewan, and Alberta. In addition to seed oil, whole seeds, and shelled seeds, Canadian hemp food companies realized that the seed cake that remained after the pressing of seeds could be finely milled and sifted into a "fiber-rich protein powder."

The trouble with the DEA around hemp seed foods began in 1998. First, a 1997 survey found THC in hemp oil made from Chinese seeds at varying levels. Then, several federal employees with positive urine tests for marijuana blamed them on the hemp foods they had eaten, and some prevailed in court. This was an obvious provocation to the DEA and other stakeholders in the growing countrywide workplace drug-testing program. The source of that problem, hemp foods, had to be eliminated!

Early tests of hemp seeds and oil from Canada then showed that THC levels were considerably lower than those in products from China. The botany of hemp explains the difference: Hemp seeds themselves contain virtually no THC. Rather, they may be externally contaminated during harvesting and processing by the sticky THC-containing resins in bracts and leaves. Studies had shown that planting low-THC cultivars combined with thorough seed cleaning after the harvest dramatically lowered THC levels on seed hulls and thus in hemp seed products, notably hemp seed oil.

The lower THC levels in Canadian hemp seeds could have settled the problem by setting THC standards for food items, but the DEA was not interested in a rational solution. The mounting retail presence of food products made from cannabis, a plant illegal to grow in the United States no matter what the THC content, must have annoyed the agency in charge of all things cannabis; the presence of low-THC residues and potential interference with workplace drug testing was the last straw. The DEA felt a sense of urgency to close a loophole through which cannabis would certainly ravage American communities. Its natural targets were the US and Canadian hemp industries.

In late 1998, expecting a crackdown, Nutiva's John Roulac and I discussed with several industry members conducting a scientific study. It would investigate whether the low THC levels in Canadian hemp seeds could still cause a positive urine test for marijuana, one of the DEA's key objections against allowing hemp seeds in food.

To have standing in an expected legal battle with the DEA, the study would have to meet scientific standards, and the results would have to be published in a peer-reviewed scientific journal, best by a group of scientists beyond suspicion of producing "sweetheart expertise." I had conducted and published scientific research since the early 1980s and, through a German friend and renowned expert on medical cannabis, Dr. Franjo Grotenhermen, had a network of scientists involved in the medical use of cannabis. I was confident we could meet these requirements.

So in mid-1999, Petra Pless, my associate at *Leson Environmental Consulting,* and I prepared the design of such a study. Franjo suggested several coauthors, all reputable scientists willing to take a critical look at the issue of hemp foods and drug testing.

Petra and I recruited fifteen volunteers in the East Bay—all without recent exposure to THC in hemp foods, or medicinal or recreational drugs, as demonstrated by a baseline urine test. Each volunteer ingested over four ten-day periods one tablespoon of four different blends of hemp oil and canola oil per day, containing known low concentrations of THC. The volunteers collected a total of ten urine samples, which were analyzed in a certified drug testing lab using the common workplace testing protocol for marijuana use.

The study found, by mid-2000, that even daily consumption of six tablespoons of hemp oil containing five parts per million of THC (the highest levels found in Canadian hemp oil) would not produce a positive urine test, with a wide margin of safety. This meant that one of the DEA's objections to keeping hemp foods legal stood on very shaky grounds.

A HEMP-BASED COMPANY

In the late nineties, David Bronner had begun his own dive into hemp education. David, too, was inspired by Jack Herer's vision of a world fueled by hemp. His experimentation with cannabis and psychedelics both at college and during time spent in Amsterdam created a deep connection to his grandfather's message of "All-One." It meant recognizing that fundamentally there was no difference between him and the rest of humanity and the world.

That vision motivated David in 1997 to join the company to advocate for social and environmental issues unrelated to soap making. Before Emanuel died that year, David shared with his grandfather that he was fully on board with his All-One activist vision as it related to the future of the company.

David summarized his position on hemp in a 2012 interview in *Inc.* magazine. "One of the reasons we liked hemp was that it was at the nexus of a bunch of hot issues, environmental issues, and also drug policy," he said.

Hemp is a remarkably useful plant: It's a good dietary source of omega-3 fatty acids; it is generally cultivated without pesticides, even in conventional agriculture; its fiber is especially strong; and, as Dr. Bronner's had found, its oil is, if used at low concentrations, a good additive in soap. The DEA had a long history of conflating hemp with marijuana, just the kind of bureaucratic ignorance that got David excited. Adding hemp to his product would make for a nice provocation of the DEA and possibly push other more constructive ideas forward.

I admit that since coming to the United States in 1986 we had entirely missed Dr. Bronner's, even though we shopped in the Santa Monica Co-op and other places carrying the Magic Soaps. Embarrassingly, when one of my hemp industry friends excitedly asked me in early 1998 "Have you heard, Dr. Bronner's will start using hemp oil?," I had to ask, "Who's Dr. Bronner's?"

Then, in 1999, David first called me. He had heard of the drug testing study and was interested in the details. Why was it necessary to involve so many volunteers to prove that hemp foods couldn't produce a positive urine test? How do you design such a study? And what worst-case assumptions should we make on the THC level in hemp oil and likely daily intake rates?

Questions not generally asked by other industry members.

We also argued other hemp issues. David found Jack Herer's "conspiracy theory" plausible—that the revival of industrial hemp had been prevented by a racket of major industrial firms and the DEA—whereas I didn't. What struck me in that phone conversation was that David combined the passion of a hemp activist with the willingness to think critically. While our study progressed, David and I talked occasionally, and I enjoyed his sharp and strategic mind and his vision.

We first met in person in early 2001 during a strategy meeting in Sacramento to discuss a pending state hemp legalization bill. A friend pointed him out to me, a tall, long-haired man in his late twenties behaving cautiously. After the meeting I drove him to the airport. We talked and I realized that he, like me, was a rather shy, sometimes awkward person. Yet during this initial chat in person, I felt drawn to his honesty, depth, and commitment—free of the common hype. And I felt that of all the hempsters I had met so far, he'd be the best bet to beat the DEA. I was ready to participate in the battle.

Meanwhile, after a somewhat adversarial review process, the findings of our drug testing study were published in November 2001 by the *Journal of Analytical Toxicology*, just in time. We now had another strong and credible piece of evidence that the presence of trace THC in hemp foods did not justify any of the concerns raised by the DEA.

THE "POPPY SEED DEFENSE"

As expected, on October 9, 2001, in the haze after September 11, the DEA published its clarifying rules on hemp foods in the *Federal Register*. In effect, they stipulated that food items containing any measurable amount of THC were deemed a Schedule I substance and as such were banned.

But David and his legal team were ready. The Hemp Industries Association (HIA) filed for an injunction. It was granted on March 7, 2002, keeping hemp foods legal until the court reached a decision. I had submitted evidence that trace levels of THC were, in fact, commonly and naturally present in hemp seeds, even from low-THC varieties. I had also submitted the results of our study that consumption of products from Canadian seeds posed no risk to workplace drug testing, with a wide margin of safety.

In that San Francisco federal courtroom, Christel and I enjoyed the play that unfolded. One of the three judges was Judge Alex Kozinski, a Reagan appointee. He listened to our attorney Joe Sandler's presentation of the "poppy seed defense"—the fact that other legal foods, such as poppy seed bagels, were also known to interfere with drug testing programs, and that had led federal employers to raise the legal limit for opiates in urine tests. Why not do this for hemp foods? It worked. As an immediate outcome of the hearing, the injunction stayed and kept hemp foods legal pending further review. Press coverage also generated free advertising for the fledgling industry and contributed to its growth.

After this rather incredible initial success, I would meet David Bronner occasionally at industry events, such as a victory party in a dimly lit Iranian restaurant in LA where I also met his first wife, Kris Lin-Bronner. It was love at first sight for her clarity and humor, though I only later realized the extent to which Kris had contributed to shaping Dr. Bronner's vision during that period.

On these occasions David didn't boast about Dr. Bronner's, so I only learned over time what this crazy company that had led the fight for the impossible, beating the DEA in court, was all about, where it came from, what drove it. The DEA case also gave me my first glimpse of Dr. Bronner's "unselfishness" when pursuing activist goals. The responsibility of preventing positive drug tests was entirely on food, not on soap makers. But for David it was "about the cause"—not about getting his company out of trouble.

After the initial ruling in 2002 in favor of the hemp foods industry, the DEA appealed. The court issued its final ruling in 2004, again siding with the industry. Would the DEA appeal to the Supreme Court? After a few weeks of tense waiting, they decided against it, realizing that their case was weak and would have taken more time, which was not on their side. Hemp foods produced in Canada stayed legal for Americans to enjoy.

It took another fourteen years of market development, education, and lobbying lawmakers by industry and activists, with crucial support from Dr. Bronner's, until finally, in December 2018, Congress passed, with bipartisan support, the Hemp Farming Act of 2018 and incorporated its provisions into the 2018 US Farm Bill. In essence it did what we had advocated for since the mid-1990s: remove industrial hemp, now defined as cannabis with less than 0.3

percent THC, from Schedule I of controlled substances and make it an ordinary agricultural commodity. It had taken the United States some twenty extra years to reach the point where EU countries and Canada had arrived in the late 1990s, and from where small yet dynamic industries producing foods and fiber products had emerged.

That ultimate victory didn't end our involvement in cannabis. For one, we continue to use hemp oil in our soaps, now from organic sources in the United States. Dr. Bronner's also carries on backing meaningful new cannabis projects and campaigns. An example is the support for the Sun & Earth certification of cannabis, grown by small farmers in Northern California, using the principles of regenerative agriculture and social fairness.

As for me, cannabis has been the plant that first took me to altered states of mind and connected me to several of my best friends. One of them, Bernd Frank, taught me much about business and the challenges of building vertical agricultural supply chains—from farm to finished product. And ultimately, hemp linked me up with David Bronner and his family. Quite a pivotal role for a humble, versatile plant.

The first two chapters will have given you a flavor of what drove Emanuel Bronner and drives his family today to make soap with a positive societal impact. Now, before taking you into the construction of tropical supply chains, let's spend a chapter to better understand soap itself—its ingredients and its history, one that's profoundly connected to the history of the Bronner family.

David Bronner on leading an activist organization

Why keep hemp oil in a product that didn't *need* it?

"Technically we could have argued that body care products weren't covered by the DEA's rule and the government would have let us off the hook," David explained. "But that wasn't what we were in it for. We were in it to keep hemp in the culture."

David was a sincere believer in hemp as a versatile and sustainable rotation crop that didn't need much pesticides and fertilizers, as well as passionate about opening up cultural space and acceptance for cannabis generally.

"I remember having a hemp shirt with stylized cannabis on it," he said. "People's response: 'Oh my God! I love that.' You know, you're creating a space for the de-repression of the culture."

Over a decade later, Dr. Bronner's continues to carry out one of David's chief missions: challenging stigmas. These days, that means education and activism around plant medicine, and his work with the Multidisciplinary Association for Psychedelic Studies (MAPS) and Veterans Exploring Treatment Solutions (VETS).

David knows well that he could not have done any of this work alone.

The organic process in which several of the company's key leaders came from activist collaborations generally—and hemp collaborations, specifically—tells important lessons about the leadership and strategy that has driven Dr. Bronner's growth and success, especially on where you find talented people and how you retain them.

I'm not the only person that Dr. Bronner's has hired full-time after cooperating on special projects. In fact, it's a hallmark practice that David has employed and that has emerged in Dr. Bronner's evolution. David calls those of us he's brought on Dr. Bronner's "aces"—we're all responsible for implementing the company's mission and ensuring projects and work stays mission-aligned.

David has replicated this approach by "identifying the Ryans, the Adams, the Christinas, and Les's"—all members of our leadership team who were originally brought in as consultants on crucial projects: Ryan Fletcher, director of public affairs and media relations, and Adam Eidinger, director of social action, both came on board during Dr. Bronner's early hemp activism days; and husband-and-wife team Christina Volgyesi, VP of marketing, and Les Szabo, director of constructive capital, had cofounded the hemp food brand Living Harvest.

"It strikes you when we work so well together and make awesome things happen," David said. "That as we grew as an organization and needed to onboard key high level people, that it was natural to bring in these aces."

Traditional soap production in
Nablus, Palestine

CHAPTER 3

The Dirt on Soap

Chicago, 2008

MUCH OF WHAT I KNOW ABOUT the history of soap I learned from Luis Spitz, one of the world's foremost experts on soap technology, both by talking to him in person and from the books he has written and edited.[1] I first met Luis in 2008; at the time, he was advising Dr. Bronner's on our move to bring the production of bar soap in-house—and so David, Kris, and I traveled to his Chicago home to learn more about how this mix of alkali and fat became such a universal consumer product.

"Home" does not give full credit to Luis's residence: it also houses a large private collection of "soap memorabilia," making it a veritable soap museum. Picture an open, atrium-style living room and a mezzanine filled with posters, postcards, boxes, and soap bars all narrating the story of soap—how it transformed from a smelly chunk of goo to a lifestyle product offering magic cleansing power.

A native of Hungary, Luis and his family were hidden in Nazi-occupied Budapest by a Christian neighbor and barely survived the Holocaust. Now in his mid-eighties, Luis is a wealth of knowledge on the history, technology, and the marketing of soap, and has advised the US soap industry since the 1960s.

Why does humanity need soap anyway? For millennia, water served as the main cleaning agent for most earthlings—jumps into lakes and rivers were the refreshing, or chilly, occasion. Food was rinsed and clothes were washed with water and a little bit of sand.

But water has its limitations. It removes water-soluble contaminants—sweat, urine, vegetable matter, and soil—reasonably well but not entirely. Water *really* fails at removing grease or dirt, ingredients that are hydrophobic—or as afraid of water as your cat. You can't just wash them off, since they don't dissolve in water.

And so, after figuring out how to control fire and forge metals, humanity developed one of its earliest consumer goods: soap.

As with fire, the discovery of soap was likely accidental and independently occurred in several places. A common myth goes like this: hunters love roasting animals over wood fires. Naturally, some fat would drip onto the ash in the process. After a few nights of barbecue, you'd find a paste in your fire pit that could be dissolved in water, brought to a meager foam, and then used to remove fatty dirt that was otherwise difficult to wash off.

And that, to this day, is the basic chemistry that produces natural soaps. If you want to make soap (a process called "saponification"), remember the early hunters. You'll need a fat and an alkali. First the fat. Virtually all molecules of any oil or fat are built from three fatty acids, connected by a glycerin backbone. These compounds are thus called "triglycerides." What's the difference between fats and oils? Chemically, none. Oils are generally liquid at room temperature, fats are solid—the difference in melting point (higher for fats, lower for oils) is caused by their fatty acid composition.

Then, the alkali. Sodium hydroxide produces hard—or bar—soaps, whereas potassium hydroxide is used to make soft and liquid soaps. Traditionally wood ash was a main source of potassium hydroxide. Today, both sodium and potassium hydroxide are produced through the electrolysis of a solution of sodium chloride—table salt—or of potassium chloride, mined from salt deposits.

Soap molecules have a unique property. One end loves water (is hydrophilic), whereas the other loves fat (is lipophilic or hydrophobic). If you whip up a foam from an aqueous solution of soap, the dissolved soap molecules penetrate the dirt film on a surface needing cleaning, turn oily substances into an emulsion, and thus pull them into the wash water. Water alone just cannot do that unless you apply it with high pressure and remove the dirt physically. Chemical compounds, such as soaps, that overcome the "surface tension" of greasy dirt films are called surfactants, or "surface active agents."[2]

Soap has been the proto-surfactant through much of human history, but there are many other natural, plant-based surfactants—for instance, those found in the ground-up pods of an acacia tree known as Shikakai in India, an agent traditionally used by women to wash their hair. (Dr. Bronner's uses it in our sugar soaps and hair rinse.)

Much like many of civilization's great achievements, the first documented use of soap-like products hails from Babylon around 2800 BC. From there, the concept spread, over the next three millennia, throughout Europe, Asia, and Africa. Germans and Gauls produced soap during the first centuries AD, and Arabs later developed castile soaps from olive oil, which lacked odors, both the off ones from animal fats or even the pleasant ones of fragrances. The area now called Syria was an early exporter of soap of fine quality, and in the West Bank city of Nablus, soap making had become a significant industry by the fourteenth century. Anyone who has recently checked soap labels in a home goods store will suspect that Provence, a region in the South of France, was another such center: soap makers there used olive oil and produced soda ash for hard soaps from saltwater-tolerant trees.

Why, then, did it take until the late 1700s for soap to become a widely available mass item, even though the idea "cleanliness is next to godliness" is ancient, promoted in Babylonian and Hebrew religious tracts?

For one, despite the apparent simplicity of the soap recipe, its two main ingredients were not readily available everywhere, certainly not in good quality and in large quantities. Animal fat—usually beef or mutton tallow and pork lard—was the predominant soap ingredient. The process of rendering this fat often stank, and so did the soap it produced.

The Mediterranean was blessed with olive oil as a feedstock, one key reason why much of the better-smelling soaps came from Syria. Arabs, in their conquest of Southern Europe, accelerated the dissemination process. Produced from olive oil, a strong alkaline salt, and the essential oil of laurel berries, the famous "Aleppo soap" became the model for the production of Marseille soap in France and castile soap in Spain. The latter became the synonym for soaps made exclusively from plant oils, such as Dr. Bronner's iconic liquid castile soap—no tallow or lard allowed.

Yet "Aleppo soap *sounds* nicer than it worked," Luis told me. While it smelled better than the alternatives, because of poor recipe control and reliance on olive oil, it didn't lather well, and contained high amounts of water.

It would take another few hundred years for soap to really take off.

SOAP GROWS UP

A profitable soap industry existed around London by the mid-1700s. But just like bathing, only rich people could pay for soap. No wonder people and cities reeked, and cleanliness was not of particularly high value among the general population—it was mostly unaffordable.

One key challenge to the widespread production and use of soap was the scarcity of the obligatory alkali. Filtering water through barrels of wood ash to produce soda or potash is a labor-intensive process with poor quality control.

Another less technical hurdle was that high-value consumer goods tend to attract monopolists and the tax office. The issuance of exclusive manufacturing licenses suppressed competition and created oligopolies whose members overcharged for their soaps. To add insult to injury, soap was heavily taxed.

All that changed in the late 1700s. First, in 1787, the French chemist and surgeon Nicolas Leblanc developed a process to produce alkaline soda from table salt—sodium chloride—and sulfuric acid. This boosted productivity, and new soap makers sprang up in England and especially the United States, where the emergence of a meatpacking industry also guaranteed soap makers an ample supply of fat.

The most famous example of the pioneers of "big soap," Procter & Gamble, was founded in Cincinnati in 1837 by the English candle maker William Procter and the Irish soap maker James Gamble. At the time, Cincinnati, known as "Porkopolis," was the largest meatpacking center in the United States, which gave P&G ready access to the animal by-products—lard and tallow—critical to the manufacture of soap and candles. Their predecessor William Colgate had set up a candle and soap production in New York City in 1806, followed by Colgate & Co.'s large soap plant in Jersey City, supplied by fat from a large hog yard.

But the great soap leap forward came only in the mid-1800s, when improved productivity met with growing demand for a product that not only cut back on odor and made your dresses look nicer but was also good for your health. When in the 1850s the Crimean War saw nine hundred thousand soldiers perish largely due to infectious diseases (typhus, typhoid, cholera, dysentery) rather than battlefield injuries, the British nurse Florence Nightingale and other volunteers sought to improve hospital conditions by prioritizing cleanliness of rooms, towels, and linens—using plenty of soap. These lessons were heeded during the American Civil War when Procter & Gamble, at that time a company of some one hundred employees, supplied soap to the Union Army.

In the early 1860s, after extensive research on fermentation, Louis Pasteur developed the germ theory of disease. He showed that removing germs may prevent infection—and soap was one readily available agent. The Solvay process, invented in 1861, then allowed industrial production of sodium hydroxide—a strong alkali and, to date, the key chemical in the production of hard or bar soaps.

At the same time, the supply of plant-based fats grew vastly. Notably, tropical colonies supplied coconut and palm oil, key and concentrated sources of lauric and oleic acids; in the United States, cottonseed oil became available as a by-product of cotton production—and soap was turning into a real consumer product. This kicked off a wave of sanitary improvements: with indoor bathrooms and bedroom washstands, bathing became more common—a status symbol, even.

THE HEILBRONNERS ENTER MODERN SOAP MAKING

In 1858, as soap production finally grew up, Emanuel Heilbronner Sr.—the grandfather of Emanuel Bronner—started his production of soap and candles in Laupheim in Southern Germany's Swabia region, just as Colgate, Procter, and Gamble had done in the United States in 1806 and 1837. Emanuel Sr. sensed the growing business potential of both products—and the small production he'd set up in the basement of his residence became a success and part of the first wave of "modern soap making" in Germany. His initial source of fat was beef tallow, as pork lard was not an option for a Jewish soap maker. Coconut and palm oils were added as they became available in the 1860s.

Across the pond, the US soap industry had begun to scale vastly with a proliferation of manufacturers and brands. Soon production capacity exceeded consumer demand, and industry leaders realized that one couldn't rely on wars or the slowly emerging desire for cleanliness to drive the market. Rather, the industry became, as is well documented in Luis Spitz's museum, one of the first to realize the potential of branding, packaging, and targeted messaging that we'd now call "lifestyle advertising."

Beginning in the 1880s, advertising budgets became a significant portion of the total cost of making and selling soaps and, by the 1920s, the sponsorship of radio programs by major soap companies became a widely known advertising tool—hence the term "soap opera."

In the late 1800s, the first liquid soaps had appeared in the United States. Made from blends of coconut, palm, and olive oil and saponified with potassium, rather than sodium hydroxide, liquid soaps made the cleaning of clothes, bathrooms, and floors much easier and swiftly found markets.

Their development strongly influenced the history of the Heilbronners. Around 1903, three of Emanuel Sr.'s sons—Sigmund, Berthold, and Karl—moved from Laupheim to Heilbronn, a city some 100 miles (160 km) north and likely the origin of the family, to start their own soap production.

Karl already had much practical experience manufacturing soap. He had visited the United States during adolescence, learned how to make liquid soap, and took the idea back home. The three brothers' Madaform Soap Factory (a play on the English "Made of Foam") would go on to specialize in the production of high-quality liquid castile soaps for high-flying customers, such as the bathrooms in Zeppelin airships, and low-flying end users in public restrooms.

They optimized the recipe to produce an ample and stable lather by varying the type and the composition of oils and fats used. That recipe also minimized the fundamental drawback to all castile soaps: they react with the high levels of calcium and magnesium ions in hard water, forming a scum called "calcium soaps" that deposits on clothes and bathroom walls.

It was that liquid soap that Berthold's son Emil Heilbronner, who later renamed himself Emanuel Bronner, would take with him to the United States and turn into Dr. Bronner's famous liquid castile soap.

ADVERTISING AND ACTIVISM

Advertising for soap boomed in Germany in the 1920s, too. Yet it was more modest than in the United States, and stiffer—more educational and product-related. The first soap opera on German radio was broadcast only in 1949, long after the United States.

While their soaps were embraced as the popular and affordable source of cleanliness and respectability, US soap companies hadn't rested on their laurel berries. By the early thirties, several had embraced a German technology to create the first synthetic surfactants—chemicals that cut grease more powerfully and worked better in hard water than soaps. DuPont and P&G launched the American detergent industry in 1932. Dreft, the first laundry detergent (a term for a surfactant or a mixture of surfactants with cleansing properties), appeared in 1933, followed in 1934 by Drene, the first detergent-based shampoo. Dove—the first bar soap made from synthetic detergents—appeared only in 1955.

As a result, natural soaps—roughly synonymous with castile soap—today are but a minor contender in the global surfactant market. Synthetic surfactants dominate the markets for laundry, household, personal care, and technical detergents. Many are petroleum-based, while others are derived from vegetable oils—mostly coconut, palm, and palm kernel oils—but are converted in complex chemical reactions to compounds such as SLS (sodium lauryl sulfate). For economies of scale these processes require large reactors. Depending on the product, the reaction requires high pressure or temperature and involves catalysts or solvents. You cannot run these at home—or even in a soap factory.

The potential risks caused by synthetic surfactants to your skin, body, and the environment are furiously debated. Some are skin irritants, while some are toxic to animals, ecosystems, and humans. They may be poorly biodegradable or cause foaming when discharged into rivers, and their surfactant properties may increase the diffusion of other environmental contaminants. Such effects vary widely with the chemistry of a particular surfactant.

For many applications, such as, say, cleaning greasy engines and transmissions, a synthetic surfactant will be your choice over castile soap. Naturally, Dr. Bronner's surfactant of choice is soap. Soap is simple in formulation and production—we can control its performance through the selection of the fats and oils used as ingredients, it's effective and agreeable with our skin, it can be made with minimal environmental impact—and soap is our tradition. (The only exception is our Sal Suds general purpose cleaner, which represents only a few percent of sales. Its main ingredient is plant-derived SLS.)

The period of gradual synthetization of detergents and replacement of soaps in many traditional markets coincided with Emanuel Bronner's formative years in the growing US soap industry. He worked for a successful soap and cologne maker in Milwaukee and later consulted for several other soap makers in Wisconsin.

As a young man in his mid-twenties, he enjoyed the relative freedom in the United States, with its prevailing "just give it a try" attitude, far away from his overbearing father. Yet he did not embrace the two powers of modernity that by then were driving his industry: ubiquitous over-the-top advertising in all media, and the drive toward technological progress and synthetic surfactants. Instead, he emphasized the necessity to stick to natural soap formulas and rely on word of mouth for discovery. Judging by his consistent refusal to advertise his Magic Soaps in the fifties and sixties, something must have turned him off when watching and listening to soap ads.

Emanuel ignored all the rules "Big Soap" had come to live by. He used virtually the same simple recipe for his liquid castile soap that Madaform had developed in Heilbronn in the early 1900s. And he applied highly nonconventional methods to sell his soaps, insisting on promoting a message of truth that inspired people to reflect, if not act, very much unlike the soapy-bubbly stuff attacking consumers from billboards and airwaves.

Emanuel's audience in the 1960s was the many members of an emerging counterculture who also looked for meaning and purpose in a world threatened by nuclear annihilation and the emptiness of the promises of consumerism. As they embraced his unifying activist message and the simplicity and versatility of his soaps, the latter became a staple of natural food stores, and he a frequent speaker at counterculture events.

All in all, Emanuel was so far behind the trends of his modern times that he ultimately came out way ahead!

So what's the secret behind the recipes for Emanuel's and his ancestors' natural soaps—which have changed little since he made the soap a cultural icon in the 1960s? That would determine where our quest for "clean raw materials" would eventually lead us.

His secret was a simple, science-based blend of ingredients.

The liquid soap is made from potassium hydroxide and a blend of coconut and olive oil. That mixture of the two main fatty acids—lauric from coconut and oleic from olive oil—makes the soap molecules more water-soluble, even at low water temperatures, and improves lathering. Saponified olive oil acts to moisturize the skin—one more feature to distinguish Dr. Bronner's from other liquid soaps. Finally, unlike most commercial soap makers, Dr. Bronner's did not skim off the glycerin yielded as a by-product of the saponification reaction, as glycerin acts as a moisturizer, too.

Our bar soap is made from a different oil blend, to balance lather stability and the hardness of the soap bar. Including saponified palm oil keeps the bar soap from rapidly softening and dissolving in the soap dish, a disadvantage of pure coconut oil soaps. Olive oil is added for the same moisturizing skin feel as with liquid soaps. Since Dr. Bronner's still does not have sufficient FTO coconut oil to feed our fast-growing soap production, we use some organic and fair trade palm kernel oil, or PKO, as their fatty acid composition and performance are very similar. (If you doubt that palm oil and palm kernel oil can be produced sustainably and fairly, read on.)

Fatty oils are the foundation for our soaps, but they're not the whole story. What distinguishes Dr. Bronner's from most other soaps, natural as well as synthetic, is a good, punchy shot of essential oils. Peppermint soaps are our bestselling flavor worldwide. Lavender and lavandin, citrus, eucalyptus, tea tree, and almond are our other traditional flavors. And we do offer fragrance-free liquid and bar "baby soaps," too.

One important change to the soap recipe was the addition of hemp oil in the late nineties. It made the lather smoother and increased moisturization of the skin. It also added a dose of symbolism and gave us a stake in hemp activism, though for soap stability we eventually limited the hemp oil content in liquid and bar soaps. Two more ingredients: jojoba oil as an emollient in the liquid soap, and tocopherol, derived from non-GMO sunflower oil, as a preservative.

Since 2007, Dr. Bronner's has added several new products to our liquid and bar soaps, so we now use a growing number of other agricultural ingredients in the recipes for our creams, lotions, toothpaste, hand sanitizers, and lip and body balms. They include avocado oil, beeswax, sugar, and ethanol—the most common alcohol, present in all alcoholic drinks and, in our case, made from sugar cane.

All of these products are made from mostly organic and fair agricultural ingredients and are based on very simple recipes.

It was the simplicity of the formulation of Dr. Bronner's products that attracted Lisa Bronner, Mike and David's sister, to become involved in the family business. While she'd spent time at her granddad's during summer vacation and had watched Trudy and Jim rescue Dr. Bronner's, Lisa hadn't been directly involved when her mom and brothers took over the company. But with her own growing family, she had faced the question of how to clean your house and everything that's in it.

The concept of using simple methods and products, as preached and practiced by Dr. Bronner's, appealed to Lisa, and she became an advocate of green cleaning. She proposed to her family to support the company's philosophy through a blog, *Going Green With a Bronner Mom*. It would reflect on Dr. Bronner's vision and offer hands-on advice on natural personal care and cleaning.

But just where do our raw materials in our products come from? Who grows and processes them, and how can we ensure that their production benefits the people and the land along the way? As I'll share in the next chapter, those were the questions the Bronners started asking themselves in 2003, and that prompted their shift to organic and fair trade ingredients.

Mike Bronner on balancing "soap and soul"

After he graduated from college, Mike Bronner wasn't sure what he wanted to do. What he *was* certain of was that he wanted to do something impactful—and his travels abroad helped him set his sights beyond the United States.

"One of the toughest things to witness is poverty in Ethiopia, where I studied during college," he told me. "You can be consumed by that because there's no way that I am in the position to solve that. It's like, the world is breaking. What difference can I make? It can overwhelm you."

Today, he gets to bring his passion for making a global impact by leading the expansion of Dr. Bronner's sales overseas. Talk to Mike and you'll be struck by his warmth and genuineness when discussing the importance of balancing "soap and soul"—in other words, matching the desire to do good in the world with a great product that customers love.

"You see so many companies who are either 'all product' or 'all soul' become imbalanced," he said. "A lot of companies may have the financial resources but they don't necessarily have the spirit, the mission, and the desire to give back and use their company for humanitarian ends. Then you have the people who want to change the world, but don't know how to set up proper margins and a proper balance sheet to get a business going."

Working hard to achieve that balance has helped Dr. Bronner's grow without taking on outside equity, thereby preserving the company's right to reinvest profits into environmental, social, and activist initiatives without the interference of shareholders who do not share its vision.

Mike also refers to "soap and soul" as a "very useful rubric" when it comes to his work setting up distribution partners worldwide. The goal is not just to sell the most soap, but to find "ambassadors of Dr. Bronner's spirit and soul."

Of course, which aspects of the Dr. Bronner's soul these ambassadors focus on will vary a bit, depending on each culture's values, needs, and shopping habits.

"We are very fortunate in America to be custodians of a legacy that goes back to 1948 when my grandfather first started making soap. He never advertised and was a pioneer of the natural products industry, and was finally able to succeed on word of mouth alone when the counterculture discovered his soaps twenty years later," he said. "That's amazing, but when we launch in new countries we have to be able to break through a little quicker!"

In Asia, Mike explains, customers are certainly drawn to the organic nature of the products—in other words, the "soap" side—whereas in Germany, the company is definitely leading with its "soul," the family history and the 5-to-1 executive salary pay cap. Recognizing the uniqueness of each market and the need to globalize not just the company's sales, but its philanthropy and activism, too, Dr. Bronner's launched its All-One International Initiative in 2019, with pilots in Germany and the UK, and expanded to ten additional markets in 2020. The program's goal is to ensure a minimum of 1 percent of sales is donated to local nonprofits advancing efforts for social justice, animal rights, and environmental sustainability in each market the company sells in.

Under Mike's leadership, sales in international markets have grown from less than 1 percent to as much as 20 percent of the company's total revenue. And like so many of us at Dr. Bronner's, his work has helped him connect more deeply with his personal goals and passions.

"When I was a teacher in Japan, it was my dream to come back and help bring our soaps to international markets," he said. "When I lived in Ethiopia, it was my dream to achieve ongoing structural improvement in people's lives. All the chapters of my life may seem a little episodic at first glance, but I think, as is the case in a truly regenerative, truly fair trade, truly organic company, everything connects."

Dr. Bronner's production team at the liquid
soap reactor during coronavirus pandemic

CHAPTER 4

How to Make Clean Soap

I N 2003, UNDER THE LEADERSHIP OF David, Mike, and Trudy Bronner, Dr. Bronner's had started its persistent growth in sales. Honoring Emanuel's vision, they had agreed that being profitable while treating their employees as family and supporting philanthropy and activism would continue to be the ultimate purpose of its production of soap. The team also included David's first wife and current director of the Bronner Family foundation, Kris Lin-Bronner, who helped shape the company's vision. Applying that vision to the company's operations naturally led them to the materials used in their soap. They wondered, *Where do our agricultural ingredients come from, and how does making them affect lives along the supply chain?*

To Emanuel Bronner, this had been an afterthought. At the time of his death in 1997, the plant-based oils one could buy from brokers had no verifiable redeeming ecological or social qualities—but there were also no alternatives. Exposure of farmworkers to pesticides was a growing concern in the United States and a cautious—in other words, organic—approach to production of our main raw materials (coconut, palm, olive, and mint oils) in developing countries seemed sensible.

As the Bronners pondered this issue, organic foods were emerging as a commercial chemical-free alternative to conventional foods. It was an obvious idea to shift the company's main agricultural raw materials, all of them also used in foods, to sources certified under the USDA's National Organic Program (NOP). Its rules for organic food had, after heated public debate, been finalized and published only in 2000.

In a nutshell, these rules require the use of certified organic ingredients if one wants to make an organic claim on the product label. Depending on its percentage content of organic ingredients, a finished multi-ingredient product may be labeled *"100 percent organic," "organic,"* or *"made with organic ingredients [specified ingredients]."* Organic farming famously prohibits the use of virtually all chemical fertilizers, pesticides, and herbicides. But that's not all: the postharvest processing of agricultural products is also limited to physical processes, such as heating, cooling, drying, and filtering, with minimal use of explicitly permitted process chemicals, such as the alkali materials used in the production of soaps.

Determined to shift to more ecological raw materials, in 2003 Dr. Bronner's started working with a brokerage specializing in the sourcing of organic ingredients. The leap in price was steep. Organic grades of our key ingredients typically cost 50 percent more than conventional ones. To avoid scaring consumers off with the significant rise in price all at once, the shift was done in two steps for different bottle sizes.

Unfortunately, NOP decided to exclusively regulate organic foods and abdicated its responsibility to regulate "organic personal care" products. In fact, Dr. Bronner's even had to file a complaint with USDA in 2005 for the right to use NOP language and seals on its soaps. This regulatory vacuum allowed opportunistic brands to hijack the term "organic" and use it on personal care products that contained little to no organic ingredients.

By 2003, David saw signs of rampant consumer deception soon to come. Notorious examples included body washes using synthetic cleansers and moisturizers made without organic agricultural material as main ingredients, while adding "organic floral water" or "hydrolate"—the by-product of the distillation or extraction of herbs. These products would thus contain minimum concentrations of organic plant-based matter but take credit as if it were all organic—in other words, as if they were using "organic water."

That part of the story ended in 2008 when Dr. Bronner's sued several offending competitors for falsely advertising their products as organic. The large natural products retailer Whole Foods stepped in and gave the offending companies an ultimatum: to clean up their act within twelve months or risk losing their place on the shelves. An early sideshow in our battle for meaningful organic standards—albeit an important one.

Back in 2004, the Bronners were more concerned about maximizing the use of certified organic ingredients in a meaningful way. It didn't take them long to realize that "buying organic" gave no insight into the social conditions of the farmers who grew the crops, their farmworkers, and the production workers who turned them into oils. Our organic brokers bought them from large suppliers in the tropics; for some materials we had two or three middlemen between us and the farmers—not very transparent.

One day, during a battle with competitors on organic integrity, someone asked David, "How do you know you don't have kids picking your organic coconuts?"

He realized: we need to know.

Because neither the NOP nor EU organic standards included any social requirements (their rules instead focused on fertilizers, pesticides, and herbicides), Dr. Bronner's decided not to make claims on social conditions in their supply chain unless they were independently verified by a credible and consumer-facing third-party certification system. Ideally, such certification would provide transparency on the origin of our raw materials—all the way to the farm.

The Bronners began asking themselves: Do the farmers who

grow the nuts for our coconut oil, the palm fruits, and olives make a profit? Do workers in the oil mill earn at least the mandated minimum, preferably a living wage? Are they treated with respect, and are working conditions safe? Does the production of oils for export benefit farmers' and workers' communities?

David had researched social certifications and expected that *fair trade* certification of tropical produce would make social conditions transparent. He also hoped that, by eliminating middlemen, one could pay farmers and workers higher prices and wages and still avoid prohibitive increases in the cost of raw materials.

There already were corporate role models to copy: David was inspired by Guayakí, which responsibly sourced the raw materials for its Yerba Mate teas in the South American rainforest; and the Equal Exchange cooperative, a leader of the US fair trade movement. Likewise, several German companies had engaged in their agricultural supply chains and made them more ecological and fairer. They included Rapunzel, Germany's oldest and largest organic brand, which purchased organic materials exclusively, often from co-ops in Latin America; there was GEPA, Germany's largest fair trade organization; and there were Weleda and Dr. Hauschka, which produced high-end natural personal care products, using some organic raw materials bought from groups of small farmers.

Ever since they started buying organic main ingredients, the Bronners at least knew what country they came from: coconut and oil palms produce fruits only in the tropics, countries such as the Philippines, Indonesia, Sri Lanka, and parts of Africa. Olive oil grows in more moderate climates with a heavy stronghold in the Mediterranean. Mint oils largely hail from northern India.

But they wanted to get closer and build stronger relationships with the people growing and processing our ingredients. Luckily, we had a relatively simple family recipe to work from. The pie chart in Figure 1 illustrates total annual consumption and relative shares of our major ingredients: coconut (and palm kernel), palm, olive, and mint oils account for some 90 percent by weight of the agricultural raw materials used in all our products.

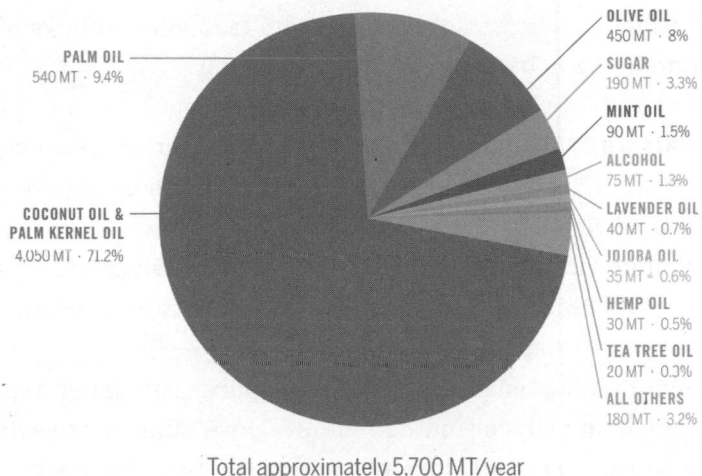

DR. BRONNER'S USE OF AGRICULTURAL RAW MATERIALS
In metric tons per year (2019)

OLIVE OIL
450 MT · 8%

SUGAR
190 MT · 3.3%

MINT OIL
90 MT · 1.5%

ALCOHOL
75 MT · 1.3%

LAVENDER OIL
40 MT · 0.7%

JOJOBA OIL
35 MT · 0.6%

HEMP OIL
30 MT · 0.5%

TEA TREE OIL
20 MT · 0.3%

ALL OTHERS
180 MT · 3.2%

PALM OIL
540 MT · 9.4%

COCONUT OIL &
PALM KERNEL OIL
4,050 MT · 71.2%

Total approximately 5,700 MT/year

Figure 1. Dr. Bronner's annual use of agricultural materials

This chart looks wildly different from the agricultural ingredients profile of most other natural food and personal care companies. They may use *hundreds of* raw materials, most in small percentages. Such a structure would certainly complicate a wholesale shift to using FTO ingredients.

In comparison, our predominance of just four main ingredients gave us focus and promised a swifter shift to FTO supply chains. To be sure, partnering with even a handful of organic and fair trade projects in several remote areas would still be a challenge.

FAIR TRADE STANDARDS AND CERTIFICATION

How did we approach the fair trade certification of our ingredients? Initially, by trial and error. In 2005, there was just one credible program for the fair trade certification of agricultural ingredients or products: that of the Fairtrade Labeling Organizations (FLO), known today as Fairtrade International. Formed in 1997, this grassroots organization had since adopted rules, minimum prices, and inspection and certification protocols for the fair exchange of a few globally traded agricultural commodities between farmers and buyers. The FLO approach was based on four major tenets:

1. Fair trade must build direct long-term business relationships between farmers in the Global South and their buyers in the Global North.
2. A global minimum price must be set for these commodities to be paid to farmers in case of a price crash and to ensure that they can produce profitably.
3. A fair trade premium is added to the purchasing price and used democratically to fund community development projects.
4. Fair trade can only take place between farmers organized in democratically run cooperatives and their buyers.

Back in 2005, FLO had promulgated rules for just a few key commodities grown in the tropics and highly relevant to Western consumers: coffee, tea, sugar, and cocoa. FLO had also set up, in 2003, FLOCERT as an independently governed subsidiary that inspected and certified farming projects.

When first meeting with FLO, headquartered in Bonn, Germany, and their US licensee Transfair International, in Oakland, California, our question was simple: "Can FLO certify our main ingredients—coconut, palm, olive, and mint oils?"

The answer was straight and slightly arrogant: "Come back in 2010. By then, FLO may adopt global minimum prices and standards for these ingredients; or maybe not."

We were taken aback by FLO's unwillingness to look at the commitment by a credible company as a great opportunity to expand the scope of fair trade beyond a few commodities, to make fair trade a truly global system. We sure were not willing to wait until 2010!

Fortunately, there were other brands looking to "go fair trade" with nontraditional products. Like Dr. Bronner's, they found that

FLO's narrow approach limited their vision of "fair trading everything."

Sensing the demand for universally applicable and stringent standards, several visionary organic certifiers in Europe developed alternative fair trade standards without FLO's shortcomings. One such example was the Fair for Life (FFL) standard initiated by the respected Swiss organic certifier IMO (Institute for Market Ecology).

I had first found IMO through an internet search for organic certification options in Sri Lanka. There, I discovered a Mr. Rajasingham, nicknamed Raj. A freelance inspector for both IMO and FLOCERT, Raj would become our first organic and fair trade inspector in Sri Lanka—and, later, an ally and friend. He knew FLO's weaknesses firsthand, but also gave us a dose of realism about implementing a new standard such as FFL. He cautioned that inspectors would always take a while to become familiar with a new standard, and that IMO would need to invest in proper training of new FFL inspectors.

I checked IMO's credentials and found them highly compatible with our philosophy—founded by a group of visionaries, including the late Rainer Bächi, they were more interested in promoting fair and sustainable agriculture than just in running a certification business.

Serendipity struck again in early 2006 and sent Florentine Meinshausen, IMO's program manager for FFL, and her family for a few months to Berkeley. Over coffees, Florentine and I discussed provisions that could make the envisioned standard more practical—notably during the first years of a certified project. This was an excellent opportunity for me to watch the development of a standard firsthand and understand its provisions in light of its vision of fair trade. (Dr. Bronner's has, as a member of the Fair for Life review committee, since continued to provide input to the periodic revisions of the FFL standard.)

Fair for Life was modeled after FLO's standards in all substantive requirements, with several major differences, some of which FLO has since improved upon:

1. Rather than setting a global minimum price for each commodity, certifiers would assess cost of local production and whether market prices paid to project farmers would allow them to be profitable. If not, buyers would have to pay a floor price guaranteeing profitability.
2. Project operators, such as our sister companies and partners, can buy from individual farmers or informal farmers associations—not just from formal cooperatives, which are much less common in Africa and Asia, compared to Latin America.
3. Project operators must ensure the fair compensation and safe working conditions of farmworkers *and* production workers, to be verified during inspections, an initial weak spot in the FLO certification.
4. To carry the FFL logo, a product had to meet an ambitious content requirement: preferably over 70 percent of all agricultural ingredients, excluding water, had to be fair trade.

Notably, FFL also certifies entire *companies or brands* as "fair"—not just individual products. Thus, Dr. Bronner's entire operations are audited annually for our commitment to be a "fair employer" and responsible "corporate citizen" and to grow the share of fair trade raw materials in our products. In contrast, FLO's product certification allows large consumer goods companies to offer a single FLO-certified product in a sea of utterly conventional non–fair trade products, signaling to consumers that they are "not so bad"—a typical strategy called "fair washing."

PICKING UP FAIR SPEED

In 2006, after we had chosen Fair for Life as our route to fair trade certification, we began to gather speed at all our first four FTO projects, a journey I'll share in the chapters to come.

Looking back, Dr. Bronner's close involvement in by now some ten FFL-certified projects has given us a unique perspective on fair trade. Our most important lesson: do not bother with FFL certification unless you are serious about building an "ethical" supply chain. Some requirements seem onerous or bureaucratic, and project operators may complain. Ultimately, though, FFL wants to ensure that you operate a responsible project that considers the needs of all stakeholders in the chain. We consider the standard a baseline upon which one can improve by carefully adding benefits, if they make economic and social sense.

To us, fair trade was never primarily about complying with FFL standards, which can be a challenge during the first two years of a project. It's about creating a lively, site-specific system that engages people and provides tangible benefits to everyone in our supply chain, including their land and communities. We view and welcome the annual FFL inspections as a checkup, to ensure that our management on the ground does not overlook critical aspects in our ever-expanding projects.

We have also taken fair trade much beyond the narrow issue of using certified ingredients. As David commonly does when engaging in a new area, we used our involvement in fair trade to tackle other burning fair trade issues. In 2008, we joined forces with Dana Geffner and her NGO Fair World Project, a fair trade watchdog and network builder across regions, products, and certifications. Since no legal guidelines exist for fair trade claims in the United States and almost all of Europe, one must evaluate and scrutinize not only the language but also the implementation practice on the ground of the now almost ten available fair trade standards.

And fair trade isn't just for tropical operations. Michael Milam, our COO, reminds me occasionally that Fair for Life also certifies brands, not just products. Thus, the question "What is fair in the US workplace?" is on his agenda a lot, more in the interest of being an empathetic and supportive manager than for compliance reasons.

In addition to "fair" you will also encounter the term "regenerative" or "regenerative organic" throughout this book. The term, which first started gaining wider traction in the United States around 2014, represents the explicit focus on improving soil health in agriculture. It has since become the intent and reality of Dr. Bronner's own and partner projects.

Regenerative agriculture loosely refers to the growing of field and tree crops and the grazing of animals in a way that increases the biodiversity of species while enriching the soil with soil organic matter (SOM), humus, or organic carbon—these terms being used synonymously. Increasing SOM improves soil fertility and moisture-holding capacity, productivity, and resilience to increasingly frequent catastrophic weather events—notably droughts and deluges.

And since all SOM is made by plants, via photosynthesis from atmospheric carbon dioxide (CO_2) and sunlight as the source of energy, any increase in soil carbon or SOM concurrently reduces excessive levels of atmospheric CO_2—the most important greenhouse gas.

Yes, that means what you think it does. This process—known as sequestration of atmospheric carbon—has the miraculous-seeming potential to mitigate climate change. (You will hear all about the challenges we encountered when taking this miracle to the field.)

While the planet's accelerating shift to renewable energy will slow down greenhouse gas emissions, it will not *reduce* atmospheric CO_2 levels. For that, we have to put the carbon back into plants and soil, notably long-lived trees and their dense root systems. Regenerative agriculture and agroforestry can do just that—and only needs sunlight as its source of energy, atmospheric CO_2 as its source of carbon, and a living, fertile soil to host it all.

To promote the concept and to ensure that the term "regenerative agriculture" was used truthfully, in 2017 an alliance of farmers, progressive brands, and experts in soil health, animal welfare, and social fairness formed the Regenerative Organic Alliance (ROA). Dr. Bronner's, Patagonia, and the Rodale Institute (the United States' most respected practical organic research institute, located in rural Pennsylvania) were founding members.

The ROA helped create the Regenerative Organic Certification (ROC) system, a standard that rewards and certifies organic farming projects for meeting high standards of soil health, social fairness, and pasture-based animal welfare criteria. Released in 2019, that certification has been awarded to a growing list of agricultural projects that meet its strict and far-reaching requirements.

In late 2019, our projects in Sri Lanka, Ghana, and India successfully passed ROC pilot inspections, becoming the first regenerative "smallholder" projects worldwide. The definition of a smallholder will vary with country and product. As a general rule of thumb: for field crops, anything less than 5 acres (or 2 ha; 1 hectare equals approximately 2.5 acres) is considered "small," compared with the farms or plantations that are hundreds or even thousands of acres in size that are common in North America, Europe, Asia, and South America.

Working with and buying from smallholders has been one key pillar of Dr. Bronner's shift to regenerative raw materials. Why bother? Because most of the world's more than 570 million farms are small and family run. Small farms of less than 2 hectares make up about 10 percent of the world's agricultural land. Family farms, including larger ones, account for 75 percent.[1]

Farmers are entrepreneurs who have a chance to shape their own fate and that of their families. Most people worldwide will prefer such entrepreneurial life, however hard and unpredictable, over the lot of a farmworker—if one can make a decent living. By helping to improve soil quality, fertility, profitability, working conditions, and sustainability of small farms, we have the potential to reach some 30 percent of the global population—and affect global impacts of agriculture. Many smallholders need technical support and economic incentives to expand standing in their communities, become better stewards of their land, increase its carbon stock, and thus help counter global climate change.

My excursions into the world of soap making and fair trade certifications will have explained Dr. Bronner's approach—what raw materials we prioritized and what certifications we choose. Now it's time to set off on the journey to our organic and fair trade projects. In the next chapter, let's start with Serendipol in Sri Lanka.

Michael Milam on bringing fair trade principles to the modern office

Not long after our chief operating officer Michael Milam traveled to Sri Lanka to visit our first FTO coconut operations, he discovered Matthew Crawford's book *Shop Class as Soulcraft*.

"It was written by this political science major [who] worked at a DC think tank and just was about to pull his skin off."

Crawford left the job after five months to open a motorcycle shop in Richmond, Virginia. His experience informed the book, which argued that, unlike the trades that have objective standards, most modern office work lacks those standards. Organizations are so complex that no one really knows what they're working for.

With the insights of that book and others in mind, Michael began to look at operations at our Vista headquarters through that lens.

"In parallel to developing our own fair trade supplies abroad, I've become very concerned for the last couple of years about what fair trade looks like for the modern office worker in the US," he explained. "I think they are often full of angst and uncertainty—partially because people don't get real feedback on how they're doing. Getting feedback from your boss or coworkers, per Crawford, is often a popularity contest. People don't know how they're really doing or if they're contributing to the team's or the company's goals and vision. . . . Most people as kids didn't want to grow up to be milquetoasts or of dubious value; they want to have an impact, to be an active part of something meaningful."

When Michael began asking himself "How do you apply fair trade principles in an office environment?" he realized that it's crucial to create a culture where people feel psychological safety. They must know more or less what's expected of them and that they won't be randomly rebuked for claiming a personal life.

"We rent space in people's heads all the time," he said. "And employees tend to be bit players in their workplace play. But when they clock out, they need to be the star of their own show. My report cannot think about me during the weekend. . . . And so, I don't text, call, or email them. I don't expect that they do work. And I expect them not to do it to their reports either. . . . In our Operations team we expect of each other that we unplug. If you still can't, that's on you."

Michael has worked hard to internalize fair trade principles into a Western operations environment and apply them to everyone he works with. It's culture building. "It's not about safety, it's not all working conditions and things like that—but it's about people feeling valued. Like they're worth more than just the salary that they get, you know?"

Personal experience shows that Michael's approach is effective. Since my team, known as "Special Operations," in effect supplies all our fair trade ingredients, I frequently meet, work, and chat with Michael's Operations team—about volumes, delivery schedules, product quality, financing. What amazes me is that his Operations staff is hugely productive, if measured by output and value per staff involved. They produce and package growing volumes of some two hundred products; they constantly respond to changes in demand, specials required by international distributors, bottlenecks in raw material supplies, and, more recently, a pandemic that doubled demand for soap and hand sanitizers virtually overnight.

Yet when I watch the flow of the operation from the upstairs conference room or meet with Ops staff, one does not sense stress or chaos. Rather, there's a constructive attitude to "challenges"— the atmosphere is one of calm, goal orientation, and mutual respect. There's also plenty of room for Michael's notorious dry puns and jokes, even when discussing solutions to the minor disaster at hand. Being valued, feeling secure, and part of a larger show is clearly good for working atmosphere, shop morale, and productivity.

Crown of a coconut tree

CHAPTER 5

Serendipity in Sri Lanka

Negombo, Sri Lanka, November 2005

I N NOVEMBER 2005, I STOOD WITH Bernd and Gordon, whom you met in chapter 1, in a large, dimly lit shed watching some ten workers producing copra oil, the kind of coconut oil Dr. Bronner's used in our soaps. The workers first unloaded bags full of the dried, darkish pieces of coconut kernel—known as copra, some showing unappetizing signs of mold—then carried it to an expeller press; the oil dripped into a greasy tank and the defatted seed cake was shoveled away.

This was the first time I saw copra oil made—or any coconut oil, for that matter. The mill, located near the city of Negombo on the country's west coast, had an atmosphere of early industrial revolution about it, and I could not see how this process would qualify for production under "fair conditions."

I knew firsthand—or by mouth—that in Sri Lanka some restaurants used that darkish copra oil, unpleasant-tasting to Sri Lankans as well as me. I had also tasted the pleasurable opposite of a coconut oil made using a different process. In 2002, John Roulac of Nutiva had first introduced me to its counterpart, virgin coconut oil—or VCO—with its mild coconutty aroma. I was an immediate convert to this novel coconut product.

To be sure, the copra oil Dr. Bronner's had traditionally used in our soaps had a very light color and was bland and odorless. For that, it had been refined, bleached, and deodorized (RBD), as is virtually all coconut oil. Yet when David and I discussed plans for our own mill in Sri Lanka, we concluded that it would make sense to cooperate with other brands who wanted organic and fair VCO. They would take the better quality of our VCO production, Dr. Bronner's would use the lower-quality cosmetics grade for our soaps, and the resulting scaling and efficiency would benefit all. Because of our hemp ties with Nutiva and because John shared David's vision of an organic planet, Nutiva was an obvious candidate, and John was interested in partnering.

After our peek at copra oil production, Bernd, Gordon, and I went next door, where the coconut cooperative had built a mill that produced grated or desiccated coconut (DC)—the coconut flakes used in macaroons and many other confectionery items. Prominently featured were several dryers that turned the wet, ground up kernel into delicious DC—but some of the equipment was rather ancient.

The DC plant hadn't been run in a year, but Asoka, the president of the co-op, explained the process: after removing the hard outer coconut shell and thin brown skin, or parings, the white ball-shaped kernel was ground and the small flakes dried in hot air, rather than in smoke or by the roadside—as was done with copra. Speedy air-drying right after deshelling the coconuts maintained the delicate flavor and avoided mold infection.

"Why don't you just take the DC from the dryers and press it into VCO?" Bernd asked. "You already have the first process step right here, and it looks like it may taste just right."

I hadn't thought about how VCO was made, and Nutiva didn't know either. There was much VCO mystique at that time—and suppliers were tightlipped. Some brands even offered extra virgin coconut oil, but no one I asked could tell me the difference from "just virgin."

Just how was VCO made, and how was the production different from making the copra oil we'd just observed?

I called my friend Werner Baensch, a German food technologist whose company Ölmühle Solling successfully developed and marketed products from organic oils—including VCO and hemp seed oil. When I told him about Bernd's idea, he said, "Well, that's actually the process virtually all producers in the Philippines use." You dry the shredded, oil-rich coconut kernel into desiccated coconut and then squeeze out the oil in an expeller press.

Now I knew for sure!

Werner also set me straight on two other questions posed by VCO labels. Some enthusiastic brands called their dry-process VCO "raw" because the oil was not refined and supposedly "cold pressed." Yet the common definition of a "raw food" is that it wasn't heated to above 118° F (48° C) anywhere in the process. Coconut kernel exceeds that temperature in the dryer, where it typically reaches 212° F (100° C) for some fifteen minutes; definitely too hot for raw! And how about brands that call their VCO "extra virgin"—a term used for the highest grade of olive oil? In fact, there is no definition of "extra virgin coconut oil"—no standard to differentiate it from VCO—and the production process is exactly the same. A good example of label confusion.

Werner also told me about several wet process alternatives for VCO. They produce a nice buttery oil—but it is often unstable and develops off-flavors. He recommended using the dry route.

By the end of this trip to Sri Lanka, we were clear on how to produce VCO.

BUILDING A TEAM

After David and I had decided in July 2005 to explore project options in Sri Lanka, the key question became: Who will be our partners, and who'll be on the team? My cooperation with Gordon and Sonali on SecondAid in early 2005 had convinced me: if I ever do anything commercial in Sri Lanka, I'd want to do it with the two of them. Gordon knew the coconut industry inside out. He and Sonali were respected professionals; they had great networks, were direct, and both had a good sense of humor. To my great joy, when I asked them, both agreed on the spot.

In hindsight, the idea of a medium-sized, family-owned US company going into a foreign country and setting up a vertically integrated, commercial-scale coconut oil farming and processing company—all without any experience in the business and its regulatory framework—seems megalomaniacal! It was, and that's what it took. It certainly rendered the early days of Serendipol exciting times—often more exciting than we cared for.

I believe our story is typical for any team embarking on a project in an area that's new to them. After a few months of project planning, it started feeling less exotic and rather normal to encounter problems, chew on them, and eventually solve them. To be sure, none of us had ever worked in any capacity with three crucial pillars of the project: the organic and fair trade certification of more than a thousand smallholder coconut farmers; the design and construction of a coconut oil factory for food-grade VCO; the building and operation of a meaningful fair trade community system.

In fact, we had no clear idea how to implement fair trade along a complex supply chain—from field to factory to port. Yet we were confident that with a little help from our friends—and Dr. Bronner's— we could do it.

And Gordon swiftly went into action. He soon met Asoka, the president of the oldest Sri Lankan coconut cooperative, or co-op, whose mill I described earlier in the chapter. The co-op had been founded by his father and originally had helped farmers organize sales of coconuts to users in Colombo, thus bypassing collectors.

Since cooperatives are the pillars of many fair trade projects in Latin America, we thought joining forces with the co-op would guarantee a built-in fair trade structure and benefit supplying farmers.

We were prepared to invest; we liked Asoka's old gentleman style and began talks about cooperation and a joint venture.

At the same time, Mr. Rajasingham, or Raj—the freelance inspector we met in chapter 4—introduced us to the world of international organic certification. We needed an organic certifier with presence in Sri Lanka, so we checked out available options, and IMO and Raj came out on top.

Not long after our team first visited Asoka's mill and co-op in Negombo, Raj joined us there to train its staff and board on how to operate an internal control system (ICS), the core piece of any group certification for organic smallholder farmers. This gave the lay audience an inspiring insight into the principles and practice of organic farming and the required bureaucracy and documentation required for certification. He was honest about the potential pitfalls and volunteered his time to us while providing value.

The coop's staff now was ready to start recruiting farmers for organic conversion. To minimize the conversion period, we recruited only farmers who had not used farming inputs prohibited under organic rules—chemical fertilizers, pesticides, and herbicides—in the last three years and could provide credible evidence.

This was not difficult in Sri Lanka since the Coconut Cultivation Board distributed subsidized fertilizer and documented it. Furthermore, very few farmers bothered to use pesticides or herbicides— and the latter would have easily been detected during internal inspections.

Over time we became savvier with our selection criteria for supplying farmers. As we would discover, the past nonuse of agrochemicals should not be the only criterion for recruitment, as it does not mean that farmers are "organically minded." Rather, it often indicates that their farms are "organic by neglect," as Raj likes to joke.

One easily recognizes such neglected coconut farms, or estates, as Sri Lankans call them, typically 10 to 20 acres (4 to 8 ha) in size. Weeds grow high, and trees are tall and visibly senile, with no sign of recently planted palms. Leaves may be yellow, indicating a deficiency or imbalance in the supply of minerals, and nut bunches contain few small nuts. There is no visible mulching—no manure and compost around the trees.

We've since learned to also watch out for degraded land, absent landowners and management, small fields of less than 2 acres (~1 ha), and plots surrounded by rice fields sprayed with pesticide: all signs that farmers are either not engaged or that farms are at risk of exposure to "pesticide drift."

In all our projects, farmers initially had little to no awareness of organic agriculture as an opportunity to improve land and income. So when Raj suggested that "going organic" provides just that opportunity, by helping farmers improve soil and tree health, Gordon, Sonali, and I jumped at it.

Raj's take, later confirmed by many practitioners: unless you work with your farmers to improve quality and fertility of their land, you shouldn't call the project "organic." We took Raj's lesson to heart and to all our projects. In Sri Lanka, this involved the distribution of subsidized compost, nudging farmers to mulch trees with leaves and branches, and replanting senile trees. And we were rather proud when, around 2014, the concept of "regenerative organic agriculture" became popular in the United States. One of its tenets: "Organic isn't just about not using chemicals, it's about improving soil health."

We were already ahead of the regenerative game!

Back in 2006, Regenerative Organic Certification was still over a decade away, but we were laying the groundwork. While recruiting farmers, we simultaneously planned our factory. I reached out to a good friend, Markus Gröber, who had built and run an organic farm and oil mill in southwestern France since the early nineties. He had no experience with coconuts—but plenty with sunflowers. He also knew how to design, build, and fix almost anything and, like many friends of my generation, had fond memories of earlier visits to the tropics. He immediately jumped at the idea of collaborating on a real project and taking his experience to Sri Lanka.

In early 2006, after screening options for expeller presses, silos, and elevators for the raw materials, Markus joined us in Sri Lanka. At the same time, serendipity brought another old friend to the project. Norbert Wansleben and I had been best friends off and on since preschool in our hometown of Cologne. We had made our first two-month trip east to Greece and Turkey in my old VW Bug in 1973, permanently shaping our perspective on wealth, poverty, and happiness.

We'd lost contact in the mid-eighties, reconnected in 2005, and found we still had lots in common. When I told Norbert of our plans in Sri Lanka, he asked, "Can I join?" I had no budget for a successful architect, but Norbert offered to do the work for travel expenses. How could I refuse? He and his wife, Ulli, became, over the next fifteen years, our advisers on how to design and build commercial edifices that connect to local architectural traditions, use common building materials, and are functional and aesthetically pleasing.

Working with personal friends on "real projects that matter" and under nonstandard conditions has added new dimensions and meaning to our relationships. It surely also caused occasional friction, as you need to find the right language to argue, especially when your friends are working for little pay. But it's been very much worth it, and we couldn't have completed Serendipol without the help from competent and motivated friends.

As important has been working with Christel, my "chief consultant" who, as a visual artist, sees things I don't and then some. We had always found each other's work fascinating and collaborated on projects, often involving travel. A luxury we could afford since we do not have children and do not separate our personal and working lives.

During our time in Sri Lanka, it was Christel who would also take note of things like the way the air would change right before rain would come, or the plop of a jackfruit falling from a tree and hitting the ground. We took frequent hikes with the wild yellow dogs that quickly became friends, and as we walked, new ideas for projects would emerge, we'd ponder how to handle the idiosyncrasies of collaborators, and we'd sometimes vent to each other—but not too often.

Eventually, it was time for David to visit Sri Lanka and see firsthand. I'd presented the project concept to his family and their trusted financial adviser Ken Hugins in late 2005. From my days in environmental consulting I was used to meetings with company directors. This meeting felt different, more personal, more visionary, with targeted no-nonsense financial questioning from Ken. David's and my ideas convinced the Bronners, and they gave their approval to continue.

David arrived in February 2006, got a solid sense of the landscape, the team, the challenges ahead of us. He was encouraged, even excited. After all, it is quite an adventure for a family company to start its first foreign company—and one with a high impact.

It was one evening over beer during that trip that we finally came up with the name for the project—and the Sri Lankan sister company of Dr. Bronner's that needed incorporating as project holder: Serendipol.

I knew *Serendib* as the old Arab and Persian name for Sri Lanka. That word is also the root for the word "serendipity"—a concept that I had come to cherish, as most major developments in my life had a strong dose of serendipity to them. My finding Gordon and Sonali was a good example. Add the word for coconut in Singhalese, the main language in Sri Lanka, and "Serendipol" was born. We liked this name so much that it became the naming model for all our projects: Serendipalm, SerendiKenya, Serendimenthe, SerendiCoco Samoa . . .

The spring of 2006 then got busy as Norbert and Markus coordinated architecture and processing design for conversion of the coop's DC mill into a VCO mill. Meanwhile, Gordon, who had discovered the co-op in the first place, began to express growing frustration about their lack of business acumen.

We could not come to an agreement on the terms of cooperation, and the level of interference by the board did not bode well for business partners in such an innovative project. We also were beginning to realize that they did not engage much with their farmer members.

One day in August 2006, Gordon called me in Berkeley and said, "I broke up with the co-op."

Apparently, the board had made unreasonable requests, there was shouting, and Gordon rose to the occasion and walked out. I wasn't surprised, but still shocked, as our entire fair trade concept had relied on partnering with a "real" co-op.

To be sure, this co-op wasn't so real—but what to do now? Reconsider the whole project? What were our alternatives? This was the first of many situations in my Serendi career where a disaster became an opportunity. By then we knew what we needed: an idling DC mill with functional equipment to get started and enough land for expansion. We had to hire field officers, recruit farmers, convert to and certify them organic; meanwhile, Markus and Norbert would have to adapt their architecture and process design to a new building and start buying equipment and prepare for construction.

We had selected Fair for Life as our fair trade standard. We were certain that creating a private sector company was likely the best way to run a vertically integrated organic and fair trade coconut project with eventually over 1,200 farmers, a sizeable and modern production with some 300 staff, and a meaningful community development program. Partnering with a noncommitted co-op with poor management and no experience producing VCO now seemed like a certain route to trouble—without any benefits.

Around this time, Gordon had engaged two new team members: Milton Fernando, an experienced and versatile engineer to oversee building construction and installation of equipment, and Dhanoj Meegahapola, a young entrepreneur who knew the coconut triangle—the center of Sri Lankan coconut production—and its inhabitants like the back of his hand.

We all visited four candidate DC mills and swiftly found our favorite site, a rundown DC mill in a village near the town of Kuliyapitiya, owned by Mr. Yoganathan, a Tamil businessman who was ready to retire. While we had received an alternative offer from a large producer of DC to form a joint venture for the production of VCO, by then we preferred the idea of controlling our own destiny without interference by external partners, companies, or co-ops.

The Bronners approved our new project concept in September 2006. We first leased and later bought the 5-acre (2 ha) piece of land, then incorporated Serendipol Pvt. Ltd. We tendered the construction of the main production and storage buildings, based on Norbert and Ulli's architecture, integrating some elements of the existing operation, and selected Lal Fernando, an inspired and reliable general contractor with a well-managed team of site managers and workers.

Yet it took two months to come to an agreement with "Yoga," the site's owner. He thriftily avoided review of our lease agreement by a lawyer and rather had his entire family weigh in. Sonali, who managed the contractual work, was often close to madness. We finally signed version 8 of the contract, and by February 2007, we started construction.

LIFE IN SRI LANKA

Sri Lanka was the first tropical country where I spent months on end, sometimes with Christel or friends, sometimes by myself. From the beginning, we knew we needed our own house, as no hotels were to be found within driving distance. Thus, starting in February 2007, we rented a roomy 1930s bungalow, in a village, to accommodate "working visitors" and me. It fit up to eight people, with a large kitchen, one tiny bathroom, and an extended veranda. I settled into my commuting routine and enjoyed driving my van, usually filled with visitors eager to go to work, through the rice paddies and coconut groves of Sri Lanka's northwestern province.

Our local partners thought we'd need a house maid—but we didn't. I could not imagine having a person doing chores in the kitchen and house, telling them what to do, especially without speaking their language. Also, it was much more interesting to shop in local markets and small stores—supermarkets barely existed in the area before 2011—with an amazing supply of vegetables and fruits. A treat was the Sunday market in the nearby village of Yakvila, with some hundred stalls offering everything from fruits, veggies, lentils, and dried fish to household appliances to Wades, crunchy spicy lentil dumplings. Christel figured out swiftly how to incorporate savory curries and vegetable dishes, prepared on our two-flame camping stove, into the menu. Our favorite discoveries were jackfruit, bitter gourd, and dal curries.

On Poya days, the Buddhist celebration of the full moon, we'd sometimes go to the local temples, quietly chat, and watch the candlelit scenery. Sometimes team members brought their families to Sri Lanka for joint tours and evening parties. Later, members of the Dr. Bronners team would visit. We'd go on to take the footage for the video *Journey to Serendipol*, to give our sales and marketing staff a close-up view of the diversity of our projects.

The evergreen lushness of the country and the simple hamlets endeared me to Sri Lanka, more so than the beaches. In my opinion, of all countries we've since worked in, Sri Lanka overall has the best food. The mainstay, rice and curry, spicy or mild, is always tasty, whether you stop at a simple roadside lunch buffet or dine at a hotel in Colombo. It's tough to find rice and curry for dinner in the countryside, as Sri Lankans prefer "fried rice" Chinese or Indonesian style, so we had curry dinners at home.

As obvious foreigners in a rural area, we were watched, as happens in small villages or towns anywhere, whether in Sri Lanka, Iceland, or Germany. Yet when walking through town, there wasn't the unwanted attention one may receive as a prospective customer. I wasn't "one of the locals," never would be, but felt respected and comfortable, receiving curious and open smiles everywhere. Being with the largest and most well-reputed employer in town, I received encouraging feedback on our work and even the occasional piece of fruit as a gift.

My largest regret is that I never learned even rudimentary Sinhala. While the older generation of Sri Lankans, at least those in business, often speaks English at home, governments shifted to a "Sinhala preferred" policy in the sixties. Thus, many college graduates do not practice English and feel uncomfortable speaking it. This has made it hard for me to do what I enjoy most, direct talks with locals who "know stuff"—notably with our agricultural field officers, whose insights I never got to value fully.

Yet living for weeks and months on end around Kuliyapitiya, although challenging and tiring after long workdays in the hot and humid climate, was one of the most enjoyable experiences in my life. Gorgeous visuals were a key part of the fascination. I marveled at many pieces of beauty: the wide vistas across rice paddy fields into coconut groves, bicycle rides through lush backroad villages and around wewas—small irrigation lakes, centuries old and often covered by lotus and water hyacinths. We'd visit a local temple with its line of stunningly lifelike plaster statues of Buddha's disciples in walking meditation. Or climb up a giant rock slab behind the Tissawa temple, then gaze from its top across the patchworked landscape three hundred feet below. The most dangerous thing that happened to me was when, one Sunday afternoon, reading *The Economist* in front of the bungalow, something tickled my feet. I looked down and it was a huge python slipping by in a hurry, as surprised as I was.

During my stints as a USAID consultant, driving myself in Sri Lanka was unthinkable. This had been made clear by the security officer at the US embassy. It's nice to be driven in chaotic traffic, but you don't develop a sense of where you're going. I also couldn't get used to having a driver waiting for us and managing him.

And so as soon as we started construction, I asked for a rental, usually slightly beat up but functional. Driving in Sri Lanka is a riot. First, it's left-hand traffic—easy to get used to, dangerous only in the morning when getting on the road. Traffic itself is anarchic, notably when it comes to passing. There's little attention given to oncoming traffic; one expects that it moves to the side if needed, and no one argues.

Trickier are the motorbikes and three-wheelers who pull into traffic without looking back. Watching entire families (up to five) on a single motorbike was at first nauseating—the kids without helmets in between the helmeted parents—but then you accept it. Since 2009, roads have much improved, and driving appears more disciplined. Yet the vastly growing stock of the slower three-wheelers, used for taxis but also as the family coach, make long trips on two-lane roads demanding if you are in a hurry.

Ironically, it ultimately did not affect the project and our life much that Sri Lanka was, until May 2009, in a bloody domestic war between the central government and the Tamil Tigers (LTTE), the self-appointed liberation army of the large Tamil minority in Sri Lanka's north. While the Tigers' basic cause—more justice to the often-disenfranchised Tamils—was supported even by many liberal Singhalese and Muslims, the Tigers used increasingly brutal recruitment methods and suicide bombings.

Against the pleas of international mediators, notably Norway, Mahinda Rajapaksa, newly elected as president in November 2005, started an all-out war against the Tigers in 2006, just as Serendipol got going. Military action was limited to Sri Lanka's north, but during my often months-long stints I constantly saw signs of a country at war. Military and police road checks everywhere, parts of Colombo were wire-fenced off, newspapers largely patriotic and supporting the government's approach.

Yet the war felt muffled. I was never in fear, and the only relevant impact of the war on our work was in February 2007, just as we were ready to start installation of the oil presses and silos. Hours before Markus was to arrive in Colombo, the Tamil Tigers bombed the military airport next to the international airport. No damage to the airport, but all incoming flights—including Markus's—were diverted, and no information on their new ETA was available.

Bernd and I later drove to the airport on speculation, and, miraculously, Markus walked out of arrivals exactly when we showed up. He had a bad cut on his hand, contracted while finishing work on his farm before rushing to the airport in Toulouse. We took him for bandaging to the Negombo hospital, which was full of people injured during the Tigers' attacks.

And that, for the next two years, was the most of what we felt of the war. Of course, visits by tourists had dwindled to an all-time low. One of our dry jokes was that, during the war, there were hardly even the typically ubiquitous German tourists in the empty beach hotels where Bernd, Markus, Christel, and I occasionally spent our weekends.

In May 2009, the army overran the last positions of the Tigers—not without killing, in the weeks prior, up to forty thousand civilians, sometimes apparently deliberately.

While there probably was no peaceful alternative to a military end of the conflict, I have no doubt that the violence committed on Tamil civilians was uncalled for, brutal, and ultimately planted the seeds of continued animosity between the two ethnic groups—including recent talk of a renewed northern threat. And the end of the war did nothing to end the ridiculously partisan politics of a country with genuinely friendly—often visionary—people, stunning scenery, and great natural resources.

I've loved Sri Lanka since I went on my first USAID assignment in 2001. Yet the wasteful and often corrupt management of the country makes me cringe. Most other countries we work in have similar or worse problems, and our job is to support fair and sustainable development from the bottom. At times that job is hampered by politics—including the occasional polite requests for bribes—but our projects' mission and obvious integrity have served us as a protective shell.

A vacation trip to Sri Lanka will not readily reveal that the country has squandered much of its potential (after achieving independence in 1948) on infighting and corruption. Sri Lanka's infrastructure is vastly improved now, trash-littered and pothole-filled roads are gone, and tourist services are usually up to Western standards, for better or worse. Where will Sri Lanka go in an uncertain world? I'd rather not even speculate—but hope.

STARTING A COCONUT BUSINESS

Immediately after its incorporation in early 2007, Serendipol applied for the status of a "preferred export business" for the benefits offered by the Sri Lankan government to stimulate foreign investment for export: duty-free import of machinery, a ten-year holiday on income tax, and protection from the capriciousness of any future government.

Similar, albeit much bigger, packages are offered to the Amazons and Apples of the world. In contrast, none of Dr. Bronner's sister companies abroad were designed as big moneymakers. Rather, they were set up as sources of reasonably priced "clean raw materials," with social and environmental improvement as an important by-product. Accordingly, pricing was structured to generate sufficient profits and the capital for expansion and a modest dividend to its shareholders.

As the war ended in May 2009, barely two years after start-up of production, Serendipol had grown vastly. All major buildings— production, canteen office, and wastewater treatment—were completed. We employed around two hundred staff, bought coconuts from seven hundred organic farmers, and produced VCO, 95 percent of which went to Dr. Bronner's for soap production. With the fair trade premium collected from Dr. Bronner's, Serendipol had already implemented over one hundred smaller and larger fair trade community development projects.

Pricing to Dr. Bronner's was reasonable and guaranteed a profit. Sonali and I had managed, despite our previous losses, to obtain a working capital loan from the Dutch ethical bank Triodos. The purchasing commitments made by Dr. Bronner's were valuable collateral, and Serendipol no longer depended on Dr. Bronner's for financing.

In addition to the oil for Dr. Bronner's, we sold smaller quantities of food-grade VCO to Nutiva and Werner Baensch's company in Germany. Serendipol looked ready for growth when we were hit by a disaster.

Which, as disasters sometimes do, ultimately turned into an opportunity.

Financing and structuring a fair trade project

How was Serendipol financed and its ownership structured?

Building the project required capital and a committed team. The recipe David proposed was simple—and Gordon, Sonali, and I accepted. Dr. Bronner's would provide an initial $750,000 in capital, and the three of us would spend a year of our own time without pay in return for an overall 25 percent stake in the operation. The balance would be held by Serendiworld LLC, owned by Mike and David, and later also the parent company of Serendipalm and Serendimenthe. Ultimately, the concept worked well because all partners were committed and capable, and Serendipol eventually became commercially successful.

There were pitfalls. First, we had underbudgeted the cost of setting up the project, and once Serendipol was in full production Dr. Bronner's had spent some $2 million versus the originally budgeted $1 million. We had underestimated the cost of constructing a set of elaborate, functional, and good-looking buildings designed and planned by our architects Norbert and Ulli: main building, storage, office, and canteen—ultimately, still a bargain. And we had wildly underestimated start-up losses caused by the flaws in our pricing structure.

How do you price a product that you sell to your parent company—in our case, how would Serendipol price the coconut oil it supplied to Dr. Bronner's?

Both cost plus and market pricing have pros and cons. The first option—cost plus pricing, in which you let your subsidiary charge a fixed markup—is fair as it guarantees a company a profit. But it can be risky. Partners with the wrong attitude may not care about efficiency, as they can pass on higher costs to the ultimate owner and customer. This will make a project noncompetitive when it wants to sell to third parties.

In contrast, pure market-based pricing bears the risk that a project makes large unjustified profits for its minority shareholders if market prices are far above cost of production. Conversely, if the market price isn't adjusted for a project's structurally higher cost, the project will lose money unfairly. That may not be of concern to a random third-party customer, but it sure is if you literally own a project, as Dr. Bronner's does, and want it to be sustainable.

The latter happened to Serendipol during its first year of operation. Unfamiliar with the cost structure of the competing commodity copra oil, we pegged the price of Serendipol's soap grade oil to the copra oil price—plus allowances for organic and FT premiums and the higher cost of production labor.

But we hadn't considered that global copra oil prices fluctuate with global supply and demand—which had no bearing on the price of coconuts in Sri Lanka, driven as they are by high and growing domestic demand. Serendipol also hadn't achieved economies of scale, and the high cost of professional staff, notably field officers to operate the organic internal control system and provide agricultural services, caused high overhead cost per output. The price Serendipol fetched for its VCO from Dr. Bronner's simply did not cover the cost of production, however efficient we tried to be.

We ultimately shifted to a basic cost plus system with annual reviews of dividends paid to Dr. Bronner's and third parties to ensure the pricing wouldn't be considered a ticket to a guaranteed dividend for minority owners. More on cost plus pricing in chapter 9.

Serendipol also taught Dr. Bronner's lessons about ownership on "remote projects." A common belief is that offering shares to key project promoters inherently incentivizes a sense of ownership and desire to perform.

It depends. For trustworthy, competent, and driven partners, such as Sonali and Gordon, it will enhance a sense of ownership and motivation to improve performance—that's what you want. Yet owning shares or receiving large bonuses will not magically produce any of these qualities in people who do not already have them.

In retrospect, we used intuition and were very lucky at Serendipol. As we would discover at other projects, blindly following this model of coownership would have caused disaster.

Coconut dryer at Serendipol

CHAPTER 6

Riding the VCO Wave

California, 2010

THE MOOD WAS TENSE ONE DAY in early 2010 as David, Christel, and I drove back to Escondido from Victorville, where we had visited the fabricator of our new liquid soap reactor. Eventually, David said, "Listen, Gero, we can't keep doing this. Serendipol's oil tastes great, but it is much too expensive for our soaps. It will bankrupt us."

I understood David well. He wasn't just thinking about the salaries of Dr. Bronner's officers that day. They had, in fact, forgone their bonuses that year, as cash was tight. Rather, he was concerned about the long-term viability of the entire company.

When the project started, Serendipol paid its farmers between fifteen and twenty rupees per nut (then about thirteen to eighteen cents). The end of the war stimulated consumer demand, and, over a few months, nut prices more than doubled. Several other factors contributed to that rise. For one, prior to Serendipol's start-up, nut prices had been below ten rupees—barely enough for farmers to make money—which meant there was not much incentive to replant the largely overaged stock of coconut palms. As a result, nut supplies had stagnated or even declined.

Next, unlike in the Philippines, Sri Lankans consume some 30 percent to 50 percent of the domestic coconut production with their food: mostly as milk for curries and oil for cooking. An increase in domestic consumption after the war ended had to come at the expense of nuts for export production.

Sri Lanka also had protectionist policies for coconut products and did not allow import of copra oil—cheaper and better—from the Philippines. Any drop in annual nut production due to lower rainfall would upset this fragile balance—and so it did in 2009–10 when a severe drought reduced island-wide nut production by 20 percent. Since Serendipol had by then achieved reasonable economies of scale, some 75 percent of the total cost of production was nut-related, and a rise in the nut price translated into a significant escalation of the oil price.

Nutiva jumped first. As much as John Roulac loved our project after he had visited in late 2007, his company's growth was based on lower-priced "organic only" oil from the Philippines, and he no longer could afford ours.

Next, the escalating price of coconut oil supplied to Dr. Bronner's soap production increased the cost of production by far more than $1 million per year, very challenging for a medium-size company that had enjoyed a period of sustained annual growth in revenues of 15 percent to 20 percent but faced tight cash flow. Our dream of producing cost-competitive fair and organic coconut oil didn't seem feasible after all.

"What if we moved our operation and learnings to the Philippines, where the nuts are much cheaper?" David asked. "One year of savings will allow us to pay for the move and provide our three hundred employees with generous severance packages that will secure their livelihoods."

"But this is a fair trade project," I argued. "And fair trade is about long-term commitment. Plus, setting up a project in a new country involves a little more than just putting oil presses into a building."

Then David had one of his flashes of genius. Why couldn't we start our own brand of food-grade virgin coconut oil? The demand for organic VCO in the United States and EU had been rising since 2007. Dr. Bronner's had an excellent reputation within the natural products industry and a committed sales team. Why not expand the company's magic and our fair and organic supply of raw materials into the food aisle?

By the end of the trip we agreed: let's market VCO under the Dr. Bronner's brand.

We also decided to make use of our firsthand knowledge of the production process and modify the product just a little. All competitors make VCO from desiccated coconut. This involved, for aesthetics, the manual removal of the brown skin (the parings) that protects the white kernel. This additional production step required extra staff and wasted some 15 percent of the overall oil content of the kernel.

We had never removed the parings to make cosmetics grade oil for Dr. Bronner's. The slight yellow tint they produced was perfectly acceptable in liquid soap. At the bungalow, we would use the same oil for cooking, very tasty. Why not produce a food-grade VCO from that whole kernel, see whether it tastes any different, and assess whether it contains other nutrients?

The flavors of the two grades were about the same, with the whole kernel containing possibly slightly higher levels of antioxidants (but that was difficult to prove). Why obsess over the whiteness of white VCO—especially since it raised cost of production by some 15 percent? It's not as if white sugar and flour are symbols of nutritional quality!

And so we launched Dr. Bronner's VCO in 2011, with a white and a "whole kernel" grade, and within just one year, it became the best-selling brand of VCO in the US market for natural products—against well-established competition.

As David had projected, our reputation in personal care, the commitment of our sales team to promoting a "real organic and fair trade" VCO, and, of course, the oil's great flavor were all important ingredients of this successful expedition into foods.

No sooner had we launched our oil than the VCO wave accelerated in the United States and, a bit delayed, the EU. This wasn't the first oil wave, though. Eating minimally processed, tasty oils had become a trend on both continents in the nineties—VCO was just the newest oil to fit the bill.

The majority of vegetable cooking oils sold today are commodity oils. You've seen or bought them: the light or clear soybean, canola, and corn oils in plastic bottles on supermarket shelves and used in processed foods. These oil seeds are expelled in large presses at temperatures above 212° F (100° C), which turns the oil dark and creates off-flavors.

Industrial oil mills often use a two-stage process: seeds are first pressed into a meal that is then further extracted with the petroleum-based solvent hexane to maximize oil yield. For consistency in color and a "neutral taste" they are then refined, bleached, and deodorized, just as is copra oil. Such oils contain little or none of the healthy ingredients or micronutrients of unrefined plant oils—vitamins, phytosterols, lecithin, polyphenols. And, of course, they have no taste.

Olive oil had been the exception. Unprocessed virgin or extra virgin olive oil had been used around the Mediterranean for millennia. Since the 1970s, it had gradually conquered cooler climates—first, because its taste recalled idyllic vacations, and, later, because its fatty acid spectrum and high levels of polyphenols made it *the* healthy cooking oil, one of the elements of the Mediterranean diet.

Olive oil helped along the early wave of more natural oils in the 1980s, when consumers wondered what other oils may taste like if made from high-quality seeds and fruits that don't require refining. Natural oil brands such as Spectrum Naturals, founded in California in 1986, sprung up. And a market for unrefined, "cold-pressed," often organic oils—linseed, safflower, canola, hemp, pumpkin—was born.

Then, in the late 1990s, the world discovered that coconut and palm oils are also quite tasty. In the United States, a VCO wave gradually started around 2003 and picked up real speed around 2010. What drove it?

Many people simply embraced VCO as a versatile and tasty oil for cooking, sautéing, frying, and inclusion in desserts. Yet there were the usual hucksters who promoted VCO for weight loss and a "healthy metabolism." Others saw eating VCO as a way of standing up to old but increasingly controversial claims by the "health establishment" that fats rich in saturated fatty acids, such as coconut oil, raised blood levels of "bad" LDL cholesterol, and, correspondingly, the risk of cardiovascular disease (CVD).

That doctrine had been promoted by nutritional scientists and doctors since the late 1950s, initially based on research by Ancel Keys, an American physiologist. High-fat dairy products and beef became suspect as key risk factors in the promotion of CVD, and so did "tropical fats" like coconut and palm oil.

A substitute for these fats had to be found for use in margarine, spreads, shortening, and baked goods. The hydrogenation, or hardening, of liquid oils—corn, soy, and canola, grown in the Midwest and the Canadian prairies—seemed an excellent solution. Basically, hydrogenation converts the unsaturated fatty acids in liquid oils into saturated ones. Most common became the "partial hydrogenation" of unsaturated fatty acids. It made liquid oils sufficiently solid at room temperature, without converting all of them into the feared saturated fats.

No wonder industry and well-meaning health advocates promoted partially hydrogenated fats as squaring the circle.

The "partial-hydrogenation high" crashed in the nineties. While it had been known that the process also created so-called trans fatty acids as a by-product, now mounting clinical evidence showed that these were much more detrimental than saturated fats to blood cholesterol levels and cardiovascular risk. They swiftly became a pariah of food science. First, they had to be listed on food labels. Producers saw the writing on the wall and made process changes to reduce trans levels. By 2019, the FDA banned the use of trans fats in virtually all foods.

Quite a turnaround! The inconsistency in the demonization of tropical oils followed by the complete elimination of their praised substitute certainly contributed to the almost religious embrace of coconut oil by many consumers.

Then, around 2010, anecdotal but credible evidence emerged that the high concentrations of saturated medium-chain fatty acids in VCO may slow down the progression of Alzheimer's disease. Who wouldn't want to try that?

As of this writing, the fog hasn't cleared. In 2017, the American Heart Association restated its position that eating any saturated fats increases "bad" LDL cholesterol more than "good" HDL cholestrol, thus raising the risk of CVD. Other research shows that this risk depends on the *type* of saturated fatty acids, with the medium-chain fatty acids present in VCO actually offering cardiovascular benefits.

As for the Alzheimer's connection, new studies suggest that a high-fat ketogenic diet or the use of medium-chain triglycerides (or MCT oils) has promise. It may benefit patients suffering from mild to moderate Alzheimer's by supplying their brain with ketones as an "alternative source of energy." Although VCO is not as effective a source of ketones for our brains as MCT, it has shown a path ignored by earlier Alzheimer's research.[1]

As VCO sales in the United States went through the roof—first in the natural foods channel, then in mass supermarkets—Dr. Bronner's did not engage in the hype. As with hemp products, our line was: VCO is a healthy and tasty oil, but no oil is a cure-all. Hemp and VCO are great ingredients—in a diverse and balanced diet. Yet Serendipol and Dr. Bronner's sure rode the VCO wave by growing, producing, and selling fair and organic VCO from a project people could actually visit. Rather unique.

By 2016, Serendipol's annual VCO output had reached 2,500 metric tons (MT), which sounds like a blessing—but it also created huge challenges. We needed to continuously convert new farmers and juggle the growing and competing demands by Dr. Bronner's and third parties, including, by then, Rapunzel, Germany's largest organic brand. They had discovered Serendipol through Raj and were happy to finally have an organic *and* fair coconut oil.

We assumed the wave would last a bit longer, made plans to double capacity to 5,000 MT per year—and then it broke. Between 2016 and 2020, the US VCO market shrank by over 50 percent. The collapsing market was not the only trouble. Another extended drought struck Sri Lanka and reduced the 2017 crop by some 50 percent; nut prices escalated to over fifty rupees, their highest level ever; and Serendipol had to retain old and recruit new customers at prices twice those of Philippine VCO.

Gordon and Sonali had to curtail production. Thankfully, the guaranteed income for those working on piece wages minimized the frustration among workers. A brutal period, but, again, we learned from it and were able to make the necessary changes.

First lesson: nothing beats committed buyers. Dr. Bronner's, Rapunzel, and several smaller customers continued buying from us for their brands—both out of loyalty and because we had the only credible fair and organic VCO—and it tasted good.

Yet several of these customers had also supplied our VCO as brokers to other brands for their private labels. At the high price of our VCO, these brands gave up on fair trade and authenticity and switched to other "organic sources."

We stopped our plans to double VCO capacity—rather, it was time to diversify. We had evaluated diversification options before and rather swiftly decided to add organic and fair coconut milk, cream, and chips to our menu, and bought and installed equipment. By 2019, with nut supplies recovered and nut prices back at thirty rupees, our global VCO sales recovered—though still far below the 2016 peak—and we began trial production of milk and chips.

How to find customers for these new products? Talk to existing ones, remind them of what sets you apart from your competition: for us, that meant our active promotion of soil health practices, an extensive and effective fair trade program, and a customer-oriented attitude—transparency and avoidance of exaggerated claims. Serendipol's visible record of community engagement impressed customers. So did the fact that we've been practicing regenerative agriculture since our early days. Becoming the first ROC-certified coconut project had already attracted ROC-friendly US brands.

By mid-2020, Serendipol was on track to expanding again—diversified, but true to our original goals, and a bit wiser and more relaxed.

A PERFECTLY ECOLOGICAL PRODUCTION

After operating Serendipol for some five years and improving trees, soil, and processing, I increasingly marveled at the "inherent sustainability" of the project. Its raw materials, coconuts, are now grown in a manner that improves farm soils and eschews their contamination; all by-products of processing at Serendipol's factory have value-added uses, and our production generates virtually no production-related waste. That makes our VCO production almost sustainable by design.

As for the production itself, it uses no aggressive or toxic process chemicals. Peracetic acid is used to sanitize the storage tanks, but that's about as chemical as it gets at Serendipol.

The main consumption of energy is in the drying of the kernel. Today, the dryer is fed by steam from a boiler that runs on our wasted coconut shells and on wood waste. No better way to generate essential process heat than from a waste material or by-products in an efficient boiler!

A walk through the production of VCO will demonstrate the versatility of the coconut plant. After the harvest, huskers first remove the outer brown husks—the raw material for the coconut fiber, or coir, industry, which had brought me to Sri Lanka in 2001 in the first place. Founded during British rule in the 1850s, the industry still turns coconut husks into high-quality "bristle fiber" for brooms, brushes, and doormats, and mixed fiber for mattresses, twine, ropes, erosion control mats, car seats. We sell good husks to smaller local fiber mills; damaged ones are returned to the farms for use as potassium-rich mulch.

The peat-like material in between the fibers, also called coir pith or dust, makes for a soil amendment with a very high moisture-holding capacity. Coconut husks, fiber, and pith have an unusually high content of lignin, the "glue" in the cell wall of trees and other woody plants. It makes cell walls more rigid and, unlike cellulose, resists biodegradation. That's why coir is so suitable for door mats and erosion control: it lasts three to five years when left out in the rain—compared with one to two years for other fibers.

The next step at the factory is to remove the hard brown shell that looks at us with its three eyes. It is filled with small pores and can be converted into "activated carbon." With its high internal surface, it is one of the world's universal agents to absorb and remove pollutants from water and air. Shells also make a great fuel. Serendipol crushes and then burns some 25–30 percent of our shells in our boiler; the balance is sold at attractive prices into the local market as the raw material for charcoal and activated carbon.

The seed cake that remains after expellers squeeze the oil from the desiccated coconut flakes is tasty and nutritious. We still sell it predominantly to compounders of chicken feed. After some modifications to our presses, we now market it for the production of a specialty milk and coconut flour.

The only other production-related waste is the coconut water—the clear liquid that is drained from the coconuts before shelling them. Coconut water is already past its prime as the latest "miracle drink" in the United States, and Europe and makes for an interesting lesson in developing value-added markets for by-products. Until the early 2010s, producers of DC and VCO considered coconut water an annoying process waste. It is high in sugars, immediately ferments once drained, and soon stinks, first like vinegar, then as if rotten. No wonder large DC mills who discharged the coconut water onto their land or into creeks eventually got into trouble with government regulators—and their neighbors!

As Serendipol grew, we first took the water to the coconuts farm as manure. Then, in 2009, we installed a biological wastewater treatment plant. Around that time, large DC and VCO producers in the

Philippines and brands in the West realized that this wastewater had nutritional value, and coconut water started its boom.

Most people I know love drinking coconut water from fresh, immature nuts. In Sri Lanka, receiving an orange-colored King Coconut as refreshment during a farm visit beats a Coke or Sprite. While the water drained from the mature nuts used in DC and oil production has less sugar and flavor, most Westerners don't know the difference, and, with a bit of marketing hype and adding sweetener or fruit flavor, the sale of "coconut wastewater" took off!

Today, it comes mostly from large DC and VCO mills in the Philippines. They drain the water before cracking the nuts, then either concentrate and ship in bulk or package the water on-site. This was not an option for Serendipol's smaller scale. Thus, we currently sell some of our "wastewater" to a local competitor for export and treat the balance before irrigating our lush factory garden with it. And who knows what it'll be good for down the road?

The bottom line on coconut production ecology: Sri Lanka has established markets for everything that a coconut palm can produce. At Serendipol, this avoids production-related waste streams. Instead, they become raw material for valuable by-products. Their sales are sizeable. As Sonali says: the sale of by-products about equals our profit margin. You can make money from selling your waste!

Sonali and Gordon had been managing a growing staff and group of farmers posing constant challenges efficiently, with energy and with heart. By 2012, after having spent some two years in total at the project, it became clear that I now added little value to day-to-day operations or expansions—and was, in fact, getting on Sonali's and Gordon's nerves. Ghana, India, and Kenya also required more and more of my time. I had to make a conscious decision to let go, then sharply reduced my visits. Instead I began to focus on finding new customers, supporting Sonali on her communication with them, resolving quality problems, supporting on key hires and on expansion plans.

My gradual withdrawal surely improved our relationships. I now enjoy scheming with Sonali and Gordon on product diversification and new marketing opportunities, the ROC certification of Serendipol, staff development, and thoroughly enjoy my annual visits to Sri Lanka, often accompanied by Dr. Bronner's colleagues. A highlight was the 2018 gathering of an entourage of some seventy people for the annual symposium of Dr. Bronner's growing family of international distributors. There were key Vista staff and good friends, such as Nasser Abufarha of Canaan Palestine, our olive oil partner in the West Bank, and his son Karmel. The group marveled at what Gordon and Sonali's team had built since 2007 and took back some inspiration for how to communicate the All-One spirit in their home countries.

FAIR TRADE: PRICING, PREMIUM, AND PROJECTS

Once we gained more insight into our project setting, we swiftly agreed with Raj that fair trade should not be about creating "an island of happiness in a sea of misery." It is about designing and monitoring your entire supply chain such that every stakeholder group can make a decent living, have a chance at personal development, be treated with respect, and live in communities engaged in their betterment.

Yet this also shouldn't cause envy among neighbors who do not work directly with one of your projects. Serendipol taught me that operating a fair trade supply chain is in essence running a well-managed company with a heart and a strong focus on developing people, communities, and their land. Trite but true. If making money is your main goal, fair trade isn't going to happen.

The implementation of these lofty goals varies from project to project, from culture to culture—and it's up to the project operator to identify the weakest stakeholders and their priorities. That said, the basic principles are the same, and we've applied them to all other fair trade projects:

PAY FARMERS, AT A MINIMUM, A PRICE THAT ENSURES THEY CAN MAKE A PROFIT. If nuts are certified organic, pay an organic premium high enough to reward extra management efforts—but not so high that the temptation will arise to comingle nuts from noncertified farms.

Keep in mind that yields will actually rise, not drop, when taking coconuts and other neglected *tree* crops to an actively organic production. In Sri Lanka, most farmers are middle class and have other sources of income than coconuts. So what will increase their income most effectively is consistent care of the land and targeted replanting of aging coconuts, thus achieving higher yields.

As an FFL project operator, one must also ensure that supplying farmers pay their helpers and contractors at least the legal minimum wage and that they do not employ children or pregnant women for more than small family chores.

PAY ON TIME—OR IF YOU KNOW YOU'LL FALL BEHIND DURING PEAK SEASON, LET YOUR FARMERS KNOW EARLY. Traders often don't pay smallholders on time, or at all. Understandably, farmers do not like it much! Reliable payment is a sure way to establish trust.

RUN THE PRODUCTION OPERATION—MILL OR FACTORY—AS IF YOU WORKED THERE. Make sure staff have a predictable fair income, are able to organize and be heard by management, enjoy a safe working environment, and have opportunities for personal and professional development.

Any benefits—health insurance, contributions to retirement programs, vacation, sick and maternity leaves—must meet applicable legal requirements. By how much to exceed them—and when—is one of the key decisions when designing a fair trade system for staff. One needs to be deliberate about balancing the needs of individual groups of staff with the need for productivity and financial viability. Thus, it is wise to expand benefit programs over time.

As Gordon told me more than once: "Be careful what you give— you cannot take it back without serious consequences."

REGENERATE BY REINVESTING. And finally, ensure that the fair trade premium you collect from your customers—such as Dr. Bronner's or

Rapunzel—goes to fund meaningful and collaborative fair trade projects.

YOU MAY STILL BE UNCLEAR about two key elements of any fair trade project: that farmers fetch *fair prices* and that project customers, such as Dr. Bronner's and Rapunzel, pay a *fair trade premium* for community projects. Here they are in a coconut shell.

The first key tenet of fair trade is for farmers to receive prices that allow them to make a profit. Thus, each project periodically reviews the farmers' unit costs of production, adds a 10 percent markup for profit, and uses that as guaranteed floor price, subject to review by the FFL inspector. The floor price is only invoked if market prices fall below it; otherwise, farmers receive the local market price, plus an organic price premium of typically 10 percent or a premium for superior quality. (Don't let it confuse you that a rate of 10 percent shows up in several spots.)

We also offer our farmers indirect incentives, such as subsidized compost, special tools, and interest-free loans for replanting with high-quality seedlings. This improves productivity, yields, and incomes, and in effect reduces cost of production. It also provides a disincentive to comingle, as only certified supplying farmers are eligible, and, unlike a cash premium, these goods cannot reasonably be passed on to a nonorganic neighbor.

As for the "fair trade premium" for community development projects?

That is calculated as 10 percent of the cost of nuts and nonexecutive labor. For example, if Serendipol spends $10,000 on coconuts and labor to produce a shipment of coconut oil, it invoices Dr. Bronner's and other customers an additional $1,000 in fair trade premium, as part of the cost of VCO. That formula is simple, transparent, and effective. The premium is not paid directly to the farmers. Rather, it flows into a fair trade fund that is democratically administered to community development projects by a committee with representation by all stakeholders: farmers, farmworkers, production workers, professional staff, and management.

One of Serendipol's many fair trade projects is a vocational center that provides shelter and skills training to abused girls. The living quarters were built by the provincial government, but vocational training was not offered. Gordon came along, saw the need and opportunity, and spoke with the facility's management. Our fair trade committee agreed to hire a textile teacher who, over the years, has trained several hundred girls in skills that will help them find employment once they come of age. I've visited several times, and I'm always moved by the impact the simple concept has had on the girls' lives and futures.

Another key theme of Serendipol's fair trade program is supporting elementary and middle schools in villages with a poor rural population. They are chronically ill-equipped with teaching materials, and often lack toilets. We typically add classrooms, books and libraries, toilet facilities, playgrounds, and water supplies. One could argue that fair trade shouldn't take on the government's responsibilities. But then, who will?

Our employees are naturally key stakeholders in community development. Most production workers own modest houses in villages near the factory. Grants of up to $1,500 per person have allowed them to add rooms, replace roofs, and improve toilet facilities. Their pride in such improvements shows when you visit.

We've learned that, to meet their objectives, all fair trade projects should be executed as if they were commercial projects, with budgets and deadlines. Yes, they should encourage volunteer labor, if appropriate. And communities must eventually take on operational responsibility, such as for schools, water wells, and toilet facilities. But simply throwing money at a project without having a strong hand in the implementation is a recipe for trouble.

Wanting to maintain control of the execution of fair trade projects may sound paternalistic. Yet this is not about knowing better what the community needs; the fair trade committee, where management is represented as a minority among other stakeholders, prioritizes and decides democratically which projects are funded. But as far as the execution, it's about efficient implementation of an agreed-upon project, and Serendipol employs a full-time fair trade coordinator. At times, this requires making unpopular choices, such as picking a contractor with a demonstrated track record instead of using one favored by farmers with ulterior motives.

Finding the balance between encouraging responsible, democratic, and community-focused behavior and making sure "things get done" is a never-ending challenge in fair trade. That's where Gordon's and Sonali's business experience and their practical approach to philanthropy and community development shine.

Early on, Sonali had been skeptical of whether one fair trade company, such as Serendipol, could have a meaningful impact on rural communities, calling it a "drop in the bucket." Gordon, an experienced doer, was excited by the opportunity to "make things happen in the village." The ability to spend significant amounts of money thriftily and effectively has turned both into social entrepreneurs.

"I never expected this project to go to this level, shift people's attitudes the way it has and become the agent of change it is now," said Sonali in a 2015 interview. To hear her and Gordon express such attitudes was a great personal joy for me and sure has impressed our visitors.

Many coconut farmers on the fair trade committee became advocates for projects that did little for them but benefit their poorer neighbors. One farmer who also sat on the boards of both a local hospital and high school successfully pushed through projects for an ER-monitoring unit and the conversion of a vacant plot of land into a sportsground for a high school. Not a bad way to gain status in the community! Finding such community-minded farmers and maneuvering them onto a committee is a fail-safe way of achieving meaningful community participation in project selection.

Serendipol's track record for breadth and effectiveness of fair trade–funded community development projects is convincing. Since 2007, the fair trade fund has spent some $2.5 million on over eight hundred projects small and large, with a focus on disadvantaged groups with no alternative.

One of Gordon's favorite lines is "We have spent several million dollars on fair trade projects, but we've never handed out a dime." Too often, charitable projects are not monitored, contractors take advantage, and construction is delayed. This wastes funds, demotivates communities, and undermines the very concept of community development. Monitoring planning and construction is one of many obligations of Serendipol's fair trade coordinator. Gordon also says, "We fund but we do not forget" (meaning: we do follow-up on the maintenance and performance of a project).

In the spirit of not forgetting: while my projects for Dr. Bronner's have taken me around the world, another aspect of my All-One work has taken me in an unexpected direction—back to my own roots in Germany. As I worked with the Bronner family to help them reconnect with their family history, while also helping to bring the brand back to Germany, I saw how that history intertwined with the traumatic experience of the Holocaust and ultimately inspired an activist organization that considers both people and nature wherever it works.

Tombstone of Emanuel Heilbronner Sr. at Laupheim Jewish Cemetery

CHAPTER 7

German Roots, German Connections

Mulfingen, Germany, June 2016

W E SAT, OR RATHER SQUEEZED, AROUND the dining table that had belonged to Berthold and Franziska Heilbronner, Emanuel's parents and David and Mike's great-grandparents. Across from me sat the brothers, Trudy, and Kris—all close to tears.

With us were several members of Tina Beck's family. Tina's great-aunt Agathe had been, for many years, the housekeeper in the Heilbronner's house in Schillerstrasse 48. Not long before the Nazis rounded up and deported, in March 1942, the Heilbronners and other remaining Jews in Heilbronn, Agathe had helped the Heilbronners smuggle the family jewelry and silverware plus the dinner table out of the house for safekeeping to her hometown of Mulfingen, 40 miles (65 km) northeast of Heilbronn. She had continued to visit the Heilbronners after the Nazis' increasingly strict "race separation rules" had forced her to quit their service.

The oak wood table illustrated one of many stories of bravery and kindness during the Nazi terror. It had resurfaced when, by complete coincidence, I met Tina and her husband, Stephan, through

Dr. Bronner's involvement in fair trade. Through her mother, Tina realized that the Bronners were related to the employer of her great-aunt Agathe. The Bronners visited Mulfingen in June 2016, dug into history over coffee and cake, and were moved by this most unlikely coincidence and connection to a tragic past.

Later that day, we visited the Heilbronners' Madaform soap factory in Heilbronn, from where Emanuel had emigrated to the United States in 1929. We met with the Frank family, who had started a metal casting operation in the factory in the 1950s and with whom Mike Bronner had become friends a few years earlier. And then we stood silently as David conjured up his ancestors' spirits in front of Schillerstrasse 48 where three simple cobblestones with a bronze plate commemorated the fate of Berthold, Franziska, and Berthold's sister-in-law Friederike. Initiated by the German artist Gunter Demnig in 1996, this *stumbling block* project has by now placed some 75,000 memorial stones across Europe.

The tragedy of the ancestors of David, Mike, and Lisa Bronner, like other entrepreneurial Jewish families in Germany murdered by the insane but brutally effective Nazi terror, also involves the gradual integration of Jewish people into Germany's mainstream society. It started in the early 1800s and climaxed after World War I, only to be destroyed irreversibly between 1933 and 1945.

Emanuel and his sisters Luise and Lotte had kept family documents. Thus, the course of events is well documented. It played out in Laupheim and Heilbronn, the two cities in southern Germany where the soap making history of the Heilbronners—the name carried by the family in Germany—began in 1858 and tragically ended in 1939.

When I began working for Dr. Bronner's in 2005, I became fascinated by the family history and its many aspects that related to Germany's history and to my own. One of my special projects was to help the Bronners explore and document their German roots.

During the first few years as a Bronnerite, I realized that Dr. Bronner's vision and history related more to my personal agenda and history than I could possibly think a job could when I was young, especially in two areas. For one, several of Dr. Bronner's missions and core causes coincide with what I have believed in since my teens and twenties: social justice, drug policy reform, an ecological transformation of society, and fair international development. In retrospect, my personal history is the backdrop to what motivated me to help build Dr. Bronner's clean supply chain.

Further, I strongly related to the tragic history of the Bronners as a Jewish family in Germany, and Emanuel's dream of a peaceful, unified planet eventually taking root. I knew in detail about the Holocaust as a young boy but did not know any Jews personally until we moved to Los Angeles. As I'll share in this chapter, my involvement in the Bronners' rediscovery of their German roots and the return of the brand to "the old country" has had a strong emotional and intellectual impact on my life.

THE HEILBRONNERS—ONE GERMAN JEWISH TRAGEDY

The origins of the Heilbronner family can be traced back to Laupheim in the early 1800s. Their family name, usually assigned by a local government, suggests that the founders of the "Dr. Bronner's" line of the family may have migrated earlier from Heilbronn, where Jews had suffered frequent expulsions and restrictions to their place of residence and trade. The migration of Emanuel's father, Berthold, and his brothers Sigmund and Karl in the early 1900s from Laupheim to Heilbronn also supports that theory.

People of Jewish faith in what's now Germany and most of its neighboring countries had suffered prosecution and pogroms throughout the Middle Ages and into the period of the Enlightenment, starting in the 1700s. Jews had been routinely banned from academic professions, crafts, and agriculture, leaving banking and trading as key sectors. They were at the mercy of local rulers and time and again were driven out of their hometowns and had to move elsewhere. Then, in the late 1700s, they gradually were granted rights and became, first in larger cities, important catalysts of German culture.

Unlike in Heilbronn, the rulers of the small Swabian market town of Laupheim had begun, starting in the 1720s, to grant Jews the right of permanent residence, of course in return for a tax and the expectation that Jews would help grow commerce. By the 1820s some five hundred Jews accounted for almost 20 percent of Laupheim's population. Conditions became even more tolerant as Laupheim was annexed by the Kingdom of Württemberg, and, in 1828, the Jews Act allowed Jews to freely choose their profession and place of residence.[1]

This was the setting where Emanuel Heilbronner Sr. started, in 1858, his soap and candle making business in the basement of his family home on Judenberg 2. Emanuel Sr.'s sons Sigmund, Karl, and Berthold moved "back to Heilbronn" around 1900, built the Madaform Soap Factory, and thus ultimately created the foundation for Dr. Bronner's.

Berthold was responsible for finances. He had married Franziska Rosenstein, and their children—Emanuel (1908), Luise (1912), and Lotte (1916)—were, according to Lotte's moving narration during our 2006 interview in her Haifa home, rather well integrated. Yet Emanuel also reported anti-Semitic bullying in school.

He learned the profession of soap making at Madaform in Heilbronn and with his uncle in Laupheim. His father, Berthold, was religious—socially liberal but critical of Emanuel's more radical Zionist leanings. It was the conflict with his autocratic father and the gradual rise in anti-Semitism, fueled by the strengthening Nazi movement, that prompted Emanuel to emigrate to the United States in 1929 and start a new life.

Anti-Semitic sentiments had never disappeared in Germany, and the Nazis fanned these sentiments. Brownshirt Sturmabteilung (SA) thugs organized boycotts of Jewish retail stores in 1931–32, before the Nazis came to power; larger companies, such as Siemens, stopped hiring Jews. Anti-Semitism was an increasing issue globally: at the same time there were "buy Christian" campaigns in the United States, and many of Germany's neighbors also showed hostility toward their Jewish population. In Germany it was organized and orchestrated from "the top," and Nazi propaganda portrayed

Jews as the source of everything bad in Germany. From all I've learned, I surmise that while many Germans were annoyed or disgusted by this ignorant hatred, as the Nazi propaganda machine kicked into high gear, many more thought: yes, the Nazis have a point. Those Jews just have too much power, and many are communists, too. Karl Marx, wasn't he Jewish? And so it goes.

Forgive me for casting the unfathomable and atrocious impact of the Holocaust in a few dry numbers. By early 1933, 520,000 people who declared themselves as Jewish lived in Germany, about 0.8 percent of the population. Despite a persistent undercurrent of anti-Semitism, they had achieved a level of integration into society as never before. Marriage between Jews and non-Jews was now common. Although German Jews continued to encounter some discrimination in their social lives and professional careers, many were confident of their future as Germans. They spoke German and regarded Germany as their home.

That over 100,000 German Jews had served in WWI was seen as proof of their loyalty to the country. That fourteen out of thirty-eight Nobel Prizes awarded to Germans between 1905 and 1936 went to Jews suggests that they contributed disproportionately to science and culture (of course, Nazis spun this fact into their propaganda about the power of Jews).

This situation changed dramatically when Hitler was appointed chancellor and the Nazis came to power in January 1933. First, they swiftly eliminated political enemies and Jews from public service. Most affected were lawyers, schoolteachers, professors, and medical doctors. The latter were increasingly subject to restrictions on the patients they could treat in private practice. Public servants who had fought in WWI received a deferment—until 1935.

In April 1933, the SA carried out a one-day national boycott against Jewish stores. Many Germans ignored it, but it further poisoned the atmosphere. So did the public burning of books of "un-German spirit" in many cities in May 1933. Many of the authors were Jewish. The Nuremberg Laws of 1935 then stripped Jews of their German citizenship.

Seeing the writing on the wall, Lotte and Luise Heilbronner followed their brother Emanuel's example and emigrated to Palestine and the United States in 1936 and 1938, respectively. During their last joint summer vacation in Switzerland in 1938, all three children pleaded with their parents to emigrate. Yet Berthold and Franziska did not want to leave Heilbronn even then. They thought Nazi rule would blow over, and they had reasons to be naive. The Nazis feared that forcing Jewish entrepreneurs to leave would have serious repercussions to the economy, so spared Jews in German industry from the increasingly vicious harassment and discrimination of Jews in public service and retail.

This relative safety from direct persecution and their age—Berthold and Franziska were sixty-five and fifty-five, respectively—made them want to sit things out. Yet conditions turned much worse after Kristallnacht, the national mob action organized by the Nazis on November 9 and 10, 1938. More than seven thousand Jewish businesses and one thousand synagogues, including the one in Heilbronn, were destroyed all over Germany. Then began the process of removing Jews from their last bastion in manufacturing. The federal "Decree on the Elimination of the Jews from German Economic Life" banned Jews from operating virtually all businesses effective January 1939. Company assets had to be "aryanized"—sold to a non-Jewish owner.

The Heilbronners' Madaform Soap Factory was among the remaining twenty Jewish-owned businesses in Heilbronn whose owners had not already sold and emigrated. In May 1939, Berthold's older brother and partner, Sigmund. died; his younger brother, Karl, had emigrated to the United States in 1936, so Berthold was left as the sole owner of the company. He had no choice but to sell his entire company in the summer of 1939. A letter by the new owner proudly announced to Madaform's customers that the business was now Aryan-owned, but they could still expect the same quality and customer service as always, and he signed with "Heil Hitler."

The loss of their business and the confiscation of most of their remaining assets left the Heilbronners no options, and, in 1941, they finally applied for a US visa. Luise paid their fare on a steamer, and they received the necessary documents in early December 1941. This tragically coincided with the Japanese attack on Pearl Harbor; America and Germany declared war on each other on December 11, after which Jews were blocked from leaving Germany.

Now the deportations of the remaining Jews in Heilbronn to extermination camps in Poland began. In March 1942, Berthold, Franziska, and Friederike, the widow of Berthold's brother Sigmund, were first deported to Haigerloch, an already evacuated nearby Jewish community. In August they were then transported to Theresienstadt, which served as a ghetto and an assembly camp for Jews who were later transported to killing centers farther east.

Theresienstadt played an important role in the Nazi deception of the international community—it was described as a "spa town," suggesting that Jews were brought there to settle for good. Berthold and his sister-in-law Friederike both died within weeks of arriving in Theresienstadt, likely due to exhaustion and infections. Franziska stayed in Theresienstadt by herself until May 1944, then was deported to Auschwitz and killed in the gas chambers shortly after her arrival.

Berthold and Franziska, the great-grandparents of Mike and David, shared their tragedy with that of 160,000 to 180,000 German Jews who could not imagine what the Nazis were up to, did not have the means or the ability to emigrate once they saw what was coming, and were ultimately killed in concentration camps by hunger, exhaustion, disease, or gas. They accounted for one-third of the 520,000 German Jews living in Germany in early 1933 and whose majority, some 300,000, emigrated before Kristallnacht, often leaving everything behind. Some 20,000 survived in concentration camps until liberation. The number of 180,000 murdered German Jews is mind-boggling enough—yet it represents only a fraction of the estimated 6 million European Jews who were killed during the Holocaust. In addition, the Nazis and their soldiers murdered some 11 million other people—including civilians in Poland and the Soviet Union, the Roma, and political and religious dissidents of all stripes.

We know little about the trauma the Heilbronners suffered during their final years in Germany, but to imagine it, just read a few of the accounts of Jews who barely made it out of Germany or survived concentration camps against all odds and wrote about their experience. Just picture that your entire world slowly turns against you. First, it's only institutional brutality, the dismissal from your job. Then you are harassed by Nazi thugs in the streets and lose your citizenship. Your neighbors or former patients no longer talk to you because it's too risky. If you are lucky, you have trusted friends or former staff, such as Agathe, who continue to support you voluntarily after it became illegal to work for Jews.

Next, most of your assets are confiscated, and opportunistic bureaucrats take advantage of your weakness and extort even more money. Then all synagogues are destroyed. Up to that point, the threats to Jews had largely been "administrative and psycho-terror." There was no need to beat up and torture Jews on a large scale. The well-planned and organized terror worked without it, and it avoided agitation by non-Jews, many of whom did not support the war on Jews and had shown this during earlier boycotts and Kristallnacht.

Then, at the very end, in 1942, the ultimate violence sets in—deportation and murder, all out of sight of a German population that knows something isn't quite right, but is too afraid of Nazi terror, and too distracted by an increasingly destructive war to care or act.

The murders of some 17 million—Jews, Soviet civilians and POWs, Roma, the handicapped, political opponents—was not the only violence carried out by an utterly sick and psychopathic leadership supported by an army of bureaucrats, party opportunists, and soldiers. Consider also the impact and trauma of this terror on all those Jews who had emigrated early enough and escaped almost certain death. It heavily scarred them and their families, too.

And there were Luise, Lotte, and Emanuel Heilbronner (later Emanuel Bronner), who had themselves left in time but then lost, despite their efforts, their parents at the last moment. Imagine the trauma that this caused for Emanuel despite or even because of the strained relationship with his father, and consider for a moment how the unfathomable loss informed Emanuel's mission to save Spaceship Earth.

Despite the brutal pursuit and loss of their parents, the siblings maintained connections to Germany, as many Jews who emigrated also mourned the German culture they knew and loved as their own prior to the Nazi madness. Our friend Dagmar, whose parents barely escaped Germany in 1938 and settled in Berkeley, told us how her Jewish father would, in the late 1940s, play Strauss on the piano, then stop and sob over the loss of his Germany. Luise wrote extensive poetry in Hebrew, German, and English about the tragic fate of her parents and the Holocaust, as well as the beloved German culture that had turned so viciously against her family and people. She returned frequently to Heilbronn and remained friends with the Loeckles, the family of the former manager of her father's factory. She later established and donated to a foundation that organizes student exchanges between Heilbronn and Baltimore. The city of Heilbronn thanked her by naming a street and a middle school after her. Lotte visited the family of their housekeeper Agathe in Mulfingen from her new home in Israel, and expressed her gratitude by bringing goods, such as Jaffa oranges, that were in short supply in postwar Germany. As for Emanuel, he also visited the Loeckle family and tried to establish business relationships in Heilbronn, though unsuccessfully.

Together, the three represent the generosity and ability for reconciliation that many Jews showed toward Germany after WWII.

A NOT ENTIRELY ATYPICAL GERMAN YOUTH

The next pages offer a sketch of my own first thirty years in Germany and my early years in the United States. I will explain what moved me to help the Bronners explore their Jewish German roots and bring our brand back to Germany. It'll also make it obvious why Dr. Bronner's way of doing business became so attractive to me, a German baby boomer transplant.

I was born in Köln, or Cologne, Germany, in 1955. During WWII large sections of the city core had been bombed into rubble. Returning soldiers, like my dad and locals who had been evacuated, came back to a place very short on housing. Papa—my dad, Willy Leson— had been drafted into the German army, the Wehrmacht, on his eighteenth birthday in July 1944. He was sent to the rapidly dissolving Western Front in the Netherlands with a battalion of eighteen-year-old kids roaming on bicycles they "requisitioned"—in other words, stole—from Dutch civilians. He had grown up in a middle-class Catholic family, despised the dogmatic behavior of Nazi-leaning teachers and fellow students, and had no interest in joining a lost war—but had no choice either.

His group luckily avoided real combat, but their final mission in October 1944 was to retake a major road near the German-Dutch border controlled by the allies after the battle of Arnhem. He often told me the story, and I have a vivid image of it. His group arrived at a large farmhouse where their major told them to drop off their backpacks with all their belongings because "you won't need those anymore." Then they approached "the enemy" through a beet field. The team was exhausted; my dad carried a machine gun, and, while taking cover on the ground, he fell asleep. Two American soldiers, friendly but firm, woke him, took his machine gun, shook their heads at his young age, and took him prisoner.

That was the end of Dad's war. He was transferred to a POW camp in Colchester, England, and joined a group of Catholic soldiers intent on becoming priests. He was released in July 1946 to return to his widowed mom. There, he joined a Dominican seminary, realized swiftly and fortunately for us kids that he wasn't made for priesthood, and returned to high school. His wartime "emergency high school diploma" wasn't valid after all. One of his classmates was my mom, Elisabeth. After school, they would occasionally meet on the tram to farms west of Cologne to trade the remaining family valuables for scarce food.

Mom, also from Cologne, had spent the war's final months in Berlin with her family. Her dad had barely made it out of the trap of Stalingrad before being transferred to Berlin. Mom often recounted the bombing raids when she and her dad took cover in fifty-five-gallon drums dug into their backyard while her mother and younger sister were in the bunker. She first encountered Russian soldiers in early May 1945 when their bunker was stormed, and she narrowly escaped being raped by one of them when a brave middle-aged woman offered the soldier a hand job instead. For several months she worked, at the age of seventeen, in a makeshift grocery store before returning to Cologne.

The years during and after the war were formative for her. Since her father traveled for work and her mother was fragile, she became her family's manager by default; she learned how to get things done, a lesson she never forgot. Most fortunately, both my parents were spared the worst of combat, destruction, and violence that caused a silent epidemic of trauma, depression, and rage in their generation. It's been rarely discussed until recently, but certainly passed on to many Germans of my generation.

My parents married in late 1950 with my sister, Monika, on her way. Papa was hired as a bookseller apprentice by the Cologne publishing company J.P. Bachem, owned by the family of one of his classmates. He spent his entire career at Bachem; moved up swiftly; became the chief editor of their multiple programs, or imprints; and eventually managed the editorial part of the company until he retired in 1991 at sixty-five. I owe his profession a lot, including my love of books and regular well-paid work as dad's typist during my teens and twenties.

With housing scarce, my parents' first modest residence was far outside Cologne, and Dad commuted to work by tram. In 1955, just after I was born, they moved to Stegerwaldsiedlung, a colony built in 1951 to 1956 on former industrial land. The "Siedlung" became my home for the next nineteen years.

Life in gray postwar Cologne was a mix of stiff restriction and budding freedom. As for all my middle- and working-class friends, our upbringing was modest. We were four kids: my four-years-older sister, Monika; me; and two brothers, Guido and Leo, two and nine years younger, respectively. My parents had no car until I was nine and, fortunately, no TV until I turned sixteen. I was fortunate to have such a modest upbringing in ways I only appreciated decades later. Since my father worked in publishing, books were currency at home. I was reading by age five, and a wide range of books accompanied me over the years. Since Dad was also a history buff, I learned about Germany's horrific history at a young age. I must have been ten when I first read, at my dad's suggestion, parts of *The Rise and Fall of the Third Reich*, a chronicle of Nazi Germany by the US journalist William Shirer, with gruesome descriptions of events in Auschwitz and elsewhere.

It took me a few more years to realize that many second- and third-rank Nazis were again in power, slightly aged—and that, despite democratic rule, there was something still wrong in Germany. As with many German baby boomers born between 1945 and 1960, this discovery laid the foundation for my leftist progressive political beliefs in the late 1960s and early 1970s. Time and experience have reshaped my ideals, made them more realistic, but my basic attitudes never really changed. Coincidentally, this made me rather compatible with Dr. Bronner's.

"Mama," as we kids called her, was strong and opinionated—she knew how to manage a six-person household, was clear about rules, and made sure we did our chores. She freely shared her commonsense wisdom with us—and our friends—often to our embarrassment. Two of her favorites were the Cologne saying "Each fool is different," and the English idiom "Make the best of it." She was spot on—we just couldn't appreciate it.

My parents were part of a postwar generation that had grown up in the 1930s and did not want their kids to be stifled by useless traditions and musty rules. This meant: no stiff visits with relatives on Sundays; instead, the whole family would take the bus to the foothills for hikes (not always loved but formative). We had the freedom to ride bikes to school and participate in sports clubs and argue with my parents' friends during their evening visits and even sip the occasional glass of beer or wine—under supervision. In hindsight, we had amazing freedom in the 1960s—including the freedom from needing to have the latest sneakers (even though I sometimes would have preferred cooler jeans).

The colony where we lived, with its three- to seven-story buildings, also offered great opportunities to make friends. Two boys I met in preschool, Norbert Wansleben and Christoph Eschweiler, became soulmates through our wilder adolescence and ultimately involved in my work for Dr. Bronner's—Norbert as architect in Sri Lanka and Ghana, and Christoph as the designer of our SecondAid website (his son Phillip now oversees technical projects in our Special Operations team).

As it was for all of my close friends, my parents gave education high priority. After four years of an inspiring quasi-Montessori elementary school, I had nine years of an initially very stuffy high school. Some teachers were left over from the Third Reich. Their teaching skills sucked, but I was bright enough to do well. I had years of Latin and ancient Greek, very useful on my later travels to the Mediterranean. We visited museums and theaters, learned to play flute and guitar, and performed with our small student orchestras.

Yet my siblings, friends, and I had developed an aversion to traditional German culture: the great writers and composers didn't speak to us and represented "bad old Germany." German pop culture was even worse—corny songs, bad humor. We became altar boys but stopped attending Catholic church at fourteen, instead fascinated by philosophy and modern literature: French existentialists, Nietzsche, then Herman Hesse, Henry Miller, Dostoevsky. We understood half of it, but it made us aware of a world far beyond our leisurely adolescent lives. High school teachers became younger and more inspiring, and we began to rebel against the idiotic ones. The arrival of first British, then American rock music in 1967 and '68 gave our emerging philosophical orientation the proper soundtrack.

Thrift and saving money was encouraged. That allowed me to buy my first bicycle at fourteen, ride it to high school across the Rhine, and then take it on a trip that would change my life. By that time, my hair had grown down to my shoulders. I felt different, like a member of a progressive cult—and my parents stopped arguing for a haircut. I'll always be thankful for their tolerance and encouragement. No sibling followed a straight path; instead, we all ventured sideways but ultimately came back, more or less, to what my parents had hoped for: responsible, slightly eccentric citizens with decent values.

LIFE-CHANGING TRIPS

So in chilly March 1970, three friends and I, all fourteen and fifteen years old, took a bike trip from Cologne to Amsterdam. My parents let me go on this two-week trip even though they knew that I planned to enjoy cannabis. That expectation of liberality was, in part, why we had selected Amsterdam as our destination. That adventure opened my world beyond what I had learned from books, school, and family vacations. The youth hostel where we stayed was particularly lively: an eclectic international group, including quite a few Americans, mostly men, with few over twenty-five. At fourteen I was about the youngest. Most details of the stay in Amsterdam are hazy, but I vividly remember our visit one night to the Paradiso, a church converted into a club and concert hall. One entered a huge dark room, found a place to sit on the ground, and then, for a few hours, smoked pot firsthand (or secondhand, as the air was thick) and watched two live bands, one of which later became rather famous. Nothing like this existed in Cologne, and definitely not for fourteen-year-olds!

The Netherlands—or Holland, as many inaccurately call it—had already been my first escape from Germany twelve years earlier. Since I was one year old, my parents took our annual family vacation on the Dutch coast. Ironically, during his wartime bike rides my dad had fallen in love with the country. German hotels and guesthouses were stiff and not child-friendly, while boarding with Dutch families was affordable and enjoyable. My parents also taught us early that being too German abroad wasn't a good idea. Fifteen years after WWII had ended, the Dutch still viewed Germans with mixed emotions. The occupation had caused death, destruction, hatred, and resentment—yet German tourists brought business, and being German wouldn't be held against you if you behaved as a decent human being. It helped that my dad had learned to speak Dutch fluently and later translated Dutch books into German, mostly theology and sociology. Naturally, we kids learned to order fries with mayo in fluent Dutch.

That attitude became essential to all my travels—adjust and put your nationality behind you. Not that this was difficult for German baby boomers. Americans or European neighbors may not realize how thoroughly non-patriotic my generation was raised. I would never have said that I was proud to be German, nor did parents, teachers, or schoolmates, at least not in public. It just didn't come up. German flags were rarely flown, except on major holidays. One notable exception was soccer, where I'd naturally side with the German team, and, yes, there was the national anthem when "we" won medals at the Olympics.

Our lack of patriotism was caused by our knowledge of the Third Reich's crimes, and because of the postwar guilt of our parents' generation, patriotism just wasn't on display. Thus, nationality didn't matter to how we defined ourselves, at least for the boys, and then young men, I hung out with. We were internationalist socialists, different, increasingly long-haired, anti-establishment—but definitely not German. By no means is this true for all Germans my age, but it is very representative of a large urban minority.

With these precautions, I was never labeled a "damn German" when, in April 1970, four long-haired German boys biked through the Dutch countryside.

It was my first life-changing trip. My subsequent participation in social and environmental movements, experimentation with drugs, and extensive travel further shaped my left-leaning beliefs—that our current system wasn't fair to the less fortunate and that "things will and must get better." Preferably as the result of a revolution, after my introduction to simplified Communist concepts and Mao's Red Book on that fateful trip to Amsterdam.

The trip further fueled my love for "the foreign," which my parents had sparked and made accessible to us. It showed me the polarity of the Netherlands—a conservative yet pragmatic society that was not wild about the open cannabis use by their children and visiting Germans. Yet it tolerated it, in line with the national consensus principle that prioritizes the avoidance of social harm over religious or social dogmatism. No wonder most subsequent adolescent trips with friends were to the Dutch coast, by bike, moped, hitchhiking, and—later—car.

In Germany, all interesting recreational drugs were illegal. Yet when hashish surfaced in high school around 1969, it wasn't its illegality or alleged hazardousness that kept me from becoming a serious pothead. How could a drug tolerated in Holland be bad for me? Rather, I had little money and didn't care for the cool older guys selling pot.

Also, my early experiences with cannabis were mixed. In the right setting—a small group of good friends—we enjoyed music and esoteric conversations. Yet when hanging out with too many people in dark basements or in public, anxiety was a common side effect. The resulting moderate approach to cannabis served me well when LSD became available via clubs in 1970. We were cautiously curious, since German media spread horror stories about Americans gone crazy on LSD. Yet the experience with hashish had turned us into skeptics of "official anti-drug propaganda," and I embarked on my first LSD trip at age sixteen in September 1971.

My high school friend Christian and I took a hit of LSD in a crowded theater as we watched the movie *Gimme Shelter*, which covered the 1969 Rolling Stones tour of the United States. We were both huge Stones fans, and their music, at the time, was still pure magic and energy. While the LSD kicked in, I noticed the intensity—the almost physical experience of music—and the tension building up to the Stones' disastrous open-air concert in Altamont, California, where an eighteen-year-old African American man was stabbed and beaten to death by a member of the Hells Angels, whom the Stones had ignorantly hired for security. I looked over to Christian, who was horrified and asked to get out before the depressing end. I had the great idea to visit a friend experienced with bad trips; he calmed Christian down, we played music, then visited a party.

I vividly remember the basement party room, dark with red lights, where I sat on a cushion for what felt like hours, listening to the English progressive rock band Rare Bird and their song "Flight." I felt a sense of complete understanding of the world and of eternity—that I'd be like this forever. Quite a program for a sixteen-year-old, but a very strong foundation for my later experiences with drugs and meditation.

Over the following decades, I may have taken psychedelics stronger than cannabis—such as LSD, MDA, and mushrooms—some twenty times, almost always on trips to the Dutch coast, Italy, or rural Germany, with small groups of friends. We had deep revelations about the universe, scrambled discussions when words didn't do justice to what went on in our heads, and beautifully distorted impressions of pink and green sand dunes, pulsating wallpaper, and yearning music alike. I occasionally felt uncomfortable tension with friends with whom I had conflicts, but never had "a horror trip."

I never had that one "life-changing trip," either. Yet I am certain that the continued but moderate opening of windows into different states of mind was essential to the person I became. Most of that impact likely came from the contemplative consumption of cannabis; stronger psychedelics occasionally added another dimension; and two periods of psychotherapy with wise older women in Germany and California cracked the door still more open.

My first verifiable experience with the performance-enhancing and mind-opening impacts of cannabis was during my first university semester of calculus and algebra: rather dry material with abstract homework problems. I often couldn't grasp what was being asked, let alone find a solution, until one evening I came home slightly stoned and had to do my homework. Believe it or not, cannabis had an "open sesame" effect. I comprehended the problem at hand, was able to visualize the abstract structure invoked, and enjoyed finding the solution. And my answers still made sense the next morning!

Not surprisingly, I followed this routine repeatedly throughout my ten years as a student—first in math, then physics. I appreciated the abstract beauty of math, but it was a bit *too* abstract, and our professors made little effort to explain how the fathers of calculus and linear algebra had come up with such complicated structures.

The first classes in theoretical and experimental physics were a mind opener, too: what I had learned in math wasn't but a high level of abstraction of the methods developed by Newton, Leibnitz, Descartes, Gauss, and others to describe quantitatively the movement of celestial and other bodies. While an "n-dimensional vector space" was difficult to imagine, set $n=3$ and you have your familiar three-dimensional space. What are the first and second derivative of a space-time trajectory but the velocity and acceleration of the body on that trajectory? Physics is still a rather abstract science, but at least it claims to analyze, quantify, and understand material reality—on the micro and macro levels.

I had found my scientific home and never regretted the choice. In my professional life, I never really practiced physics, but it became my general toolbox and inspiration for much of my later work in the environmental field and in business. True to form, I wrote both a master's thesis in physics and a doctorate dissertation in environmental science and engineering, with occasional targeted support of cannabis. Both pieces came out rather well, and an excerpt of my dissertation on biofiltration as "an innovative air pollution control technology" has become a frequently cited peer-reviewed paper. I couldn't have made it all up on a cannabis high, but that sure helped.

My experiences with psychedelics also prepared me well for another aspect of my work with Dr. Bronner's. Around 2008, David first told me about MAPS, the Multidisciplinary Association for Psychedelics Studies. Their research into the therapeutic use of psychedelics has become a key area of Dr. Bronner's activism. It took another ten years of promising global research results and the 2018 release of Michael Pollan's book *How to Change Your Mind* for the topic to receive very serious widespread consideration in media, public, and politics, notably by the US Food and Drug Administration and the Veterans Affairs Administration. For such a controversial topic, that's not too bad.

A growing body of international research suggests that psychedelics, when administered in a controlled setting and guided by a professional therapist, may improve or even heal mental illnesses often resistant to treatment by psychotherapy or conventional psychotropic drugs, such as depression and posttraumatic stress disorder (PTSD). The latter is of particular public concern, as an estimated 15 percent to 30 percent of veterans from the wars in Iraq and Afghanistan ultimately suffer from PTSD, usually at high cost to their family lives, careers, and society. I've found the sometimes firsthand testimonials of patients whose lives were turned around by psychedelics impressive and, based on my own experience, very plausible. This current wave of interest in, and documented successes of, psychedelics is rather different, more scientific and mainstream, than the understandable but shortsighted and disastrous hype of the 1960s that brought emerging and promising research into their medical and spiritual uses to a screeching halt.

Considering my own mind-altering experiences and those of close friends, I favor changing drug laws to allow the therapeutic and spiritual potential of psychedelics to flourish. I'm particularly proud that Dr. Bronner's has given significant financial support to MAPS and other organizations in the field. It relates very much to how I began opening and changing my own mind some fifty years ago. Offering the option of psychedelic therapy is an act of kindness to those who often suffer beyond imagination, be it as a result of military service for their country or as refugees escaping unbearable situations.

My personal journey was in many ways also inextricably intertwined with my growing passion for social justice and fair international development. In 1973, right after high school, my old friend Norbert and I had taken a two-month road trip to Greece and Turkey. On our expedition through rural Anatolia, we watched the hard lives of farmers. We enjoyed and were ashamed by Turkish hospitality in cities and villages. How could they be so open when Turkish guest workers were treated rudely in Cologne? On mind-blowing overnight stays in small remote towns, we had eggplant and lamb stews for dinner on quiet plazas, watching old men smoke water pipes and listening, over tea, to the chants of the muezzin.

Fair and ecological international development became high on my agenda and followed me through my university years, participation in student government, organization of seminars on ecological topics, and my stint as an environmental researcher at the KATALYSE Institute. Needless to say, I didn't consider joining the military, the German Bundeswehr—I would not have made a good soldier.

To qualify for the alternative, sixteen months of compulsory service, I had to make my case as a conscientious objector, an option not available to my dad in 1944 but established after WWII. My service consisted of visiting and helping seniors who had been released from hospital, lived alone at home, and needed support with cleaning, shopping, body care. It turned out what they needed most was someone to converse with and reflect on their lives—most were in their seventies and eighties. I was already twenty-eight when I started my service and had a master's in physics. I knew how to listen and ask questions, and was moved by the life stories I heard. Taking care of seniors in such an intimate way became another one of my formative experiences.

A TALE OF TWO GERMANYS

During the first thirty-four years of my life there were two Germanys separated by a wall. We lived in West Germany, the Federal Republic of Germany, sponsored by the Western allies, and there was East Germany, the socialist German Democratic Republic (GDR), overseen by the Soviet Union. Yet I had no concept of West Berlin as a separate Western island, surrounded by East Germany and also fenced off. That changed in 1979 when I studied physics at the Free University in Berlin for one semester. Aside from physics classes and hanging out with friends, mostly "refugees" from West Germany who had either escaped narrow-minded rural areas or avoided being drafted into the German army (West Berlin was not formally part of West Germany), I became fascinated and repelled by the wall surrounding the island of West Berlin. I visited that manifestation of the Cold War and of inhumane and well-rationalized separation many times. My first visit to East Berlin, with its decaying infrastructure and 1930s feel, gave me strong second thoughts about the desirability of "real socialism" in East Germany, which I had always hoped would exist at least in some meaningful and humane form.

The border was omnipresent, frightening, stupid—but a reality people lived with and did not expect to change—ever.

Ten years later, in 1989, the East German freedom movement, encouraged by Mikhail Gorbachev's unwillingness to back up the East German regime—as the Soviets had done before—caused the swift collapse of the regime and the wall, with ripple effects of political changes in virtually all of Eastern Europe. I couldn't wait to finally drive across East Germany and did so in March 1990. The contrast was stunning. Villages and towns in East Germany reminded me of West Germany in the 1950s and early 1960s: devoid of color.

Through the 1990s and 2000s, we visited East Germany often and were amazed by the rapid modernization—similarly in the Czech Republic and Hungary, and much less so in Romania and other Eastern European countries, where our work in industrial hemp has taken us since the mid-1990s. I enjoyed talking with people about their experience during socialism, what they liked and what they suffered from. It has been more than thirty years since the wall collapsed, and a young generation has grown up in a different system. Yet there are still visible rifts in all Eastern European countries, wounds caused by forty years of more-or-less authoritarian regimes and the persistence of former socialist elites. This is not fundamentally different than the continued presence of high- and low-level Nazis in West Germany after 1945 and illustrates the limits of bringing forced regime change to a dictatorship. Germany's reunification is unique and caused, after initial elation, much friction on both sides—and there is still a clear yet gradually dissolving political divide between East and West.

My favorite commercial anecdote on life under socialism came in

1998 from the managing director of a textile firm in Hungary that wove hemp fabric. I asked him about sales and marketing during socialism; he smiled and said, "Much easier than today. Once a year a delegation from the Soviet Union would come, order 100,000 square meters (1 million square feet) of hemp fabric, which they used as crop covers in grain fields. We signed an agreement to seal the deal, celebrated with a few vodkas and that was all." The collapse of the Soviet Union destroyed this arrangement, ultimately causing the demise of the company as well as the socialist economy in Hungary and other Eastern European countries.

ENCOUNTERING JUDAISM

Everyone my age and in their right mind strongly resented what the Nazis had done to the world during their twelve-year rule and knew, in broad strokes as well as painful detail, of the crimes committed against the Jewish people. No wonder that, in the 1960s, I didn't know anyone who questioned the right of Israel to exist, and during catechism, which at the time we took seriously, we learned that Israel was the land of the Lord. Guilt, discomfort, and curiosity shaped my relationship to the chosen people.

Yet the relationship between Germans and Judaism was also awkward—and how could it not be? I noticed it when my parents discussed Judaism with friends and when older Germans had trouble even using the word "Jew." There was a positive mystique about Israel for younger Germans, though only few of my friends traveled there, usually to spend time in a kibbutz. One had to fly to get there, which was uncommon in the early 1970s. It later became difficult to reconcile my sense of historical responsibility toward the Jewish people with my emerging political attitudes and sympathy for the Palestinian cause, as European leftists felt for Palestinian refugees and the pain inflicted by the formation of Israel. I was torn over what to think of Israel and Zionism, yet I had not knowingly met a Jewish person. I was so culturally ignorant that I did not even realize that Woody Allen's movies, which we watched with German dubbing, couldn't really be understood without knowing his love for using stereotypes about Jews.

This changed dramatically when Christel and I moved to LA in 1986. When entering the office of the doctoral program in Environmental Science and Engineering at UCLA, I met Mark Gold, a Los Angeles native who made no secret of his Baltic Jewish background. He was critical of, but not resentful toward, Germans, and he was very good at joking about anything, including Jews, Americans, and Germans. Once I learned how to take his style, we became good friends and allies for life. Mark was my first source of meta-level understanding of Jewish identity in America. He's also been my mentor on science-based environmental activism, which he now practices as the State of California's deputy secretary for oceans and coastal policy.

As our circle of friends and colleagues expanded to include many more people of Jewish heritage, we recognized that the expulsion and murder by Germany of millions of Jews across Europe had not only been the best-organized genocide in history, but had also caused an utter tragedy for Germany's future, since the country destroyed a relatively small but well-integrated, educated, industrious, and patriotic segment of German society across many fields. It wasn't just Albert Einstein and other prominent scientists! No one in Germany had told us that, not explicitly. In fact, in an effort to overcompensate for the Nazi propaganda on a "powerful Jewish conspiracy against Germany," many liberal Germans, including my dad, did not stress enough the important achievements of their less than 1 percent share of the German population.

Christel's and my relocation to the United States had not only given us new perspective on the history of Germans and Jews; it also showed Germany in a new light. We had to cross the Atlantic to appreciate the culture and the freedom we had grown up with in Cologne: the stimulating public discourse and high standard of living that allowed us a rather Bohemian lifestyle while studying and working for a living, fixing our house and old cars, and engaging in politics.

Both Christel and I immediately liked the openness and opportunities we found in LA. One true cliché: in Germany, if one had a good idea, the first response was "Yes, but . . ." In LA, it was: "Sounds good, give it a try." For two thirty-year-olds, this was a great stimulant. Christel took her portfolio of artwork and photos to galleries and prepared for her first shows, a liberty she would not easily have taken in the Cologne art scene. During my two years on UCLA's campus, I participated with fellow students in meaningful research for the State Water Resources Control Board. And once I went out on my own as an environmental consultant, I became a serial expert on biological air pollution control and then on industrial hemp. We experienced the United States as a welcoming country. It helped us grow up while allowing us to stay the way we were—as contradictory as this may sound. Yet we always knew how privileged we were, being white with a strong values-oriented upbringing at home and a solid university education.

2006-2016: DR. BRONNER'S RETURN TO GERMANY

My work with the Bronners on researching the family history was not only personally meaningful for all involved, it also became one pillar on which to build a presence of our brand in my home country. Mike Bronner had successfully set up distribution of Dr. Bronner's products in Japan and Korea, our first two export destinations, and he and David thought that it was time to go into Europe, especially Germany, and into Israel. How could they not want to reconnect and bring our castile soap back to where it came from, a country where organic foods and natural cosmetics were well established, no less?

And I sure wanted to participate, even though this had little to do with my day job of setting up organic and fair smallholder projects. As you can tell, even though I had left Germany for the United States in 1986, I had kept many close contacts and spent quite a bit of time "in the old country," much of it professionally. From California, Christel and I had watched developments in Germany, such as the collapse of the wall, and maintained friendships across all periods of our personal histories. My earlier work with the German hemp industry also spilled into the growing German organic industry. I was certain that Dr. Bronner's activist message and agenda, product quality, and authenticity would speak to motivated younger Germans and those of my age who expected more from a product than just functionality and a low price—they looked for authenticity and social impact.

We'd have tough competition in Germany, with several natural cosmetics brands of global reputation—such as Weleda and Dr. Hauschka—and many smaller ones. And how would we communicate the brand, with its unusual and barely legible label, using just PR and word of mouth as Emanuel and his family had done in the United States? David jokingly suggested an almost biblical marketing line for the German market: "The soap that will wash your conscience clean." But we knew that wouldn't go over too well with Germans young or old.

So, in February 2006 I organized the first Bronner trip to Germany with David, Kris, and their daughter Maya. The occasion was Biofach, the venue for our two BIORESOURCE HEMP conferences in Frankfurt in 1995 and '97. Biofach had since grown into the world's premier show for organic products and moved to Nuremberg in southern Germany.

We used the trip for some hemp tourism and German history, too. We first visited Cologne, where we saw a Gestapo prison and had dinner with Michael Carus, then stopped to visit Bernd Frank and his hemp fiber processing plant near Karlsruhe. It gave David an appreciation of all the trouble even the most motivated hemp entrepreneur involved in agriculture and processing had to go through. Bernd's detailed accounts inspired David, a hempster to his core, to jokingly coin the line "Hemp: I wouldn't wish it on my worst enemy." Finding food supplies for David's vegan diet was easy in Cologne and Heidelberg, but much harder in small towns in southern Germany where all a vegan could eat were french fries and sauerkraut—very tasty, though! At Biofach we caught up with

Mike Bronner and met potential distributors—but nothing clicked. David also realized that our hemp activism in the United States meant nothing to these distributors. Ten years after farming industrial hemp had become legal in Germany, it was no longer a cause, as it still was in the United States.

A year later, in February 2007, a larger Bronner's team returned to visit Laupheim and Heilbronn for an in-depth history dive. I had since phoned Werner Loeckle, the son of the last managing director of the Heilbronners' Madaform factory, who had grown up on the factory property. He took us to the cemetery where several of David's ancestors were buried; told us that his father had hoped that Emanuel or other family members would want to reestablish Madaform but found no takers. Before leaving Heilbronn we visited the old factory, snuck into the yard without meeting anyone, and Adam took a symbolic brick from the ground as physical reconnection with the past.

Laupheim was different for us, mostly since David and Mike's direct line of ancestors had moved from Laupheim to Heilbronn in 1900, and everyone else had emigrated. Yet there were many connections to the past. A friend of Bernd's lived near Laupheim and connected us with a local historian. He was generous with his time, had drawn up the family tree, took us to the Jewish cemetery, and showed us the gravestones of several ancestors going far back into the 1800s. We also visited the ancestral home of the family in the Jewish quarter where Emanuel Heilbronner Sr. had started his soap and candle production in 1858.

There is no Jewish community in Laupheim these days, but history is ever present. A neighbor to the Heilbronner's home told us that her father's job had been to accompany the remaining elder Jews to the train station from which they were taken to extermination camps in 1942.

At the impressive Museum on the History of Christians and Jews, set in a castle and showcasing the gradual integration of Jews beginning in the 1700s, we saw references to the Heilbronner family and learned that Carl Laemmle, the founder of Universal Pictures, hailed from Laupheim. He had emigrated to the United States in 1884, stayed connected with and became a benefactor of his home-town, helping many Jews emigrate in the 1930s until he died in 1939 in Beverly Hills. We learned that his studio produced and financed the compelling antiwar movie *All Quiet on the Western Front* in 1930, adapted from the book of German author Erich Maria Remarque, about the tragedy of WWI and a generation of young men point-lessly slaughtering each other. Nazis rightly saw the danger this antiwar film posed to their propaganda and, through a targeted pressure campaign, had it banned within weeks of its release, two years before they came to power.

That evening in Laupheim we got drunk on Kronen Pils, a local beer. Though we never met the brewery's owner, Paul Eble, he helped me ship a keg of Kronen to Dr. Bronner's anniversary party at Expo West in 2008, celebrating the sixtieth birthday of the brand in the United States and marking 150 years since the family's first soap manufacture in Laupheim.[2]

Right afterward, at the 2007 Biofach in Nuremberg, we finally found a European distributor for our products, a Belgian firm suc-cessful in selling their own organic coconut and palm oils and eager to bring our cult product to the German masses. I was skeptical, since just getting our soaps onto shelves in German natural food stores wouldn't be enough. The product needs explaining and PR, not a key element in the distributor's strategy. We ended up in quite a few stores but had few sales. Germans, including many friends and relatives, just didn't know what to do with a bottle covered with incomprehensible text. Once I explained, they understood, but staff in retail didn't have the time or inclination.

Thus, in 2010 we decided to start a dedicated distribution com-pany in Germany to get the message across. Through our network of friends, we found Axel Rungweber, a young man with a compatible vision and a law and business background. Over the next years he built, with Mike Bronner's and my support, the team of Dr. Bronner's Europe GmbH (DBE), our first wholly owned distribution subsidiary.

The first years were brutal for the growing team of motivated

Bronnerites. The failure of our soaps to sell in natural product stores under the previous distributor had blocked that distribution path, and new channels had to be developed. First came drugstore chains, then concept stores, next the first natural stores willing to give it another try. DBE kept growing against all odds and tough competition. I enjoyed watching how the DBE team launched stories in German media and tracked the annual feedback at Biofach, where we became regular exhibitors. If in 2011 virtually no one knew Dr. Bronner's, by 2016 we had droves of visitors complimenting us on our products and work.

From my work with Rapunzel on palm and coconut oil, and from friends and family of all ages, I knew that Germans were interested in "clean supply chains." For example, the evils of palm oil were much more well known and controversial there than in the United States. This offered me a great opportunity to argue in increasingly frequent talks at German venues that palm oil could actually be a great and sustainable crop—if one grew it properly, as we did in Ghana (discussed at length later in this book). That now five members of our Special Operations team are German has created more synergies and opportunities to train DBE staff in "regenerative agriculture" and adds to the credibility of DBE's messaging. Imagine how much I enjoy talking about our clean supply chain on my home turf!

RECONNECTING WITH LAUPHEIM

In 2016, out of the blue, a new link to Laupheim emerged. In his search for descendants of Laupheim Jews, one Micha Schick, the custodian of the Jewish cemetery in Laupheim we had visited in 2007, contacted us. Christel and I visited him and his colleagues at the Society of History and Remembrance and were impressed by their dedication to using the tragic history of their town to create ties with the descendants of former Laupheimians.

Micha—a policeman working in forensics by day—connected us with the principal of the local middle school. The following year, Mike Bronner and I spoke to some three hundred middle school students about our history and vision. We went far into recess and still received a standing ovation afterward. This showed that we could get younger Germans excited with our message of learning from—and overcoming—the past through unity. I was very impressed and elated!

In the evening we gave another talk at the former morgue of the Jewish cemetery; it, too, was well received by an older audience. The next day Micha told us that the new owner of the ancestral home on Judenberg 2, which we had visited back in 2007, had been at the talk and was moved by the Bronners' story and having second thoughts about her concept of tearing down the house and building apartments. We met with her at the house, and the rest is history. Imagine an activist California company going back to its roots and incorporating into a modern manifestation of our vision. We just had to do it, and after the meeting she agreed to sell the house at a very reasonable price.

Micha guided us through the renovation process. We selected an architect who made the house livable and modern—the existing six-and-a-half-foot ceilings just were too low for comfort—in line with the style of the old building and the Jewish Hill neighborhood. After reconstruction, we will rent the house to a Catholic institution that provides housing and work to intellectually disabled persons all over Swabia. The redesign of the house includes facilities that open it to the neighborhood—a small café and deck. Our vision is to help turn Jewish Hill into a diverse, modern neighborhood, of course with Dr. Bronner's family origin story prominent.

One highlight in the rediscovery of their German roots was the 2018 reunion of the extended Bronner family, including visits to Laupheim and Heilbronn. Laupheim rolled out the red carpet for some thirty family members, including the descendants of Uncle Ralph, Jim Bronner's brother, who'd helped guide the Bronners through the 1990s. The program was orchestrated by Micha. After a tour of the town in an old bus, the local orchestra played brass music in the museum's park. Finally, we went for an increasingly unruly tour of Paul Eble's Kronen-Brewery and joked around with his kids, who had been to the United States and wanted to know who was behind the crazy brand of soap they had used in the shower and on camping trips.

When people with Jewish ancestry visit Germany, they may still encounter initial apprehension, notably with those over forty. The awareness of the Holocaust, their forefathers' guilt, and uncertainty of what to expect from visitors still surface seventy-five years after the nightmare ended. Our exploration of the Bronners' German history has been rather different. Mike and David and their company's message are nonstandard, and both engage easily and authentically. This makes it easy to agree to remember but not obsess with the dark memory and instead move forward. (Note that none of Emanuel's descendants and their family are of Jewish faith, but Mike and David agree that they share a strong element of cultural Judaism, as did their grandfather, who ultimately created a religion of his own. He kept the membership open enough such that all of his family, whatever their official faith may be, subscribe to some or all of his All-One faith; and virtually all of the company's staff and now our suppliers of fair and organic ingredients and most international distributors connect with the ideas at the core of his vision.)

To claim that one's current grand deeds are deeply rooted in personal and family history is an overused cliché. Yet our dive together into its history has provided the Bronner family (and company) not only a strong and meaningful connection to their ancestral roots, with all their triumph and tragedy, but it also serves as a deep foundation that informs our advocacy and mission today.

We would encounter living and family history again in our quest for another essential crop—olives grown and rooted in the Holy Land.

Part 2

LEARN, GROW, IMPROVE

Olive harvest in Palestine

CHAPTER 8

Olive Oil—A Symbol of Hope in the Holy Land

On the Border, January 2007

I T WAS DARK, BUT ACROSS THE fence I made out Nasser Abufarha, standing some 150 feet (45 meters) away, by his car. What kept us from getting together was that I was in Israel and he was in the West Bank of Palestine, at the northern border checkpoint of Jalamah. It was January 2007; I was on my second visit to Canaan Fair Trade, the supplier of most of our organic and fair trade olive oil, and I had arrived at the checkpoint just before 7 p.m., when it was about to close.

The young Israeli soldiers were not entertaining arguments about letting me cross before tomorrow morning. So I called Nasser and asked him what to do. He suggested that the cab driver who had brought me from the Tel Aviv airport take me to one of the loopholes the border still had to accommodate Jewish settlers in the West Bank, and he'd send another cab with the right license plates authorized to operate on both sides of the fence. I switched cabs at the suggested place, feeling mildly conspiratorial as the Palestinian driver took me into the West Bank.

Fortunately, there were no Israeli checkpoints on the road, and an hour later Nasser and I reunited, after a 50-km detour, in his hometown of Jalamah. It was a powerful reminder that we were doing business in a place not as accessible as other countries we work in.

But let's back up a bit to how we got here.

In 2005, olive oil, our third largest ingredient by volume, was on our short list of ingredients to be switched to a certified organic and fair trade source. Simply buying organic olive oil from California wouldn't do. As with our other ingredients, we wanted to have an impact beyond just supporting organic agriculture.

Through an internet search, David found Canaan Fair Trade (now named Canaan Palestine), a commercial fair trade project headquartered in Jenin, a town in the northern West Bank. Founded by Nasser Abufarha, a Palestinian American with a PhD in anthropology, it appeared well thought through, was apparently working successfully with olive farmers, and aligned with our vision of achieving societal and ecological benefits through commerce. David was quite excited when he realized that the only fair trade olive oil on the planet came from the West Bank.

The initial suggestion by Adam Eidinger, our then PR and now social action director, was that considering the family and company's history and the fact that Emanuel Bronner's sister Lotte and her children lived in Israel, we should also buy from an organic project in Israel. This opened up a key fair trade issue: How meaningful is fair trade in well-developed Western countries, such as Israel, when you have a country next door where farmers struggle for survival?

Yet David saw a meaningful compromise: Why not buy the majority of oil from Canaan, as their olive farmers were under occupation and faced much more adversity than Israeli farmers; then purchase the balance from organic—or even fair trade—projects in Israel that were committed to coexistence with Palestine? In addition to Sindyanna, a fair trade project in Israel that engaged with Israeli Palestinians of Christian faith, David was also eager to purchase organic olive oil from the Strauss family, a distant Jewish relative of the Bronners. That way, Dr. Bronner's olive oil would be mixed from Muslim, Jewish, and Christian sources, resonating both to his grandfather's All-One vision as well as the vision of peace represented by the olive branch.

I first spoke by phone with Nasser in early 2006 about his path to organic and fair trade certification. We realized that we were both still rather green and would complement each other well. Nasser had, since he started Canaan in 2004, set up a fair trade structure, the Palestine Fair Trade Association (PFTA), and had been selling fair olive oil to several Palestine support groups, mostly in the UK. He already knew that to expand beyond that solidarity market, he needed external verification of his organic and fair trade claims, and Dr. Bronner's was very willing to support Canaan. This would include payment of all certification expenses for the first three years, something we've since done with other emerging fair trade projects.

In parallel, I was figuring out in Sri Lanka how to set up an organic smallholder system and fair trade coconut oil mill and had discovered the Swiss certifier IMO. And just as we started our collaboration with Canaan, the idea of using IMO's "Fair for Life" as our external fair trade standard emerged. I introduced Nasser to IMO, and we organized an initial organic training with IMO staff. As in Sri Lanka, we targeted accelerated organic conversion, since hardly any olive farmers used agrochemicals, and scheduled the first organic and FFL inspections for November 2006.

Unlike in Sri Lanka, Dr. Bronner's owned no shares in Canaan and would not be involved in operations. Instead, our role would be as a major customer and to lend support wherever needed.

Meanwhile, we also found a very compatible source of fair trade olive oil in Israel. The project Sindyanna had been founded by two Jewish Israeli women intent on collaborating with Israeli Palestinians, both farmers and workers. They produced fair olive oil and regional spices, such as zaatar, and like Nasser realized they needed organic and fair trade certification to stand a chance in the international market.

The Sindyanna founders had had the same experience we had

with the fair trade certifier FLO: "come back in 5 years." And so, as we had agreed to do with Canaan, Dr. Bronner's covered Sindyanna's initial Fair for Life certifications. IMO supported Dr. Bronner's approach to sourcing from "both sides of the fence" and went out of their way to help both projects prepare for their first audits. And since "olive oil from the Holy Land" would become our first purchase of organic and fair raw materials, we decided to use the occasion to produce the first of several short videos portraying our vision of a "clean supply chain" and the projects we worked with.

Tel Aviv, Israel, October 2006

In late October 2006, Christel and I arrived for the first time ever at Tel Aviv's Ben Gurion Airport. We had prepared well for this adventurous trip and read up on the history of the conflict and current conditions. And we hadn't missed radio coverage of the second Intifada from 2000 to 2005, a period of often heavy violence between Palestinians and the Israeli army in the West Bank and the Gaza Strip, as well as suicide bombings in Israel proper.

At Tel Aviv airport, we met Adam and his videographer, Robin Bell. They excitedly told us about the rave they had just attended in the Negev desert, as part of David's ongoing non-olive interest in Israel. Our first stop was Haifa, where Christel and I received a full dose of impressions.

The first was from an Israeli in his seventies who struck up a conversation as he heard Christel and me chatting in German outside our hotel. Without hesitation, he told us in German about his upbringing in and escape from Wiesbaden, near Frankfurt, in the late 1930s. In California, we had met many descendants of Ashkenazi Jews from Europe, but hardly any who had escaped the Holocaust. The openness and friendliness of the happenstance moved us, and it became the first of many such encounters that made the German-Jewish connection even more tangible than in Los Angeles. It also made us realize that many Jews born in Germany, in addition to Hebrew, spoke German rather than English.

We went for dinner in a trendy area, and our young and self-confident waitress asked about our destination. When we said "the West Bank," she was shocked. Reflecting the mood in Israel, she informed us that this was very dangerous. Numerous suicide bombings by radical Palestinians had, during the second Intifada, killed one thousand Israelis and generated an atmosphere of fear and wholesale distrust of Palestinians.

This was the first of many encounters in the not-so-Holy Land that helped us understand how effectively a decade of hostility and separation generates fear and lack of understanding.

The next day we visited Lotte Reches, Emanuel Bronner's youngest sister at her retirement home in Haifa. Lotte had left Heilbronn for Palestine in 1936, eventually joining the Ein Gev kibbutz in what would become northeastern Israel. Adam wanted to interview her for her life story and perspective on Emanuel. Her German was immaculate, but her English vocabulary had gaps that we filled in from behind the camera. At ninety, she was shockingly lucid and made Christel and me choke with the accounts of her family life in Heilbronn and her years at Ein Gev. I won't forget two of her lines: "my family in Heilbronn were Germans of Jewish faith, in that order." And on her brother, Emanuel, she said: "he was always somewhat of a rascal."

Jenin, Palestine, October 2006

The following morning, we walked across the highly secured Jalamah checkpoint into the West Bank with plenty of filming equipment, all properly authorized, and met Nasser for the first time on the other side of the fence. His welcome was warm, and we knew we'd be friends.

That we had work to do—get the organic and fair trade inspections started and shoot a video—kept us focused and made our first encounter very productive. That we were "comrades" in the battle for fair agriculture and peace created a base of trust that has made all future encounters with Nasser and his team inspirational and fun.

During the first two days in and around Jenin, Nasser gave us an engaging crash course in "What's going on in the West Bank—and how did we get to the current situation?" His family had lived for generations in Jalamah, a small town just on the Jordan side of the demarcation line initially created by the 1948 Israeli War of Independence. (In contrast, this same event is referred to as al-Nabka—or "the catastrophe"—by Palestinians, many of whom were either expelled from their homes in what's now Israel proper, and moved into camps in the West Bank, the Gaza Strip, or Lebanon, or migrated to the West.)

During Nasser's youth, the West Bank, captured by Israel from Jordan after the Six-Day War in 1967, was functionally part of Israel, legally an occupied territory. Nasser and his contemporaries enjoyed their mobility within Israel, but they felt like a disenfranchised minority without a perspective for their people. Mounting land expropriation by the Israeli Military and other agencies did not help. During the first Intifada, or uprising against Israeli occupation (1987–1993), Nasser became increasingly pessimistic about Palestine's future as an independent political entity, and in 1990 moved to the United States.

There, he first studied computer science and worked in related areas, including the management of a Radio Shack store in Detroit. He then shifted to anthropology, where his PhD thesis "The Making of a Human Bomb" researched the cultural and strategic aspects of using suicide bombings, and asked, "What makes people in conflict zones, such as the West Bank, become martyrs?"

While working on his master's in anthropology in Madison, Wisconsin, in the early 2000s, he began noticing cafés selling fair trade coffee. He became convinced that this fair trade concept could also benefit olive farmers in his home turf. Thus, in 2004 he founded Canaan to help improve livelihoods and create relevance in the northern West Bank. The combination of his naturally pro-Palestinian attitude and a desire to understand and help solve the roots of the conflict made Nasser my most trusted and inspiring expert on the Holy Land with a Palestinian perspective.

Emanuel Bronner offering his soaps to the world in 1978.

The author in 1980.

1973   1984   2005   2017 / CURRENT

Evolution of Dr. Bronner's iconic label on the one quart peppermint soap bottle, from 1973 to current.

Michael Milam and Trudy, Mike, and David Bronner
in front of Dr. Bronner's fire truck.

Gero and Christel at Serendipol nut yard. Sri Lanka, 2009.

Serendipol's team and visitors on second anniversary. Sri Lanka, 2009.

Sonali Pandithasekara, Karmel Abufarha, Gordon de Silva, and Nasser Abufarha at Dr. Bronner's international distributor symposium. Sri Lanka, 2018.

Lunch on the field of one of Canaan's olive farmers during a visit by teams from Special Ops and LUSH. Palestine, 2018.

Special Ops team at annual retreat. From left to right, front to back: Phillip Eschweiler, Jenn Rusu, Gero Leson, Julia Edmaier, Rob Hardy, Les Szabo, Ryan Zinn, Ute Eisenlohr. Jim Thorpe, Pennsylvania, 2019.

Serendipalm management team with Phillip Eschweiler, Gero Leson, and Safianu Moro in between. Asuom, Ghana, 2018.

Oil palm farmers from Abaam: Stephen Abrokwah, Daniel Nyanorm, and Charles Ohene. Ghana, 2016.

Four longtime production workers at Serendipalm: Comfort Amoanimaa, Mina Agyekumwaa, Elizabeth Buabeng Afrifa, and Linda Anim. 2016.

Fruit cleaning at Serendipalm during peak season. Asuom, Ghana, 2016.

Pavitramenthe team with visitors from Dr. Bronner's. Bareilly, India, 2018.

ABOVE: Group of women in fair-trade funded project. Dhilwari, India, 2018.

BELOW: DAF workshop in Samoa with Bastian Dreher-Pellhammer of Ecotop and group of field officers. 2019.

To warm us up, Nasser showed us around Jenin's refugee camp, founded in 1953 by Jordan to house Palestinians who had fled Israel during the 1948 war. It had been the site of clashes between the Israeli army and Palestinian militants in 2002. We saw numerous murals calling for resistance, and posters glorifying martyrs from the second Intifada that had ended only the previous year. At the same time, Jenin, whose city planning is unlike the Israel-controlled rural areas under the control of the Palestinian Authority (PA), was busy constructing office and residential buildings, most using the traditional Jerusalem (lime) stone as facades. There was a large, semi-enclosed market, or bazaar, and many small family-owned restaurants selling hummus, falafel, and other delicacies common throughout the Eastern Mediterranean.

The atmosphere was overwhelmingly similar to places Christel and I had enjoyed in Turkey in the 1970s and 1980s, just more modern, including the pervasiveness of mobile phones. We strolled through the market where we had a hummus lunch and inhaled the lively and engaging atmosphere. Then it was time to visit and film the reality in the fields.

We met entire families harvesting olives by hand with tarpaulins covering the ground. Nasser took us to vistas from hilltop fields that excluded any signs of modernity nearby. They were stunning, almost biblical. In the distance one would see Nazareth, on the other side of the fence and visibly modern. As you then looked down into the valley with its rolling slopes; reddish iron oxide soil; white limestone; and olive, almond, and fig groves, one expected Mary and Joseph coming down the valley road with their donkey, en route to Bethlehem to be counted.

Up until then, the Israeli occupation of the West Bank had been visible to us through frequent checkpoints by Israeli military, as well as by the PA police. Yet not until we visited a farming village with an olive oil press near the border did we realize the logistical difficulties that the occupation imposed on the rural population. Some of the farmers owned olive orchards separated from their village by a "finger" of well-fenced-in territory sticking into the West

Bank from Israel and occupied by several Israeli settlements. Farmers had access to their orchards only once a week and needed prior approval—a very inconvenient hurdle, especially during periods of tree maintenance and harvest. The logistics complications were but one obstacle to profitable olive oil production in the West Bank, which Nasser had taken on to overcome by going "fair trade."

Our day ended with a visit at one local olive oil mill where farmers brought their freshly harvested olives; the mill owner ran them through modern yet slightly aged Italian olive pressing and oil-processing equipment, and each farmer then fetched their oil. Dipping fresh bread in the green pungent oil, with a crowd of farmers waiting in line for their turn, was a joyful experience for the Dr. Bronner's team, allowing us to directly connect to the Mideastern tradition of producing oil for food and, to a much lesser degree, soap.

The next day we swung back into Israel to visit Sindyanna, near Nazareth. We interviewed one of the founders, Hadas Lahav, and one of her Israeli Palestinian farmers, and filmed their packaging operation. That intensive day gave us great insight into the project's concept—supporting the reconciliation between Israeli Palestinians and Jews in the Nazareth area by giving economic support to women—and the business challenges to such a project.

At night, we visited an oil mill in downtown Nazareth and learned to appreciate, for the first time, the difficulties of obeying fair trade requirements regarding working hours during the peak processing period. As with any agricultural operation, work is demanding and time-intensive during harvest time, and owners of small businesses, such as this oil mill, prefer if their staff work long shifts. Usually, so does the staff, sometimes making them exceed fair trade limits on weekly working hours. We would later encounter the same issue in a rather different setting at our palm oil mill in Ghana. I'll describe the concern and our solution to it in chapter 9.

The next day we sat in Canaan's headquarters in Jenin with the two IMO inspectors, Britta Wyss from Switzerland and David Gamrekeli from the Republic of Georgia. We scratched our heads, because the reports prepared by Nasser's team during the first set of internal inspections were all done in Arabic, which the inspectors didn't read.

This was just one of the communication headaches that our inaugural organic and FFL inspections brought with them. Fair trade concepts and extensive documentation requirements were also new to the agricultural field officers in Canaan's team. For Nasser and me, this turned these first inspections into a crash course in how organic and FFL standards view a smallholder project.

We learned to appreciate detailed and accurate documentation and the need to assess and control critical risks to the organic integrity of products—such as the use of fertilizers and the smuggling of conventional fruits into those from organic farms. One does not think about these issues when buying a bottle of olive oil, but now we knew. Both inspectors were inquisitive, and we all realized that the field officers would still need much training.

It helped Canaan's credibility with the inspectors that Nasser clearly was not interested in just adding two seals to improve marketability; rather, he was driven by effecting real change in the lives and livelihoods in the region. And there already was evidence of Canaan's impact on the ground. Nasser had helped establish the PFTA and initiated fair trade projects: prices paid to farmers for their organic and fair oil were some 30 percent higher than those they fetched in the local market. Canaan charged all customers a fair trade premium on purchases of olive oil and used it to fund community development projects with input from farmers and other community representatives. Not bad for a new project.

Two days after we had started the inspections, Canaan celebrated its annual harvest festival. In attendance were many of the (by then) 1,500 farmers, Canaan staff, and a flock of buyers and supporters from abroad, making for a crowd of more than 250 visitors. There was a mix of great food, speeches, and traditional dancing by men. That party made me realize that Nasser had well laid the foundation for becoming the world's first and soon largest supplier of credible fair trade organic olive oil, with the goal of making an impact for smallholders in the northern West Bank and their communities.

Before returning home after this first visit, Christel and I traveled from Jenin to Jerusalem—one shouldn't see the Holy Land without it—and got an appreciation of the Palestinians' everyday problems firsthand. There were four checkpoints on the main road, two of them taking thirty minutes to pass. At one we watched two young Israeli soldiers ordering a Palestinian who walked toward them (and whom they suspected of an attack) to drop his pants in the middle of the road—understandable from a safety standpoint but adding further humiliation. And we learned how many Palestinians cope: our driver knew bypasses to the main checkpoints, which were communicated by cell phone.

We realized that settlements, at least in the northern and western parts of the West Bank, are functionally bedroom communities, some looking like California suburbs. They had, during the second Intifada, drawn protests and violence by Palestinians, so were fenced in and often connected to Israel proper by secured roads which could not be used by Palestinians, thus often adding extra miles to an otherwise short trip.

Since 2006 I have been back in Jenin five times and always marveled at what Nasser and his Canaan team have built in the face of unpredictability over Palestine's short- and long-term fate. During that period, Dr. Bronner's has developed a uniquely strong relationship with Canaan. Since Nasser's situation was similar to mine, in that we both built organic and fair smallholder farming systems with value-added production and with similar challenges, there were experiences to share and alliances to build. Here are a few examples.

ETHICAL FINANCING

For Palestinian olives, the harvest starts in mid-October and extends into November. Entire families roam through their orchards, cover the ground with tarpaulins, climb into the trees, pick or comb olives, collect them from the tarpaulins, and take the olives in their pickups and cars to local oil mills for toll processing.

For many field or tree crops, such as olives, that annual window of the "harvest" or "peak" season is narrow, covering only one or two months of the year. Like any buyer, a fair trade project must purchase the farmers' produce, or the finished product such as olive oil, during that period. Yet customers for olive oil, such as food or soap brands, want supplies to match their own sales patterns— usually not in sync with harvesting patterns. They also prefer to pay on terms, typically thirty or sixty days after the oil has shipped or been received. This seasonality is at the core of the annual financing challenge of any agricultural start-up project.

But how do you finance this obvious gap if you have little credit history and no cash reserves?

Conventional banks rarely lend to socially motivated start-ups in their early days—it's too uncertain. Thus, one of the roles Dr. Bronner's took on in our own projects and those of close friends, such as Canaan and later Pavitramenthe in India, was that of a bank. From 2006 to 2008 we advanced to Canaan most of the money it needed to pay for our annual demand of olive oil, typically $2 million.

As Dr. Bronner's grew and was frequently tight on cash itself, another solution had to be found, and Nasser was on it. He contacted and evaluated several of the emerging flock of "ethical" or "sustainable" banks—those with the social mandate to lend to projects benefiting disadvantaged groups, such as smallholder farmers and small entrepreneurs in developing countries.

To compensate for the higher risk of default of such projects and the lack of easily repossessable collateral, they charge interest rates a few percentage points above those of commercial banks. Issuing working capital loans for crop purchases is, in effect, a key activity of ethical banks. They use purchase orders by credible buyers such as Dr. Bronner's as security, typically lend up to 60 percent to 70 percent of total purchase orders, and require repayment usually within six to nine months.

Starting in 2007, Nasser built relationships with several such banks, most notably Triodos, a respected Dutch organization. This took a large load off Dr. Bronner's cash flow. And when, in 2009, Sonali and I needed working capital financing for Serendipol to become more independent from Dr. Bronner's, Triodos was our first stop.

I vividly remember the first conference call with the bank: Sonali called from Sri Lanka and I was standing in our mill yard in Ghana with roosters crowing around me as we pitched Serendipol as the most sustainable coconut oil project on earth. Dr. Bronner's support and Nasser's reference helped. Even though Serendipol had only lost money so far, Triodos gave us a $250,000 working capital loan, enough to help us through the major coconut buying season.

We developed a close and productive working relationship with Triodos. Then, over time, Serendipol "matured," became increasingly profitable, and, by 2013, qualified for loans from Sri Lankan commercial banks charging much lower interest rates. (Our projects Serendipalm in Ghana and Pavitramenthe in India have gone through the same experience with Root Capital and OikoCredit, US- and German-based ethical lenders, respectively.)

In essence, ethical or sustainable banks offer professional and nonextortionist financing options to social enterprises that need much more than the $1,000 typically offered by microcredit institutions. Trite but true: unless a young agricultural project thinks early about financing its seasonal purchases of raw materials, it will end up stiffing farmers for a lack of cash—common in agriculture, fair trade or not—or pay extortionist interest to ruthless lenders; neither is good for business or reputation.

GRANT PLANS

Between 2006 and 2010, Canaan had grown considerably, largely due to Dr. Bronner's growing appetite for olive oil. In 2009, Nasser first told me of his plans to expand Canaan's operation: build its own headquarters and operational facility, bring some of the value-added oil milling and packaging in house, expand storage capacity for oil, and diversify to add new products. Financing on top of the annual working capital loans for the purchase of oil was not available, and Nasser began looking for grants to help Canaan grow and expand the impact of its work.

People aware of the uneven distribution of wealth on our planet generally support giving aid to "less developed countries." But how to do that efficiently with a long-lasting impact? To simplify, many Western aid programs from the 1960s through the 1980s focused on building roads, schools, wells, processing of agriproducts—all very important, but unless you also develop an effective and noncorrupt civic infrastructure with some promise of sustainability (things like a school board, a small "water district" that charges a fee for water, a cooperative that runs a processing unit), that infrastructure is doomed to rot.

The saying "Give a man a fish, and you feed him for a day. Teach a man to fish, and you feed him for a lifetime" increasingly became the guiding principle for aid. Aid agencies realized that private-sector companies with a commitment to their host country will, in many sectors, make more effective contributions to development than NGOs or governmental agencies. The simple reason is that they engage with farmers, workers, and community in ways not generally available to NGOs and governments: they buy goods from farmers and employ people on a commercial scale. They also contribute to select community development projects, and thus are an integral part of the economy, whereas NGOs generally aren't.

Projects such as Canaan or Dr. Bronner's Serendi projects practice, as part of their business, what the aid agencies of many developed countries love to support: the capacity-building and development of markets for value-added products, increasingly related to preventing and adapting to global climate change or pandemics. Many such agencies are financed by the national ministries for economic development; some are funded by private foundations.

Realizing that private companies can be agents of development led to the creation of programs for public–private partnerships (PPP). PPP projects typically focus on the environment, training and upskilling, workplace security, and innovation in agriculture and processing. Naturally, the sustainability of this approach depends on the profitability of the companies receiving funds—but that's not substantially different from smaller NGOs that also need to raise funds for their goals and whose "business model" may be less solid than that of a company.

More important, development without strengthening commercial activity ignores that commerce is the life blood of any society— so why not engage with it?

But having private companies as the motor of rural development is not a fail-safe, either. For one, they will often look at a grant as a way to primarily support their business goals and commit less to the development aspect of it. Understandable for young companies trying to make it in "sustainable agriculture," but it may distract from their project mandate.

Briefly, how do PPP grants work? Naturally, a project needs to be eligible—it must be located in "the right country" and its goals must match the mandates of the program. A grant may fund up to 50 percent of the total cost of an approved project; the remainder must be raised by the applicant, such as Canaan or a Dr. Bronner's sister company. Eligible contributions can be in cash or kind, including all labor and expenses, such as those by staff at Dr. Bronner's and its affiliates. In a nutshell: PPP grants allow a company to fulfill its otherwise unaffordable dreams—but you have to put up at least half of the cost, so you have some real skin in the game.

Back in 2009, Nasser came across the Dutch PSI program, a PPP administered by the Dutch foreign ministry. It required cooperation between Canaan and Dr. Bronner's, with the latter taking the role of a committed buyer and technical partner. A grant of close to 1 million euros, courtesy of Dutch taxpayers, ultimately financed a substantial expansion of Canaan's storage and bottling operation for olive oil and the diversification of its product range to include cured olives, capers, dried tomatoes, couscous, and other products.

Picture a large underground vault with a battery of one hundred stainless steel tanks, each holding five thousand liters. Storing olive oil after purchase at cooler temperatures and with a nitrogen "blanket" significantly reduces oxidation and extends its shelf life and value. Nearby, a semiautomatic bottling plant fills the spicy olive oil into the tall green bottles valued by aficionados in Europe and the United States.

Dutch taxpayers do not want their money spent frivolously, nor can a PPP grant be anticompetitive (i.e., give a strong advantage to the recipient) unless the project stimulates benefits in an entire industry or region. Most PPP programs limit their contributions to a private-sector project to some $250,000. Some have restrictions on the purchase of production hardware and who gets to own it after the typical three-year duration of a project. And there are extensive reporting and documentation requirements—as is expected when it comes to spending public money.

To date, Dr. Bronner's supply chain projects have received matching funds for PPP projects of more than $2.5 million from the two main German development agencies, GIZ and DEG, and the British FRICH and AgDevCo programs. These grants ultimately matched Dr. Bronner's generosity with our staff time and financial resources and allowed us to pursue social development and sustainability goals in Sri Lanka, India, Ghana, and Samoa for which we wouldn't have had funding otherwise. No wonder I now take a more positive view of development aid by Western countries, as long as it gives the private sector an opportunity to drive the process—with all the needed checks and accountability.

REGENERATION IN PALESTINE

To most readers Palestine will be an elusive concept; it is not a common travel destination, and few can imagine what it looks like—notably since most news footage involves air strikes, commando attacks, human suffering, and rubble. No wonder that friends in the United States and Europe look at me with concern when I suggest a visit to the West Bank and Canaan's operation as an enjoyable, educational, and "safe" vacation trip.

Driving through the northern West Bank and visiting Canaan's farmers, one sees few signs of the conflict—at least during "quieter times." Rather, between villages, one marvels at the hilly, sometimes rocky, Mediterranean landscape dotted with groves of olives, almonds, pomegranates, figs, and grape vines. The latter reduce soil erosion by wind and rain, and vine leaves make for a tasty vegetable ingredient in lamb roasts. Most villages are well-kept, and Jerusalem limestone is ubiquitous. Cities, such as Jenin and Nablus, are modern and growing with large older quarters dating back to Roman times or earlier. They feature lively markets with traditional food production (and the occasional maker of traditional bar soap). Much of the area around Jenin is fertile alluvial valleys teeming with field crops—tomatoes, cucumbers, melons, grains, and herds of sheep. An afternoon hike to an outcrop near the villages of Anin or Nsif Jabail offers stunning views of the land and villages.

What's the food like in the West Bank? Picture our breakfast in the garden of Nasser's guest house. In a crevice of a karstic rock ledge a fire was burning, and Nasser fried a handful of eggs from his own free-roaming chicken in a generous amount of olive oil. There was leban (fresh cheese), the flat bread from the local baker still warm, green onions and cucumbers, a dish full of za'atar (dried sage with sesame), and tiny cups of cardamom-spiced coffee from a thermos we had brought along.

Even more insightful and impressive are field lunches with farmers to discuss their agricultural practices and life in general. We sit at a long table in the broken shade of olive trees over a lunch of fresh bread, olive oil, boiled potatoes, hummus, cheese, yoghurt, tomatoes, sometimes lamb, with figs and sweets as desserts. One enjoys the flavor and then realizes that such a lunch is the dream of any Western foodie who savors short, local supply chains. Leave out cheese, lamb, and eggs, usually served separately, and it is vegan. Virtually all the food we ate was grown or raised within 20 km of the table—out of necessity and tradition. Yes, sugar, coffee, and the white flour in the pastry came from elsewhere, but it doesn't take away from the fact that Palestinians in the West Bank may be one of the few modern populations that largely eat local food—and thus are leading a wave of nutritional regionalism sweeping much of Western Europe and, increasingly, the United States.

As I have never visited Gaza, I can only speak of the West Bank and specifically the farmers and staff at Canaan. Much of what I describe will sound superficial, but it is meant to give my personal impression and to counteract the common perception that all of Palestine is a dangerous neighborhood.

The West Bank shares one nasty feature with socialist former East Germany, remembered from my trips to Berlin in the seventies: a fence or wall around it that few locals can cross routinely. Yet what was or is enclosed by that fence is very different. East Germany was a well-controlled dictatorial regime, one that did not tolerate political dissent and was quick to imprison. Leaving it for the West was virtually impossible, and many who tried lost their lives, directly at the fence or later over broken hearts.

The West Bank is different. You routinely meet people who have lived, studied, and worked in the United States or Europe, and returned voluntarily. One of Canaan's farmers excitedly spoke about his trip to Wisconsin on Nasser's invitation, and his side trip to Las Vegas, which he said he had to see. Canaan's IT expert had worked and gotten married in Mexico and returned with his wife to the West Bank—it was his home, after all.

Since we began buying our olive oil from Canaan in 2006, I have had many discussions with Nasser about his vision for his company and country. For him, the people, their land, and the olive trees are a symbol not only for peace, but also for endurance. He took us to several groves of trees with huge trunks, some established to be far older than a thousand years and still feeding the locals. Yet it took me until 2018 to fully appreciate Canaan's impact. Initially, I thought it was all about offering farmers who were cut off from international trade, and whose orchards are under siege by Israel, a better paid outlet for their product. Over the years and as Canaan's impact has grown, I've come to appreciate the anthropologist's wisdom Nasser shared with me early on. "Gero," he said, "it's mostly about offering people meaning and purpose."

And that's what Canaan has done. Meet their farmers and realize the motivation that Nasser's experiments in diversification generates, such as the production and export of a traditional Palestinian food staple, freekeh. Or discuss with some forty farmers the concepts of regenerative agriculture, and field their skeptical questions and thoughtful contributions. Then see the pride when realizing that some of the traditional farming practices well qualify as regenerative, such as cover cropping and intercropping in between olive trees.

A coincidental visit by Bob Quinn, a pioneer of regenerative agriculture in Montana and founder of the brand Kamut, led to engaging discussions about the rediscovery of ancient wheat varieties and their benefits—and to walks through fields of traditional wheat and spelt varieties, in trials grown by Nasser's contract farmers. The latter are also experimenting with the production of organic heirloom tomatoes in greenhouses with mesh roofs and controlled irrigation.

One morning we witnessed the drying, turning, and roasting of green-harvested wheat on a hillside. The procedure looked like an archaic dance. Young men followed each other in a line, turning and upturning and then turning again the cut wheat, throwing it with each movement by pitchforks in the wind. In a slowly turning kiln a flame burned off the chaff and straw. After another round of sun drying you have freekeh, a traditional grain with a rather modern nutritional profile: high in protein and fiber and a low glycemic index. Later Nasser tells us that he's working with a group in southern Germany that uses the same traditional process.

The next day we join Canaan's staff of fifty on their annual company outing, rolling down the road to visit Bethlehem and Hebron with singing and dancing on the large bus. You speak with individual staff about their lives and expectations and are surprised by the normality of their wishes in the face of looming uncertainty: find a loving partner, maybe have kids, have a meaningful career that contributes to Palestine's cultural heritage and the development of the country. Since one can speak openly, you'd expect outbursts of anger toward the continued de facto occupation. Not so much anymore. The silliness and provocation of allowing a handful of Jewish settlers to form an enclave in Palestinian downtown Hebron and protect it by Israeli soldiers receives an annoyed head-shaking—"yes, that's really crazy." And then you talk about more personal topics, things you can do something about, such as getting your father to accept that the choice of a spouse should be yours.

Nasser has, from the beginning, looked at the cultural significance of Canaan's work. He keeps reminding us that Palestinians have a long civilization-building history in the area.

Most Palestinians trace their ethnic roots back to the Canaanites, a group of Semitic-speaking indigenous populations of the Southern Levant, both sedentary and nomadic-pastoral groups. They had settled the area of modern Syria, Lebanon, Palestine, Jordan, and Israel beginning in the eighth millennium BC and gained significant political importance during the second millennium BC. Its ethnic groups were organized in city-states—many of the cities still stand today, such as Beirut, Tyre, and Jericho—with smaller inland kingdoms specializing in agriculture. The Greeks called the Canaanite culture "Phoenicia." During its height, between 1200 and 800 BC, this federation of city-states based on agriculture, seafaring, and trade expanded across the entire Mediterranean. Their merchandise included timber, dyed textiles, wine, and, naturally, olive oil. The city of Carthage, in today's Tunisia, was a major Phoenician hub, and Canaan deities, such as Baal, influenced the Greek religion.

By about 500 BC the land of Canaan had become the battleground of other regional powers and lost its dominance to Persians, Assyrians, Israelites, Romans, and, later, Islamic Arabs and Christian crusaders. Yet they've retained a cultural identity in spite of having the deck of power stacked against them. Maintaining this sense of cultural identity is one of Nasser's visions.

I hope very much for Nasser, his fellow Canaanites, and for the Israeli Jews who are their neighbors that this strong cultural foundation and interest in building a society connected to its culture and striving for collaboration will be the Palestinians' contribution to lasting peace in the Holy Land.

IN ISRAEL

If this chapter on "olive oil from the Holy Land" mostly talks about our work in the West Bank, it's because that's where our team thought construction of a fair and regenerative supply chain for olive oil would have the greatest impact.

At the same time, David, Adam, and other allies also became involved in Israel on similarly visionary projects, such as efforts to legalize the use of cannabis for medicinal and spiritual purposes in Israel. Furthermore, in recent years, groups in the United States and Israel have cooperated on investigating the use of psychedelics for those purposes. I believe that Dr. Bronner's backing of such efforts may well become one of our most important philanthropic projects—time will tell.

After the first two visits to the Holy Land, I had also fallen in love with Israel, as different as it was from the West Bank. I never had a real problem reconciling my affection for land and people on both sides of the fence. Aware of the Holocaust as a driving factor, I did not question the legitimacy of Israel, even though it had caused massive suffering to Palestinians. I had no illusions that the anti-Israel rhetoric and policies of the neighboring Arab countries were meant to serve their own, generally less-than-enlightened purposes, rather than the Palestinian cause. As for Israel, I had, since 1973, kept an eye on its politics and was increasingly turned off by the actions of successive governments that, under the pretense of security, caused more and more frustration among people in the West Bank and Gaza Strip, with occasional periods of hope in the 1970s and 1990s. In a nutshell, to me, Israel is a great example of how a country with the right and means to defend itself has managed to provoke those who already suffered from its deeds, causing a spiral of violence and counterviolence.

Aside from that, Israel feels rather different from Palestine. A modern, high-energy country, it is in many ways reminiscent of California's semi-arid landscapes or Southern European cities and suburbs, combined with a high ethnic diversity. And the voltage of personal and public discourse sure is much higher than in the West Bank.

During our early years in California, Christel and I had met occasional skepticism toward Germans by Jewish Californians. Yet we never experienced this in Israel. Israelis we chatted with immediately knew we were German. The conversations turned to current matters, and when we spoke about history, often involving the Holocaust, German roots were usually viewed as positive or neutral. The main reasons for this, I made out, were that those with German parents and grandparents had absorbed their connection to the German culture and deemed them influential and worthy. Moreover, Germany is perceived by Israelis as the most loyal friend of Israel in Europe, compared with, say, France or Spain.

My personal relationships to Israel vastly expanded when, in 2008, Dr. Bronner's found a distributor for our products in Israel. Shai Friedman, the founder of EcoGreen, became a good friend and ally—and someone who helped us understand the position of left-leaning Israeli patriots. Shai and his wife, Atara, hosted Christel and me several times at their house in the eccentric community Clil in the Galilee, with simple and creatively built houses, sometimes yurts, in an arid setting, with a café run by the second generation of left-leaning European Jews.

Shai showed us around northern Israel and gave us a firsthand appreciation of the visibly multilayered history of the area, including: the crusader town Acre; the Jordan Valley, site of the first settlements in the early 1900s; the circus at the Christian holy sites at the Sea of Galilee; and the modern yet history-laden Tel Aviv and Jaffa, with visible German influence. The White City is a collection of over four thousand Bauhaus-style buildings created by German Jewish architects who emigrated to the "British Protectorate" in the 1930s and created the largest assembly of such buildings on the planet.

We once met Shai's mother, an enlightened and impressive woman representative of many Jews from Hungary and Romania who barely escaped the Nazis. She was multilingual and very accomplished as a surgeon specializing in the treatment of injuries suffered by Israeli soldiers.

And I learned through Shai that in Israel, progressive attitudes are very compatible with strong patriotism, anger at the hostility of neighboring countries, and paranoia of Iran's plans. With him and other friends we had repeated arguments over politics and generally couldn't quite resolve our disagreements. But these arguments also were the foundation of a strong friendship that soon extended beyond business and soap.

I remember the first encounter of Shai and Nasser in 2008 at Dr. Bronner's Israeli market launch event at a college near Tel Aviv. Driving from the event in the same car, the two got into an argument about the right of Palestinians expelled in 1949 to return to their homes. They naturally disagreed on the facts—what crimes were perpetrated during the expulsion—and the solution.

There was no agreement during the car ride, yet also no obvious hostility and anger. I wondered whether they'd ever become friends. They did, over the years, as we all met regularly at trade shows in Germany and California and then the eventual visit by Nasser and his son to Clil. It took only ten years, but that's nothing for such a long-lasting conflict. To watch that relationship develop was a metaphor for what a mission-based company can achieve.

Personally, one of my biggest hopes is that Dr. Bronner's work in the Holy Land will create more such relationships of genuine respect and appreciation, with never-ending arguments as a reminder that the Middle East is full of historical conflicts, suffering, and trade-offs with no easy solutions. But as long as there's a potentially critical mass of people on both sides of the fence with an attitude of coexistence and respect, I'll be hopeful. So much grows from olives, an emblematic crop helping people find purpose and peace in an area torn apart by conflict.

The next two crops I'll introduce, oil palm and cocoa, are problematic in very different ways but offer the same potential for re-generation. Let's move over to Ghana for that.

Tea tree: a strong flavor and a value-added crop

Now that you've been introduced to two of our major ingredients, let's turn our attention to one of the essential oils that give our soaps their distinctive scents. Dr. Bronner's fourth strongest—or best-selling—variety is tea tree, a tall shrub in the myrtle family, native to Australia's coasts. The pungent essential oil is steam distilled from leaves and branches and credited with medicinal benefits.

In early 2017, our Special Ops team came across a fledgling tea tree oil project started by a young, white South African couple. (I'll share more about the workings of the Special Ops team in the next chapter). Oribi Oils checked all our boxes: Stuart and Lauren Bateman's vision was to help mend the growing, gloomy rift between the country's formerly ruling white minority and its black majority. Forming a cooperation between commercial white farmers and emerging black farmers while diversifying the region's agriculture would be their contribution.

The predominant regional crop is sugar cane, grown as a mono-crop with seasonal labor. Why not add a novel, value-added crop that smallholders can grow, is harvested year-round, and processed locally?

Lauren's family grew sugar cane in the Oribi Flats area south of Durban, and she had grown up there, too. She and Stuart assembled a coalition of farmers and cooperatives and took over a government-built small distillation plant. Most of the land contracted by Oribi was organic; they dreamed of "going fair trade," but didn't quite know how. After meeting the Batemans at Biofach, my teammates Rob Hardy and Ryan Zinn and I found them sincere and swiftly decided to help further develop the project—as a committed, significant customer. After all, we needed a more credible, accessible, and better-quality source of FTO tea tree oil, and this looked just like it!

First, Dr. Bronner's OSI team tested samples—they smelled just right, and we started buying from Oribi. Next, our teammate Julia supported Oribi on their path to FFL certification in 2019. Credible intention and a fair trade structure were already in place, and so the certification was straightforward.

The project now includes some 130 farmers on 220 hectares in a blend of larger, white-owned farms and some fifteen cooperatives formed by black smallholders, mostly new to commercial farming and cultivating smaller plots of tribal land. Such collaboration is still rare in post-Apartheid South Africa and not without problems. For example, Stuart's idea of the joint preparation of fields by black and white farmers flopped. Additionally, many of the large cane farmers still subscribe to an input-dominated conventional agricultural paradigm. Shifting to "regenerative" will take time.

The Batemans, now with three kids, have become realistic about the pace of progress. They understand these challenges as a natural process, just as we've experienced on all our projects. Meanwhile, Rob and Ryan support the regenerative shift: the planning of a composting plant to increase humus content, the use of mulch to protect the trees from droughts, the reduction of the depth of tillage before row planting, and the introduction of cover crops to minimize barren soil. To expand, the project also needs to diversify its crops; it runs trials with other aromatic herbs such as rosemary, rose geranium, and lavandin.

Setting and product of Oribi are very different from our other FTO projects, but the concept is the same: motivate a diverse group of people to cooperate on their livelihood, use their shared goals to improve agricultural and social conditions, and understand that it will take years to get where you want to go.

Ghanian farmworkers carrying
oil palm fruit

CHAPTER 9

Palm Oil—Redeeming an "Evil Crop"

WHEN DR. BRONNER'S DECIDED, IN 2005, to shift its major raw materials to organic and fair trade sources, palm oil naturally had to be included. It accounted for some 10 percent of our agricultural raw materials—and still does.

But by then palm oil had become the devil's oil. "You cannot produce sustainable and fair palm oil," is the conventional wisdom of many of our activist allies, leaving consumers confused about the actual problems with the crop and unsure of what to do about it.

"Why is Dr. Bronner's still using palm oil? Because it's so cheap?" some ask us.

"Don't you know it's destroying the rainforest and killing orangutans?" others say.

If we wanted to give truthful and heartening answers to these questions, then building an organic and fair supply for palm oil was particularly important. Our experience over the last fifteen years now allows us to explain to customers and the world at large what palm oil is, how it works, and what damage and benefits it can generate up and down a supply chain. Thanks to our "in house" production of FTO palm oil, Dr. Bronner's is in an excellent position to demonstrate that it is not the oil itself that native people and environmental NGOs fight against—for good reason—but rather the way it is generally grown: in large monocultures on carelessly cleared forest land.

I always add that Dr. Bronner's is not using our own palm oil from Ghana because it's cheap. Rather, as we joke, it's one of the more expensive palm oils on the planet—because we produce it in a fair and regenerative way that benefits our host town Asuom, its environs, and the planet at large in several significant ways.

Before visiting Ghana, let's understand what drove the boom in popularity and the poor reputation of palm oil.

THE POTENTIAL AND TRAGEDY OF PALM OIL

As with all our key projects, the choice of Ghana as the home for our palm oil project has a historical twist to it. The African oil palm, *Elaeis guineensis*, originated from Guinea, the traditional name for the West African region along the Gulf of Guinea, now stretching from the The Gambia in the northwest to Cameroon and Equatorial Guinea in the southeast—with Ghana somewhere in the middle.

The oil palm's natural habitat is the moist tropical forest or savanna along the coast, where it may grow up to 60 feet (20 meters) high. Although they look like trees, botanically palms are related to grasses and bamboo. Because palm oil dating back to 3000 BC was excavated in an Egyptian tomb, it must have been used by West Africans for at least five thousand years and was likely taken to Egypt by Arab traders.[1]

The palm forest on the south coast of Nigeria must have looked stunning, because the first Europeans named it "Palm Oil Coast." British traders exported the oil for use as an industrial lubricant. It also became a key ingredient of soap products, such as the Palmolive brand and, of course, the Heilbronners' Madaform brand. By around 1870, palm oil was the primary export of some West African countries until the next decade when it was surpassed by cocoa.

Colonialists also saw the oil palm's potential elsewhere. The Portuguese and Spanish exported it to South America in the 1500s, the Dutch to Java in 1848, and the British around 1910 to what is now Malaysia, where they set up modest-size plantations. Only in the 1970s was it discovered that oil palms were not primarily pollinated by wind but rather by insects native to West Africa. Their introduction and the breeding of varieties with more flesh and less kernel ultimately laid the ground for today's productive plantations in Malaysia and Indonesia. They now produce some 85 percent of the world's growing demand for palm oil and have also become the source of a global social and ecological tragedy.

Why has palm oil become so successful and controversial? Certainly not because a medium-sized company like Dr. Bronner's uses it in bar soaps!

In fact, palm oil has countless uses. Between 2005 and 2019, its global annual consumption had risen from 35 million metric tons (MT) to about 72 million MT (1 metric ton equals 1.1 short tons, or 2,200 pounds). Projections peg consumption by 2030 at 110 million MT per yr. This makes palm oil—or palm fruit oil, to be precise—the world's most sold plant oil by volume. It accounts for some 35 percent of the world's plant-derived oil production, far ahead of soy, canola, and sunflower oil, and palm oil plantations now cover some 25 million hectares of tropical land—more than half the size of California![2]

What drives its popularity? In short, its unique composition of fatty acids offers diverse uses in processed goods at low cost. Most palm oil used in consumer products (including Dr. Bronner's bar soaps) is refined, bleached, and deodorized (RBD) to yield an off-white, tasteless, and odorless product. RBD palm oil may then be "fractionated"—its fatty acids separated into two main groups: high-melting point *stearin* (which increases fat solidity and can replace partially hydrogenated fats in shortening and margarines) and low-melting point *olein* (liquid at room temperature and predominantly used as cooking oil.) That versatility makes palm oil suitable for myriad consumer products: foods, cosmetics, animal feed, and cleaning products.

Since the 2000s, the EU has used increasing amounts of palm oil for energy (biodiesel, heating oil), prompted by periods of high crude oil prices and subsidies for "biofuels." Palm oil is irrelevant in the US fuel supply; few passenger cars run on diesel, and the US approach to "green fuels" has focused on the subsidized production of ethanol from corn—as unsuitable in reducing greenhouse emissions as is palm oil in diesel.

The palm fruit offers a second, rather different oil: palm kernel oil (PKO) made from the edible seed of the oil palm fruit. Its fatty acid composition is similar to that of coconut oil, which it has increasingly replaced in technical and food applications. PKO and coconut oil both have a high content of lauric acid, which is key to the lathering of Dr. Bronner's soap and is essential to the performance of synthetic detergents. Thus, both oils are named "lauric oils" and fetch a steep price premium over palm oil.

The cut-open palm fruits in Figure 2 show the source of both oils—the outer light-colored fruit flesh and the inner white kernel and its dark shell. Note the much thicker fruit flesh and thinner shell in the tenera fruit forms on the left, bred for maximum fruit oil content, versus the dura form with a very thick shell.

Now, combine the versatility of palm oil with the economics of its production and the reason for its success becomes obvious. Of all oil crops, the oil palm is the most productive, as measured by the output of oil per hectare. It typically produces 5 MT of oil per hectare per year; compare that with canola, soy, and sunflower, which all produce less than one MT per hectare per year. High productivity and low maintenance requirements of oil palms makes for excellent economies of scale—in other words, the larger the plantation and the mill, the lower your cost of producing a metric ton of palm oil.

These low costs of production combined with income from two

Figure 2. Selection of palm fruits of the tenera and dura fruit forms

product streams, palm oil and PKO, allow for a low selling price and a good profit, even when world market prices for palm oil crash due to oversupply. No wonder that investors and governments in Malaysia and Indonesia placed their bets on oil palm's production and export. For maximum productivity, plantation operators will apply mineral fertilizers, use herbicides to knock weeds down, and utilize pesticides, if needed, to fight infestations by pests and diseases.

As demand for palm oil continues to grow, other countries in Asia, South America, and Africa are tempted to follow the same path. A great economic concept—except it favors farming in monocultures on large plots of contiguous and cheap land. One *could* plant such plantations on degraded land, formerly used for cattle ranching or other monocrops. Yet that was not done in most early Indonesian plantations—and still isn't in all.

Rather, they use forest—secondary or even primary—frequently by taking public land on a low-cost lease or through land-grabbing.

Then the clearcutting or burning of preexisting forests begins—with the well-known dreadful effects on people, animals, local environment, and global climate. National governments in tropical countries generally support such aggressive development and accept its high social and environmental cost. They are driven by the need to generate export revenues—and corruption between private plantation developers and government decision makers often plays a role. There just isn't the oversight or even the interest to protect unproductive forest; it has no economic value except for those who live in it—and they have little voice .

That's where the production of palm oil began to attract the ire of local populations and international NGOs alike.

IS SUSTAINABLE PALM OIL POSSIBLE?

In 2004, the largely uncontrolled sacrifice of forests and communities prompted a collaboration of prominent producers and traders of palm oil, banks and investors, major consumer brands, and NGOs like the World Wildlife Fund. Named the Roundtable for Sustainable Palm Oil (RSPO), it was aimed at jointly tackling a serious global environmental problem and the growing criticism of palm oil by Western media and consumers that threatened to halt the global growth of its consumption.

RSPO's key mandate: promote the production of "sustainable oil palm" through credible and enforceable standards, effect improvements to setup and operation of oil palm plantations, and engage with all stakeholders. Now, RSPO has more than 4,500 members worldwide, representing all sectors of the palm oil value chain, plus financing and NGOs.

In theory, the original RSPO standard ensured "sustainable" plantation management, including minimization of uncontrolled soil movement and erosion. It permitted only the "controlled" use of agrochemicals. It also required that plantations employ "social accountability" and "transparency" when dealing with its labor force, smallholder farmers, and local communities.

Land cleared and planted after 2004 was not RSPO-certifiable, but most of the insensitive clearing of the 1990s was grandfathered in. NGOs first routinely denounced poor enforcement of standards on certified plantations. Even many RSPO members were dissatisfied with loopholes, allowing continued deforestation. In response, RSPO adopted in late 2018 new principles and criteria, strengthening its rules on deforestation, planting, labor, and land rights. To maximize the inventory of biomass in oil palm plantations, a "high-carbon stock approach" distinguishes forests from degraded land and will allow RSPO members to plant only on the latter. A standard for independent smallholders now regulates their practices and the relationships between farmers and large palm oil mills.

So is all well with big palm oil? Not quite. Past standard violations by RSPO members—notably, large plantations—suggest an ongoing temptation to sacrifice planet for profit. The larger global concern is that still only some 20 percent of the world's palm oil production is RSPO-certified. The balance comes from plantations that are only regulated by their governments. Even worse, in 2018, less than 50 percent of that amount was actually sold as RSPO-certified. Both facts reflect poorly on the willingness of producers to follow RSPO's pragmatic rules and of brands and consumers to pay a very modest price premium that even covers the additional cost incurred by the producers to grow and mill RSPO palm oil.[3]

This situation makes it unlikely that the topic of "sustainable palm oil" and the smoke over Southeast Asia will disappear from the news anytime soon. Meanwhile, most *trusted* brands have convinced their customers that RSPO-certified palm oil is as sustainable as it gets.

So why would Dr. Bronner's start its own production of organic and fair trade palm oil in Ghana? About half of the world's palm fruits grow on small farms—in Africa, even more than 60 percent. Unsurprisingly, their yields are only about one third of those of well-planted and maintained plantations. But that can be changed, as Serendipalm and other organic projects have shown. Increasing yields through improved seedlings, farm maintenance, and mixed agroforestry can expand global palm oil production without further clearing forest.

Why bother? In chapter 5, I outlined the importance of smallholders for employing, feeding, and cooling the planet. As an SME, a small and medium-sized enterprise, Dr. Bronner's feels kinship with small farmers, entrepreneurs who have some control over their future—but require support to live up to their full potential.

This will not happen overnight, but even its possibility explains why Dr. Bronner's and other brands would pay a significant premium for an FTO palm oil from such smallholder farms.

And perhaps before judging developing nations too harshly for preferring economic development over protecting natural resources, shouldn't we think about the role Western companies have played in environmental devastation the world over? That is something my work has allowed me to witness firsthand in Nigeria, this time related to petroleum.

THE OTHER OIL—THE IMPACT OF PETROLEUM IN NIGERIA

Escravos, Nigeria, 2002

It was late 2002, three years before starting Serendipol in Sri Lanka, when I took my first trip to Nigeria. Chevron had hired me to help coordinate a research project in one of their main petroleum operations in the northwestern part of the Niger Delta.

From our helicopter I marveled at the meandering natural waterways that crisscrossed the area. There also were a few straight, obviously manmade canals, but no roads; all transport was by boats. The occasional village had twenty to fifty simple houses with sheet metal roofs and jetties.

The land was flat and low-lying, much of it covered by grass and tidal water. There were extended areas without any vegetation, strongly eroded mud flats and swamps with dead oil palms. I then saw live oil palms on knolls farther inland. Why did they do well at an elevation but die in the flats?

Satellite photos and reports from the ground showed that large portions of the local freshwater swamps and forest had been destroyed since the early 1980s. Shell and Gulf Oil, whose Nigerian leases Chevron took over in 1991, had drilled and pumped oil in these areas—yet the widespread damage to vegetation was clearly not related to oil spills.

The purpose of our project was to determine the causes and chronology of this ecological disaster and assess whether and how some of its fallout could be remedied.

I first arrived in late 2002 at Escravos, Chevron's oil and gas terminal at the mouth of the Escravos River and our base for the survey, then spent some six weeks there between January and March 2003. Our field team included Chevron Nigeria staff and consultants, several Nigerian ecologists and soil scientists, and two US experts in sedimentation and hydrological surveys. By boat or helicopter and then by foot we set out to explore preselected transects, taking soil samples, photos, and descriptions of the vegetation.

January and February are dry and mild in the delta, and I enjoyed the hikes through mangroves, then often into the mud flats filled with dead trees. Walk a little farther, and one found large green areas with alternating salt-tolerant ferns and grasses.

It didn't take a biologist to quickly grasp that the destruction and change we witnessed had been caused by the intrusion of saltwater into a freshwater habitat. In fact, Chevron scientists knew that the gradual dredging of the area in the 1970s to create access for the large oil-producing platforms called "flow stations" had also allowed saltwater to invade this very low-lying area. This gradually destroyed freshwater vegetation and fisheries—as well as the livelihoods they had once supported.

For all I can tell, this effect was not anticipated or sanctioned. It developed over time and was accelerated by a catastrophic synergy. The sand bar that had protected one of the main artificial canals,

Opuekeba, from the ocean was gradually washed away and eventually breached in the 1980s. The root cause was the construction of the first large hydroelectric dam on the Niger River in the 1960s. It drastically reduced the sediment deposits that had historically built and kept up the coastline in this area. A complex chain of events.

To inland communities who had lived off the tropical forest and freshwater fishing, saltwater intrusion was a disaster. Villages lost their fresh water supplies, the production of tropical hardwood and of palm wine, to name just a few essentials. In contrast, the beach village of Awoye benefited from the unintended breach of Opuekeba canal. Its fishermen now could navigate their boats straight into the ocean, rather than having to drag them across mudflats.

Were Shell, Gulf Oil, Chevron, and the Nigerian government, with whom all oil companies had formed joint ventures, aware of this disaster? In theory, they were. Yet, for several reasons, their response was underwhelming.

Satellite images showed that this change happened slowly. Staff expats at oil companies rarely went to the field to look at trees, and they typically rotate after two to three years. Nigerian staff may not have cared or didn't expect to be heard by their bosses.

The common responses by oil companies to growing frustration: provide boats and backup generators to communities, pay for the construction of schools and churches, make compensation payments to villages. Unfortunately, these payments often went to chiefs who "forgot" to share them with their communities or were simply bribed into silence.

It became clear during our exchanges with the communities how poisoned the atmosphere was. I never again saw as much hatred and frustration as in the eyes of people who had consistently been screwed by petroleum companies and their own governments. An informal meeting in one village turned into a shouting match as a hardcore fraction of villagers was opposed to letting us enter their territory and take soil samples, while others were conciliatory and wondered what benefit we could offer. I won't forget the image of some fifty villagers screaming at each other in their open meeting hall as we walked out.

The survey area was home to three major tribes who had feuded over access to resources before, but oil development followed by devastation made things worse as each tribe struggled for compensation. The generally dismal conditions around Escravos, Chevron's role, and the anger among villagers at foreign oil companies and their own government were publicly-known and covered—for example, in a feature article in the *New York Times* just weeks before my first visit.[4] Yet it left out the environmental and social disaster that had occurred "in the swamps." Unlike in Nigeria's south, one could not easily walk into that area and take photos.

Our survey did not end well. By late February 2003, hostility on the rivers rose—civilian and military speedboats taunting and threatening each other. One day, on returning to the terminal, a speedboat passed and forced us to land at a village jetty and debark. I did not feel threatened, notably because one of our "kidnappers" asked whether I could get him a job at Chevron or, alternatively, take him to California. We entered the village's open meeting hall and were told that we'd illegally crossed into Shell territory and had to pay ransom, some $2,000 for each of us seven.

We soon realized that the kidnappers were amateurs. They allowed the other US contractor and me to return to the terminal to fetch the money while the five Nigerian researchers stayed behind. At the terminal we were told that Chevron had a policy of paying no ransom; apparently kidnapping was a common event. Instead, we sent the boat back to collect the Nigerian researchers, who had been treated well and had left $5 per hostage lest the kidnappers feel completely humiliated.

The next day several civilian boats came speeding down the Escravos River with men brandishing guns. Minutes later, a member of the kitchen staff, who watched the spectacle from a watchtower by the river, was shot at and killed. Kitchen staff feeding some one thousand terminal dwellers went on strike. Even worse, some two thousand denizens of the adjacent village, belonging to a different tribe than the attackers, feared for their lives, tore down the fence, and came onto the terminal to seek protection and set up a camp.

Luckily, I had made friends with the aeronautics department, run by South Africans, and got our team of seven airlifted to Lagos on the second day of the turmoil. The airlift of the refugees from the next-door village by Chevron and Shell aircraft was chaotic and took much longer.

Naturally, Chevron terminated our research work—it would have been too dangerous for fieldwork, and bringing in the military (as Chevron had done in 1998, with very poor PR results) was not an option. Our work wasn't important enough.

I realize we were naive to expect Chevron could reverse some of the damage caused—powerful major oil companies are ultimately weak when it comes to rebuilding communities that were ruined by industrial actions, whether it's in the Niger Delta or in the United States. The lack of infrastructure and the sheer extent of the bad will in Nigeria just raised the stakes.

This is not to say that no one at Chevron cared. Their willingness to plan and start an expensive multiphase investigation of the event and potential remedies without external pressure is evidence they did. I also met a few Chevronites who believed strongly that their company had an obligation to make things whole and did raise the issue with upper management. Yet, ultimately, the risky, complex, and conflicted conditions on the ground prevailed and deteriorated after 2003. And, after all, Chevron and the Nigerian government needed to produce oil and make money, and one couldn't risk that.

The most haunting of all images I saw in the Niger Delta was the night view from the Opuekeba flow station where we stayed for a few days. On the canal was a never-ending stream of dug-out canoes coming from far away to fill up fifty-five-gallon plastic drums at the large tap from which Chevron provided fresh water, which most villages no longer had after seawater intruded. Three hundred feet (100 m) away, a flare lit up the night sky brightly. It was fueled by natural gas, which bubbles up with the oil, but which wasn't captured at the time and just flared off. That flare could have supplied all the energy needs of the entire area, and this was just one of many such flares.

Occasional news from the area suggests that Chevron and Shell have continued to expand oil production on offshore platforms, much easier to protect than operating in the swamps. Control over the situation on the ground is illusive: sabotage, theft, continued spills, armed insurgencies, and, at the heart of it, continued failure to share the wealth of the country with those who live in the petroleum region and endure the fallout.[5] And even the capture of the otherwise wasted natural gas and its conversion to liquid fuels, such as diesel and naphtha, and its feeding into a pipeline to supply other West African countries, has taken almost twenty years to complete.

After returning home from Nigeria, I wondered for two years what I could have done to help bring about a little change in the delta or even publicize what I had seen. I ultimately concluded that I had no realistic course of action that would help improve conditions in the delta. Once I began planning organic and fair trade oil projects for Dr. Bronner's in 2005, I thought of that work in part as my redemption from what I hadn't been able to do in Nigeria.

FINDING A ROUTE FOR ORGANIC AND FAIR PALM

Asuom, Ghana, 2006

Because Dr. Bronner's had decided in mid-2005 to "go fair trade," we had made good progress with our "clean supply chain." By mid-2006, project planning in Sri Lanka was well under way and we projected our first shipments of olive oil from Canaan in Palestine for early 2007. Now we needed a route for organic and fair palm oil. David and I had been looking for sources, and the story was no different from that for coconut and olive oil: fair trade palm oil did not exist because FLO had not developed a standard for palm oil—and still hasn't.

Luckily, we already knew that the Fair for Life standard would soon offer a credible alternative. And so, as we had done with coconut oil, we began searching for existing organic palm oil projects willing to "go fair trade" or, failing that, set up our own project.

How many sources of organic palm oil were there in 2006? Not many! Remember: globally, most palm oil is used as ingredient in undistinguished commodities like processed foods, cosmetics, and technical oleochemicals.

With such a low demand, no wonder there were, in 2006, worldwide only two relevant certified organic palm oil suppliers: Daabon in Colombia and AgroPalma in Brazil. They were plantation-based and Dr. Bronner's had bought organic RBD palm oil from both. Yet neither operation ran a meaningful smallholder program, and both seemed somewhat opportunistic about going fair trade.

Fortunately, our network offered an alternative. Jungle Products, then a brand selling organic red palm oil to US consumers, told us of a small, US-registered but Ghana-based NGO called Fearless Planet. They'd been trying to set up a women-run palm oil project in Ghana and were looking for a partner in the north.

I first went to Ghana in December 2006 to meet the NGO's founder, Danielle Gold, a socially minded American who had worked intermittently on development projects in the country since the 1990s. We drove to the area around Asuom in the Eastern Region, some 100 miles (160 km) northwest of Accra, where many smallholders grew oil palm and tens of small oil mills produced red palm oil.

The trip took four hours—just getting out of Accra took two. Sitting in chaotic stop-and-go traffic, we marveled at the new overhead highways being built by Chinese construction firms, a common sight in major African cities. In Accra these highways are now largely complete but, with growing traffic, driving into and out of the city during rush hour is hardly faster now—just easier on your vehicle.

Once out in the countryside, I saw, for the first time, oil palm plots on the ground, small monocultures interspersed with plots of oranges, cocoa, cassava, and maize, the common mix in southern Ghana. Yet there was also plenty of land with citrus and cocoa groves so neglected that the bush had taken over. Where the road had lost its asphalt topping from the heavy tropical rains, reddish iron oxide soil dust covered the trees.

We passed through villages and small towns with churches, small warehouses from the colonial era, and stalls and storefronts painted bright yellow, blue, or red, advertising for a major cell phone company. The market in Asamankase was teeming with people in tailored, colorfully patterned shirts and dresses. Many were on their phones or conducting business in the small stalls along the road. Women carried large trays loaded with loaves of white bread, ripe bananas, or pastries high on their heads, squeezing alongside the line of cars winding its way through the small district towns to offer their goods. A few tall trees that had escaped the large-scale, often illegal felling in the 1980s and 1990s towered over the hilly, fertile landscape.

This was a very different world from the fast-growing metropolis of Accra we'd just left behind.

Once in Asuom we visited three palm oil mills, and I swiftly got the picture. Such artisanal mills are called "cramers," purportedly after a Belgian engineer who set them up in the early 1980s. Facility owners usually lease the mills out, complete with equipment and a couple of strong young men.

The production is organized by women entrepreneurs who buy fruits from local farmers, hire local women for the lighter work, then produce red palm oil for use in many traditional dishes. Working conditions are not particularly comfortable, even unsafe. Mill buildings are simple, open wooden sheds with earthen floors and generally built without input from a structural engineer, conjuring up the risk of collapse. Key features of cramers are large, open, steel vats where palm fruits the size of dates are boiled on wood fires after women have cleaned them by hand from the chopped-up bulky fruit bunches.

Once boiled soft, the fruits were poured into a perforated large steel cylinder. Two young men would then tighten a screw-plate until the red liquor had been squeezed out of the fruits. Other mills use motor-driven screw presses. Batches of the liquor are boiled for hours with water, a process called clarification. The bright red oil floats on top; solids, skins, and fiber settle to the bottom with the heavier water; the oil is skimmed off; and the water is dumped, generally into nearby creeks or onto land.

None of the mills looked suitable as a partner to practice organic and fair production, but it was easy to imagine that we could set up the same process in a more comfortable, safe, and ecological way. Ultimately, this became the concept for our own cramer in Asuom.

Danielle and I were joined on our field trip to Asuom by a woman I'll call Charity. Raised in Asuom, she had moved to Accra and there sold palm oil from the village on a small scale. I was impressed by her energy but slightly taken aback by her flaring temperament, which was on display during the trip. In Asuom we met her two sisters, and Danielle and I agreed to engage Charity to eventually oversee the operation of our planned mill.

Clearly, we needed our own dedicated cramer to process organic and fair palm fruits. The risk of comingling was just too high. The technology was simple, and palm fruits were plentiful. Yet it eventually took some six years to guide the project's destiny to become a local "force of good," and for us to expand into other crops in Ghana, including cocoa, and discover our method of choice for practicing regenerative agroforestry.

THE FIRST THREE YEARS

Of course, we didn't know the rough road ahead when, during my next meeting with the Bronners in California in early 2007, they approved the project as sketched out by Danielle and me.

Danielle would be responsible for assembling the local project team, which included four part-time field officers on loan from the Ministry of Food and Agriculture (MOFA). Meanwhile, I obtained a public private partnership (PPP) grant of some $100,000 from the German development agency GIZ. Combined with Dr. Bronner's more substantive investment, it allowed us to build a small oil mill, office, and a team. We leased a plot of land in Asuom from Charity's extended family, set up a simple mill structure with equipment, and bought four off-road motorbikes so the field officers could get around to the farms.

Danielle had a diverse network in Accra, found two part-time managers for the organic internal control system (ICS), and her team started recruiting farmers for organic conversion. As in Sri Lanka and Palestine, we selected farmers who had demonstrably not used fertilizers and pesticides or herbicides for at least three years. This was not difficult, since spending money on fertilizers is uncommon and, fortunately, the small oil palm monocultures that farmers in Ghana grow on typically 5 acres (2 ha) are spaced properly and rarely suffer serious yield-dropping pest attacks. Yet, as in Sri Lanka, these farmers had not taken care of their land. As a result, yields of fresh fruits bunch, or FFB—the bunches weighing some 50 pounds (approximately 25 kilos), which feed small and large mills alike—were less than half that of a well-maintained field.

We went to work. Danielle and her partner Daniel designed a set of open-production sheds, a small office, and toilets; Daniel's brother Negash, a general contractor, built them. Our ICS team prepared for and passed the first organic and FFL inspections in September 2007 and, in spring 2008, we had enough organic FFB for trial production.

What challenges did we encounter with organic compliance? Comingling with conventional FFB is always the first concern. Once the word got out that we paid a 10 percent organic premium to farmers, based on actual not estimated weight, as other buyers do, farmers who were not ICS members tried to deliver their fruits to the cramer, and we had to reject several of the early deliveries. Fortunately, supplies were plentiful, and the mill management had little motivation to let conventional FFB slip in to boost raw material supply.

During the inspections we did not find farmers using pesticides or fertilizers on their crop, yet some farmers were found to have used herbicides instead of weeding manually. They were sanctioned and had to start the three-year conversion. However bad one may feel about being tough with smallholders, it is wise whenever they violate the basic and clear organic rule "do not use synthetic pesticides and herbicides." If you look the other way, you're signaling "it's okay" to do, and farmers will not take you seriously—a slippery slope.

Having organic fields of one crop, say, oil palm, and conventional fields of another crop, such as cocoa, *is* allowed under NOP and EU standards—but farmers must provide that information to the ICS management. Not generally allowed is *parallel production* (when you have both organic and conventional fields of the *same* crop). The risk of comingling is just too high.

Farmers must also get used to keeping records on fieldwork and sales, not a common practice among smallholders anywhere. We had to train field officers to conduct extension visits and internal inspections and put new recordkeeping procedures into place—a process that took some three years. As you've no doubt gathered, maintaining an organic ICS is a rather documentation-intensive job!

During my early visits I stayed at the modest yet comfortable guesthouse of an agricultural research station. In the evenings one heard the tropical birds and the eerie screams of the grasscutter, a cane rat common to sub-Saharan West Africa and often hunted as bushmeat. During my morning walks around the lush station, I noticed how many of the local trees species I had earlier seen in Sri Lanka, and I exchanged friendly greetings with farmworkers, women and men, who came the other way.

Initial project setup and operation couldn't have been more different between Serendipol and Serendipalm, the project's name once we incorporated it in 2009. Without experienced managers like Gordon and Sonali with their network of professionals, it took us longer to build the much simpler and smaller mill in Asuom than the larger and more sophisticated buildings in Sri Lanka. Construction and installation were slow, and our ICS managers were concerned about Charity's tendency to scream at farmers and staff she disagreed with.

We had first envisioned this project as women-led but realized in 2008 that Charity's husband, whom I'll call Kofi, had managed behind the scenes and had brought organizational and technical skills to the party. After all, the project's main goal was to benefit local women in need of work. This did not require that production be exclusively managed by women—especially since the growing team of field officers early on consisted exclusively of men. Broad participation of women in project management, including administration, production, and ICS, took several more years to come about and required a conscious and planned effort.

We began oil production on a small scale in March 2008. Danielle and her team had no experience in sizing equipment to a targeted throughput and we had to step up the equipment size several times. By late 2008, we had produced our first container: some 20 metric tons (MT) of the dark red crude palm oil (CPO).

Dr. Bronner's couldn't use that CPO in our bar soaps—it would have given them a dark color. Instead, it had to be processed at a refinery with organic certification that also met FFL rules regarding labor and was able to process smaller batches traceably. Danielle found a refinery that met these criteria but we had to truck the CPO in drums—100 miles (160 km) on bad roads. The cooperation with its owner was enjoyable, but refining losses in 2009 of up to 25 percent were high compared with 6 percent to 15 percent in an efficient refinery. We needed a refining alternative.

Fortunately, by then we had met the trusted German brand of organic food products, Rapunzel. It had built the origins of a global network of organic and fair trade suppliers and was interested in Serendipol's VCO and our palm oil from Ghana. We swiftly became allies with Rapunzel's strategic sourcing manager, Barbara Altmann.

A farmer's daughter from Bavaria, she has a practical, common-sense vision of "better agriculture." She had been key to developing Rapunzel's relationships with its organic and fair suppliers and knew the reality of organic production and commerce in the tropics firsthand; our palm oil team didn't need to camouflage that we were learning on the job.

Barbara suggested we try out ZOR, a refinery near Amsterdam— a subsidiary of Cargill, it specialized in smaller batches, including organic. Ideology would have dictated that we continue working with the small refiner in Ghana—but our desire for professional service and logistics and for lower refining losses beat ideology.

This refining experience taught us an important lesson: when building a fair and organic agricultural supply, be clear where you want your beneficial impact to be. Small really is beautiful, but quality and logistics requirements often necessitate a pact with organizations one generally loves to hate.

During 2008 and 2009, we produced and shipped four containers of RBD for Dr. Bronner's bar soap, nowhere near the fifteen (or more) containers we needed per year back then. The bottleneck was not in our supply of fruits but the painfully slow upscaling of the processing equipment, all locally made from steel.

Once we had sufficient equipment, production finally leaped.

It took three years to get there, rather than the two at Serendipol—but we now had an organic, fair, and reasonably functional supply chain for some 300 MT per year of crude palm oil, shipped in flexitanks to Holland for refining, and then to be used by Dr. Bronner's in soaps and by Rapunzel in its famous Tiger chocolate spread.

TROPICAL COOPERATION

In 2009, we finally gave our project the needed corporate framework. Until then it had been known as "Fearless Planet," named after Danielle's NGO. Now, we needed to register as an exporter of crude palm oil and build a team of professional staff with payrolls— none of which Fearless Planet and its parent NGO ORT were able to do.

In August 2009, we incorporated Serendipalm Co. Ltd. as project owner and operator. Dr. Bronner's holding company, Serendiworld LLC, owned by David and Mike Bronner and also a majority shareholder in Serendipol, initially held all of Serendipalm's shares. David, Danielle, and I were founding directors, with Danielle in the role of the "local director" required under Ghana law.

Next, we urgently needed oversight of the project's growing payroll and cash flow. Thus, Lawrence Acquaye became Serendipalm's first professional employee. A young man with an accounting degree who was recommended by Danielle's lawyer, he was short on professional experience, somewhat shy, and required training in accounting software, but was very sincere and motivated to put his civic-minded attitude to practice.

His joining created the first opportunity for collaboration between two Serendi projects. In 2010, Lawrence spent a week at Serendipol, where Sonali dedicated one of her accountants to training Lawrence in Quickbooks. That visit not only laid the foundation for Lawrence's mastery of this common accounting software, it also demonstrated to him that Dr. Bronner's had successfully built a much larger organic and fair project. This became a source of optimism and comfort for him and our growing team of professionals during the subsequent difficult days at Serendipalm. Lawrence's trip to Sri Lanka has become one of many project-driven exchanges in between projects, with Dr. Bronner's staff and with customers. I believe there is no better way to meet, cooperate in a meaningful and productive way, and create understanding between the worlds.

As palm oil production ramped up in 2010, we entered a tough period that lasted through mid-2013. With gallows humor, Serendipalm's professional team called it the "special period." Danielle had left Ghana in early 2010 for personal reasons. Fortunately, we had recruited as her successor, Aaron Ampofo, whom we had met as a freelancing inspector for IMO. A competent social entrepreneur, Aaron knows how to handle staff and farmers alike. Danielle had been instrumental in assembling the initial team and overseeing project development, but running a vertically integrated farming and processing operation was not her forte—she had always been clear about this. Shortly before she left, she said, "Gero, for me, the project is done."

For us, it had just started.

Nothing better characterizes the stereotypical difference in attitudes between NGOs and for-profit manufacturers. Considering that both organization types pursue different approaches—if not goals—that's how it should be. NGOs can play a critical role in creating alliances and executing physical projects under difficult conditions and in areas where the private sector just doesn't see a business opportunity, such as in the support of the disadvantaged, and in war zones, refugee camps, areas with poor infrastructure, and so on. (I'm oversimplifying to make a point.)

Conversely, the private sector's goal is to create long-term profitable projects that engage in commerce, including the production and marketing of goods and the employment of people. Except, of course, the private sector does that to make a living, whereas NGOs, in theory, operate to pursue a societal good.

So much for theory. In reality, both sectors overlap. NGOs also need to make money to pay salaries, usually funded by tax-deductible donations, grants, and consultancies. On the other hand, private-sector companies—such as, say, Dr. Bronner's—are free to think that a successful commercial business should benefit people, their communities, and their soils, and act accordingly. There is much room for productive collaboration between the two worlds as long as expectations and capacities are clear.

SERENDI ECONOMICS

Many FTO projects that combine farming and processing struggle with competitiveness. They benefit farmers and their communities and create fair, safe, and meaningful jobs. This raises their unit cost of production on several fronts: higher prices of raw materials, higher wages and benefits, higher overhead for professional staff, and non-production-related expenses spread over a smallish output.

Dr. Bronner's and other third-party customers will pay a premium over conventional or other "just organic" products. As long, that is, as the product has an inherent value, such as supporting fair, ecological, and effective development.

The price premium should not be perceived as a way to charge a higher margin for a "special product" without any relationship to the effort it took to make it.

How does one price such *value-added* product? After Serendipol's initial failure to survive on market-based pricing, told in chapter 5, we now use modified "cost plus pricing" for our own and close partner projects. Ultimately, our soap customers pay a premium for the higher cost of our raw materials. We then pass it on to farmers, workers, and communities upstream.

The mechanics of "cost plus" are simple. If the total fixed and variable cost to produce and land palm oil at its destination is, say, $2.00/kg, using a "cost plus 10" formula, one would sell it for $2.20/kg—a markup of 10 percent on variable cost (palm fruits, direct labor, shipping, energy) and fixed cost (administration, other overheads, depreciation of buildings and machines). This markup usually suffices to pay taxes, make capital investments, build reserves, and possibly pay a dividend to shareholders.

Cost plus has one potential weakness. In theory, managers of a company with a guaranteed 10 percent markup have little incentive to reduce their cost by improving operational efficiencies. In reality, this risk exists only if your investor, such as Dr. Bronner's, is also the sole and captive customer and you lack an efficiency-minded management. Once you sell to third parties, they will want your higher price to represent a value.

Some fifteen years of project experience also suggests that competent and likeminded project managers strive for efficiencies. This renders cost plus an effective and fair pricing method. It avoids the well-known dangers of pure market pricing, such as cutting cost by reducing wages or, god forbid, buying conventional raw materials. Yet only close suppliers of raw materials will give you full insight into their cost. Thus, keeping an eye on market pricing is one good way of motivating project operators to strive for efficiency.

Some of the higher price for Serendipalm's palm oil results from the organic and fair trade premiums, 10 percent each, we pay for FFB. We employ more workers per output than large palm oil mills, and their wages and benefits are considerably higher than in comparable small local operations. Our kitchen serves free hot lunches to all staff, adding some 2 percent to the total cost of production.

Running a labor-intensive production does not only raise cost.

Limiting weekly working hours in the fruit-cleaning department during the peak season was our initial fair trade management challenge. After all, this is the period where people can earn money and are willing to work late. Under Charity and Kofi's management, many women routinely worked more than sixty hours per week for two to three months, in violation of FFL rules.

While IMO acknowledged that these hours were not "all work" (working conditions in fruit cleaning allow for socializing, chatting, and singing), we still had to reduce them. We started logging working hours, ensured that fruit cleaners were free to leave after an eight-hour shift, often requiring backup staffing for shorter late shifts. We eventually rebuilt the fruit-cleaning section to maximize working space, thus allowing a larger number of women to work. Then we juggled Saturday shifts and made sure no one worked twelve hours per day for more than five days during the peak season.

As production grew, in 2020 we installed two FFB strippers that separate fruits from FFB mechanically. They helped us cope with the ever-increasing weekly supply of perishable FFB without causing unacceptably long working hours. These strippers now run from February to June while every space in the building is still occupied by workers. As FFB supplies dwindle in June and July, we turn them off and return to fully manual fruit cleaning.

Serendipalm could replace all 150 jobs in fruit cleaning with four such strippers operating year round, but we won't because the project's commitment is to create meaningful jobs to those without alternatives. The project's entire atmosphere is built on this concept, too. Preserving such jobs is but one example of how *constructive capitalism* may differ from textbook capitalism, which aims to minimize unit labor cost. We're not advocating inefficiencies but consider the stakes of all parties involved. Here, the advantage of a growing business is that it can mechanize key aspects without eliminating jobs. Dr. Bronner's did this by shifting to automated soap filling, whereas Serendipalm installed strippers. Training staff and offering them opportunities in other departments is the way to go.

Two other key factors raise Serendipalm's cost of production.

Most cramers suffer high variable cost for their low oil extraction rate, the percentage of oil squeezed out of FFB. In 2012, Serendipalm's extraction rate was just 12 percent—compared with 22 percent achieved by large palm oil mills. By 2020, we've raised that to 18 percent thanks to the installation, planned and coordinated by Phillip, of two new expeller presses and a high-tech centrifuge. This *decanter* more efficiently separates oil, water, and solids than the old clarifier method did. In effect, we now generate 50 percent more oil from the same amount of FFB and working hours. That sure drops your unit cost. An unexpected side effect: the red oil now tastes sweeter, less cooked, and we sell some of it as food-grade red oil.

One key factor driving up our fixed cost is our staff of twenty trained professionals: agricultural field officers, accountants, engineers, HR staff, and managers. They have been critical to building a meaningful FTO project. In fact, it is the synergy between this management team and the over three hundred production and fieldworkers that gives Serendipalm its spirit and energy. Yet the salaries of so many professionals in a project with a comparatively small output raises overhead cost per unit of oil.

The textbook solution: produce more oil and the overhead cost per unit of oil declines. Naturally, you need to find customers. We did, and annual oil output increased from some 280 MT in 2012 to over 900 MT in 2020, and demand for 1,050 in 2021. All the above measures combined helped us reduce our unit cost of production from about $3,000 per MT to $2,100 per MT and accordingly our sales price. Clearly, this is still a steep premium over "just organic" oil from larger mills, but it's going in the right direction.

Back in 2012, five years after the project started, we had to grapple with the project's greatest challenge. By then, Kofi, Charity, and her two sisters were becoming increasingly unreliable as production managers. They had resisted training in technical and management skills. Equipment and tractors broke down frequently and blocked production, and Lawrence pointed to financial irregularities in both production and kitchen budgets. Moreover, their style of management intimidated and demotivated workers and professionals.

In January 2013, Phillip Eschweiler, son of my preschool friend Christoph and a trained car mechanic, asked to come to Serendipalm for an internship for his bachelor's program in "Georesource Engineering." Over a month, he built a systematic preventive maintenance and repair program for our growing (and poorly maintained) fleet of tractors, trailers, and motorbikes. He was hands-on, swiftly accepted by the mechanics team, and built the foundation for today's maintenance programs, which he supports as our team's technical projects manager. While there, he told us that Kofi and Charity had been virtually absent from the cramer, and there had been frequent chaos in production.

We knew we had to part ways lest we put the future of the entire project in jeopardy.

We had continued to hire professional staff and built a management team around Charity and Kofi, making sure that critical functions—notably financial management and the organic and fair trade systems—were not under their control. One such staff addition was Safianu Moro, an energetic young man with a master's in agriculture. He had joined in 2010 as a field officer and collaborated well with Charity and Kofi where needed.

Safianu was clear that they would never accept a peaceful separation. After all, they considered Serendipalm "their project" even though they had no financial stake in it and didn't contribute to its growth. Safianu committed to staying on as general manager should we terminate them, and we knew that the other professionals would take his lead.

The conflict came to a head. Charity and Kofi rejected our offer of a compensation package that would allow them to start their own business, with our team continuing to provide free financial, technical, and strategic support. The local chief tried to mediate and asked that we keep Charity and Kofi on, but we had made up our minds: a continued cooperation would be unbearable for the entire project.

Our team felt compassion for the couple. They were well-meaning people who had seen an opportunity to portray themselves in Asuom as project owners and benefactors and hadn't realized that this project was not about them but rather about fair development for a community. When they saw they wouldn't become rich on their salaries and didn't have the skills to successfully manage the operation, they began helping themselves. We had seen that conflict coming and had financed them a truck and the lease for their own farm to generate alternatives. We knew that both had a rather different view of their performance, and so, doing right by them was critical to how we tried to resolve the conflict, even if it was in vain.

We ultimately resolved that when individuals place their own well-being above that of a project that benefits a whole community, one needs to make tough choices. One hard lesson for my team, to be repeated in 2014 in India: be careful with whom you partner—unless you want to spend years in court!

Yet do not let that caution keep you from exploring opportunities with local partners. Trust your intuition, engage in your operations with an open heart and mind, yet seek independent verification of what you're told, and don't give away the store. And offer shares in such a project only to people you know well and trust, lest you lose control over your project and its development potential.

The years of the "special period" also focused us on a key challenge for any company: in the face of adversity, how do you motivate a team and keep professionals in a project location with little evening entertainment?

When telling the Serendipalm story, I always mention that we have built a team of over twenty professionals in a simple oil mill, whose offices have fans but no A/C, in a town with one decent bar, no restaurants or movie theaters, and a three-hour drive to the capital. And yet we have kept adding professionals, and not one has resigned since 2013 (knock on wood). Many of them are in their late twenties and thirties, got married while at Serendipalm, had children, and stayed in town.

Contrast this with the "rural exodus" common in many areas and ask: What keeps these young professionals in Asuom? I've asked most of them in person and their response is consistent: as small as Serendipalm is, it provides meaning, purpose, and hope to a team of now over three hundred of our farmers and a whole community of ten thousand to which we offer engagement and openness. Naturally, we also insist on our rights if need be: with banks, the police, and contractors. Being a fair trade company doesn't mean you're a pushover.

Because the management team had been crucial to Serendipalm's success, we further invested in team building and coaching, and empowered staff to make joint decisions. I once heard in a radio program on happiness that nothing, even a fantastic salary, makes employees happier than the freedom to make decisions. That's been my personal experience, too, but naturally, one needs to be prepared for such decision-making power.

Aware of Safianu's leadership potential, we suggested he attend a program by the London-based WYSE International, a charity specializing in the education and development of emerging leaders. The programs were recommended by Rob Hardy, who in 2011 became my first teammate on our officially named "Special Operations" team; Rob's a big fan of coaching, his wife's profession. Safianu returned highly inspired from WYSE and began translating his learnings into the building of a seven-person management team. A bit later we offered Safianu the position of managing director and a minority share in the company.

A simple recipe has worked for all projects we've watched up close: give people a meaningful job and the authority to act; be respectful and listen to their concerns; offer growth opportunities and training, notably on building teams and leadership. Pay team leaders competitive salaries, yet paying top salaries to engage superstars never occurred to us—it would be ineffective without the other pieces, create envy, and drive our cost of production through the roof.

How about production staff? It is one thing to motivate managers and operators through responsibility; motivating workers performing physical repetitive work is different. Paying more than competitive wages and offering uncommon benefits is a first good step—that's what Dr. Bronner's did in California when the company got serious about staff welfare in the 1990s. Yet real motivation requires more. As Safianu and his new team grew, I routinely asked him how they motivated production staff.

"Not too difficult," Safianu said. "We hold regular meetings, ask staff to raise concerns, and respond in earnest but also don't let anyone pull a fast one on you. Our workers now say 'you are a listening company,' the best compliment one can get where hierarchy still rules."

His advice: "Treat people with respect. Don't yell at them. If someone steals, which does happen, consider circumstances and use judgement but make sure you act consistently. Anything else is considered favoritism."

Nothing earth-shattering, but many managers could take a lesson from Safianu's team.

Staff enthusiasm is on display during events, such as Serendipalm's holiday party. Teams of workers present singing, dancing, and theater pieces, self-organized without prompting and management oversight.

How does our Special Operations team fit in? Its members and the increasingly frequent interns and international visitors are mostly white, both women and men. With the exception of two Mormon missionaries, no other white people live permanently in Asuom. We usually walk from the cramer to our guesthouse through backroads to the friendly excitement of little kids shouting to their siblings, "Obroni, obroni" (meaning, "Look, a white person"). Older kids may say, "Obroni kokoo maakye" (meaning, "White person, good morning"), to which one may respond in Twi, the local language. Both acknowledge the difference in skin color in a curious, friendly, and engaging way and leave it at that.

As in all our projects, it took about two years for farmers to understand our agenda: to pay fair prices that would make money for them while supporting community development.

Early farmers' meetings were held in churches, with arguments and threats of boycotting the project if we didn't dramatically increase the price. Yet after the meeting, we would smilingly shake hands with our foes and the air was cleared. We've gone through many meetings with farmers since. They follow a routine: start with a prayer led by a Christian or Muslim; an hour or two of heated, often circular arguments; usually a conclusion—and then a closing prayer. I've come to appreciate that tradition and always join in the "Amen."

Another ritual we've enjoyed participating in, as morbid as it may seem, are funerals. At least for Christians, it's likely the biggest party in their lives. Their relatives have to pick up the tab, and social pressure to attend is high. To minimize financial stress and demand on time, many areas in Ghana now pool funerals and make them monthly events. In Asuom this may involve four ceremonies at once on the funeral grounds. Corpses are refrigerated in a district town, then on Friday guesthouses fill with visitors from Accra.

During the ceremonies, many guests wear black or red, while the mourning members of the church of a departed often dress in congregational outfits. This includes choruses and condolences to the family. One funeral I attended was for one of our farmers, pooled with three other deceased, whose coffins were all on display on a large open funeral field. How joyful and ecstatic the guests were—in sharp contrast to the widow of our farmer, who was heartbroken.

And there are the dedication ceremonies for brick-and-mortar fair trade projects, such as the maternity ward in Asuom, water wells, school expansions, or the apartments built for hospital nurses in Abaam. Local dignitaries—the chief and elders—attend in their official attire. The programs are usually organized by the receiving community: fiery speeches and giving of thanks. As with our holiday parties, I most enjoy the choral singing by Serendipalm's production workers and the dance performances by youth groups. They are pure spontaneity and dedication—and all that without a drop of alcohol (or maybe just a few). The future of Serendipalm will include the expansion of regenerative farming practices and product diversification—notably into cocoa and cassava—as well as the implementation of several major community development projects. This would exemplify how regenerative agriculture can support rural development—in an All-One spirit. Much of our plans are covered in the following chapter.

Building a "Special Operations" team

By the time Serendipalm stabilized in 2013, the number of our Serendi projects had grown and so had the size of my team. Since 2006, when we started Serendipol, I had been the only full-time team member. As our realm of FTO projects expanded, we have grown to nine people, several part-time and/or working mostly elsewhere in the All-One empire. We are four women and five men: three Americans, five Germans, one Brit; we reside in the United States, Germany, Spain, and the UK. No two live in the same city. We work mostly in our home offices making ceaseless conference calls with teammates, project teams, and external allies, commercial and otherwise. We meet in person at our tropical projects, trade shows, retreats, and odd events.

We started calling ourselves "Special Ops" once Rob Hardy, Ryan Zinn, and Les Szabo had joined in 2013. Julia Edmaier, Phillip Eschweiler, Jennifer Rusu, Ute Eisenlohr, and Anke Buhl followed over the years.

What exactly do we do? Primarily, Special Ops is a "full-service provider" that initiates, builds, and supports several smallholder farming and processing projects in the Global South. Our involvement varies by project. The main projects are those three in which Dr. Bronner's has ownership, plus a growing number of close partner projects. (By now, you've met our projects Serendipol and Serendipalm, and our partner Canaan.) Dr. Bronner's is the largest customer of most all of them, but not the only one. Thus, our team also builds, expands, and smooths operational links between these projects and our headquarters in Vista on finances, logistics, quality control of products, storytelling—whatever is needed.

To help these projects grow and diversify, we introduce their marketing, sales, and customer service staff to regeneration-minded companies in the United States and Europe. We educate the latter on the projects; learn about their hot buttons in quality, certifications, and price; and then help the projects find solutions. In essence, we offer young projects a custom-made service package in technology, financing, construction, team building, and marketing that others don't have access to. All that in good personal spirit and at no extra charge. Eventually and gradually we step back from operational involvement, just monitor overall progress and finances, and support growth, development, and commercial relationships with third parties, mostly from a distance.

Dr. Bronner's ultimate vision is to use only *regenerative* ingredients. Thus, we continually scout for, discover, evaluate, and integrate new promising projects that share our vision and could use a good new customer. Cases in point are our recent encounters with new suppliers of avocado and arnica oils. If we are compatible, a cooperation emerges, and we'd pass leads on to likeminded brands needing *good* ingredients.

Naturally, we use our hands-on project experience to tell "the regenerative story." In a world of hollow commercial propaganda, nothing beats Dr. Bronner's word-of-mouth approach; our authentic jungle stories are a growing facet of it. We speak at conferences and trade shows, present to retailers, train Dr. Bronner's staff, and cowrite marketing and PR materials.

What makes the relationships with our suppliers most special is the extent to which we get involved in "almost anything." We put a strong focus on team building, then eventually step back for local teams to run their own show—but we're always available to support.

Serendipalm cocoa farmer in Ghana

CHAPTER 10

Cocoa—The Path to Regenerative Chocolate

Ghana, 2006

O N MY FIRST DRIVE TO ASUOM in late 2006, I met a new plant. In the bush next to the road I discovered a grove of trees that carried, on their trunks and major branches, ovoid fruits the shape of an American football, though about half its size. Held only by short connectors, they grew in clusters, with colors ranging from mottled green through deep yellow to a beautiful dark orange. I had not seen anything like it.

"What are they?" I asked our driver, Collins.

"Cocoa," he said. "It's peak harvest season."

Yet another crop whose products I had consumed for years without bothering to think about where and how it grew! But it didn't take long to develop a working relationship with the plant that grows chocolate. We would learn, even before we purchased our first palm fruits in 2008, that many of our oil palm farmers also grew other tree crops, such as cocoa and citrus, and field crops, including cassava (manioc) and maize. We knew because farmers in an organic ICS must report all plots they farm, organic or not.

Virtually all cocoa in the area was grown with a strong dose of synthetic pesticides, which are prohibited in organic production. It was obvious. Driving to and from palm fields, we would see farmers and farmworkers on their way to spraying their cocoa, carrying yellow canisters featuring hoses and spray nozzles. We would see them in the field, where they handled the toxic chemicals rather casually. Many farmers are not aware of the health risks and were told by suppliers and government extension services that there is no viable alternative; unfortunately, short of fundamental agroecological changes to the dense monocrops they were typically planted in, there usually isn't.

The spraying of cocoa and the drift of pesticides had spelled trouble for our production of palm oil since our first organic inspection in late 2007. (This is one of the often unmentioned costs of conventional agriculture—the potential value destroyed on neighbors' certified organic land by pesticide drift.) And so we agreed with IMO to establish sacrificial safety zones of two rows of oil palms. Farmers had to harvest them separately and sell the FFB to other cramers. Since enforcement of that prohibition was time-consuming, we stopped recruiting new oil palm plots smaller than 5 acres (2 ha) and bordered by conventional cocoa fields.

Why didn't we immediately persuade cocoa farmers to abandon the use of pesticides, convert their cocoa fields to organic production, and find customers for these beans? After all, organic and fair cocoa beans fetch premiums of typically $500 per MT, depending on origin and quality. And cocoa would have diversified Serendipalm's operation.

We avoided such an early entry into organic cocoa for two main reasons. One, we were preoccupied with the challenges of building a functioning palm oil production system. The second reason goes to the heart of the complex trouble that cocoa production finds itself in in West Africa, by far its largest producing region worldwide.

To understand why, let's explore a bit of cocoa's history.

COCOA: NOT A HAPPY WEST AFRICAN CROP

The cocoa plant originally hails from Central and South America, where it was highly valued in pre-Columbian times and where much of the world's cocoa is still grown. The Spanish conquistador Cortés brought cocoa and the knowledge of its use by the Aztecs back to the Spanish court. The bitter taste prevented an immediate boom, but by the 1540s, adding sugar or honey produced a pleasurable and stimulating beverage. It was a luxury drink, for sure.

Colonizers grew cocoa, first using enslaved indigenous people. After decimating their populations through disease and violence, plantation owners turned to West African slaves. More cocoa production shifted from Central to South America, mostly the Atlantic side, which was easier to reach by ships bringing slaves from Africa and taking cocoa to Europe.

Since the 1970s, the two neighboring West African countries of Ivory Coast and Ghana, with their suitable soils and climate and a solid foundation of cocoa experience under British and French colonial rule, gradually became the largest cocoa-producing area on earth. Combined, they now produce over 60 percent of the global crop of dry cocoa beans.

In the 1980s, escalating cocoa prices drove large planting campaigns, reflecting the world's growing appetite for chocolate products. A great opportunity for West African smallholders, yet the story didn't pan out as farmers and their governments had hoped.

West African farmers often planted their cocoa trees hastily, the quality of seedlings was poor, and many farmers broadcast seeded (scattering seeds by hand). This created orchards with tree densities of 1,500 to 2,000 cocoa trees per hectare, much higher than the 1,100 to 1,300 considered optimum for a cocoa monoculture.

Farmers also routinely omitted the planting of recommended shade trees; and once trees had grown up, they stopped pruning and thinning them out, fearing that would reduce bean yields. Weeding and harvesting was often their only maintenance. Yet densely planted unpruned trees make for poorly ventilated orchards, very susceptible to attack by insects, such as mirids or capsid bugs, or by the *Phytophthora* fungus, which forms black mold that destroys the infected pods.

The overall result was miserably low cocoa yields. Such typical conventional smallholder fields in Ghana now yield between 350 and 400 kg/ha of dry beans. Compare this with the 800 to 850 kg/ha average yields when planting from quality seeds or seedlings at the right density, including shade trees, and maintaining crops with the modest use of agrochemicals. Simplistically, this is at the core of the poor state of Ghanaian cocoa farming.

The post-harvesting treatment of Ghanaian cocoa beans—fermentation and drying—also used to be inconsistent. Farmers first ferment the beans to change the flavor of cocoa beans from bitter to their characteristic fruitier flavor. For that, they scoop the pulp-encased beans out of their pods, pile them up in small heaps, and cover them with banana leaves for five to seven days—turning them twice or thrice to keep them from overheating and for aeration. Since farmers are in a rush to sell, they often cut fermentation time short, making Ghanian beans generally under-fermented.

Most critical for bean quality is the next step, the proper drying of beans, to a moisture content of about 7 or 8 percent. If beans are stored too moist, they become moldy, the one flavor even heavy roasting can't remove.

To control the quality of a promising export commodity, the British colonial government had created, in 1947, the Ghana Cocoa Marketing Board. Later renamed Cocobod, it took control of the purchasing and marketing of cocoa beans and gave Ghana cocoa a reputation for quality. Reforms in 1984 engaged the private sector and authorized licensed buying companies (LBCs) to ensure proper drying of beans, collection, and initial warehousing. Cocobod fixed a farm gate price and paid the LBCs for the beans, who in turn paid the farmers. In other words, in Ghana, purchasing and export of cocoa beans is a government monopoly.

Cocobod then sells the beans to cocoa importers worldwide,

naturally at a profit. Seemingly, that approach worked well; today cocoa beans from Ghana are considered of good quality, widely used in commodity and specialty chocolates, and fetch a modest premium over the world market price. Farmers benefited from guaranteed sales of their entire production at reasonably stable producer prices.

Yet Cocobod did not address the underlying agricultural problems that caused low yields in the first place. Increasing pest attacks coincided with the collapse of the world market for cocoa. The extensive global planting had driven up production faster than demand grew. Thus, nominal global cocoa prices crashed from $4,400 per MT in 1977 to between $900 and $1,500 per MT through most of the 1990s—great for buyers in the West, terrible for cocoa growers.

Rather than attacking the cause of the problem by helping farmers to thin out, prune, and replant trees, Cocobod placed its bets on agrochemicals, notably pesticides. It began issuing free insecticides and copper-based fungicides. It also set a national farm gate price paid to farmers that was well below the world market price. Simplistically, it used the balance, often half of the beans' export value, to fund its operations, international promotion programs, one round of free pesticide sprays, and some farmer support programs, such as offering motorized pruning tools on loan.

Was it a successful program? It sure helped raise exports of Ghana cocoa from 200,000 MT in 1985 to 815,000 MT in 2018. Yet it didn't solve—and instead further contributed to—the underlying agricultural problems. While Cocobod considerably raised its farm gate price for the 2020/21 season to around $1,800 per MT, Ghanian farmers with low-yielding cocoa fields still make little, if any, money once you figure in all costs. Naturally, farmers will continue to harvest since the beans now grow "for free," but many can't afford to spend money on the replanting and pruning needed to improve yields: the dreaded low-yield trap.

Moreover, many cocoa farmers are aging and not fit for demanding fieldwork. Without external support their farms are condemned to minimum farm maintenance and spraying of free pesticides, with many farms engaging child labor, usually their own, as workers to save on cost. In Ivory Coast and Ghana, farmers hoping for a future price increase have even planted many new cocoa plots illegally into protected forests.

Could all this be true? That more than half of the world's chocolate is made from cocoa beans largely grown in jam-packed, poorly maintained farms—sometimes planted illegally on supposedly protected land? That these farms show poor bean yields and are barely profitable? That farmers use pesticides rampantly, often carelessly, and child labor is prevalent in some areas to help farmers get fieldwork done at low cost?

This sketch sounds like an overstated cliché—unfortunately, it isn't.

To be sure, there are many well-run cocoa farms in West Africa, but by and large cocoa is not a happy crop. Serendipalm and our varied collaborators and advisers had since 2012 experienced this reality firsthand in Ghana; our Special Ops teammate Ute Eisenlohr knows it well from her experience as cocoa certifier. It's that aggregate experience that taught us about the trouble in West African cocoa and gave us a vision of what we could realistically contribute to improving, or even revolutionizing.

WHY IS THERE CHILD LABOR IN COCOA?

The lousy economics of growing cocoa in West Africa are at the core of pervasive child labor, a problem most chocolate eaters hopefully have heard of.

When we talk about child labor, we may be referring to cocoa farmers who bring their own or a neighbor's kids to help out with fieldwork. Some of it is light work, such as scooping cocoa beans out of the pods. Other tasks may be dangerous, especially for younger kids: land clearing, weeding and breaking cocoa pods with machetes, working near a pesticide sprayer, or carrying heavy loads.

Anyone who's learned their family trade by helping out at a young age knows there can be benefits for both sides—as long as the work doesn't put children at risk, clash with school attendance, or deprive children of their right to play. Yet there is a vast difference between minors helping with nonhazardous tasks after school and groups of children being taken from their homes in poor rural areas and sent as cheap labor into cocoa plantations—a nefarious form of child labor that the industry has become known for.

Studies suggest that by far most child laborers work on their parents' cocoa farms. Only a fraction of minors work under forced indenture in Ivory Coast and Ghana. Their recruitment in rural areas where parents are desperate for income is organized by traffickers and predominantly benefits illegally planted farms that need cheap seasonal labor.[1]

Depending on working conditions, the parents' farm scenario may or may not cause physical harm, deprive children of their education, and be considered child labor under conventions of the International Labor Organization (ILO).

The indenture or slave labor scenario, on the other hand, is always inhumane and deplorable.

Given that most at-risk children work for their family, one can begin to tackle the problem through direct education of our farmers. In cooperation with Serendipalm staff, our teammate Julia Edmaier started in 2020 an awareness and training campaign in the Asuom area about risky tasks, such as the use of machetes. Julia had joined our team in 2014 after running the operation of IMO's Fair for Life program for four years.

When it comes to indentured labor, only government action combined with serious pressure from foreign customers will make a dent in the infrastructure of the slave trade. Yet, ultimately, addressing the problem of child labor problem at the root requires a systemic improvement to cocoa economics in small farms—including that farmers need to be able to hire adult farmworkers.

READING THE BEANS

With all the trouble surrounding cocoa, no wonder we were reluctant to produce it early on in the Serendipalm project. The control of Ghanian cocoa exports by Cocobod posed a further hurdle. Companies like Serendipalm or even cooperatives cannot simply buy and sell beans from farmers to their known customers abroad. Yet this "traceability"—the assurance to customers that their beans in fact come from a particular project—is a key tenet of organic and fair trade production. Compare these cocoa-specific hurdles with the ease of buying FFB, making and exporting fair trade and organic palm oil to known customers, and you'll understand why Serendipalm did not seriously consider organic cocoa until 2012. As Ghana opened to organic cocoa production, we eventually found a licensed buying company and a European importer that can ensure traceability—in line with Cocobod rules. Rather time-consuming!

Back in 2012, one evening at the guesthouse, while Barbara Altmann of Rapunzel was visiting, we speculated about converting the cocoa our oil palm farmers were growing to organic production. After all, chocolate bars and spread were among Rapunzel's most successful products.

Traditionally, Rapunzel had bought its cocoa from organic and fair sources in Latin America. Yet beans grown on certain volcanic soils there had a high content of cadmium, a toxic heavy metal that the EU was planning to limit in cocoa and other food products. And with the growing threat of catastrophic hurricanes in Central America, Rapunzel considered shifting some of their cocoa demand to a credible organic and fair supply in West Africa where both risks were minimal. And it wouldn't hurt Serendipalm and its farmers to diversify its menu of value-added products.

Rapunzel's first bean tests from Serendipalm's farmers were encouraging: the cadmium content was much lower than in Latin American beans, and their quality was quite good, if a bit under-fermented. With Rapunzel as an interested customer, we gave it a try, recruited the first one hundred cocoa fields into our ICS in 2013, and started farmers on their conversion to organic production and certification. Serendipalm's cocoa adventure had begun!

Unlike for their oil palm fields, these farmers had previously sprayed "prohibited inputs"—which meant they had to undergo a full three-year organic conversion, a period full of challenges for any crop.

Unsurprisingly, farmers cannot overnight correct their planting and maintenance mistakes in order to reduce pest pressure. We had to offer a backup solution in case of an infestation. Fortunately, Cocobod began noticing organic cocoa as a novel export market and supplied to each farmer one free application of pyrethrum—a pesticide extracted from the flowers of the chrysanthemum daisy—with most formulations accepted by organic rules. The quick "bug knockout" action of the pyrethrum pleased farmers but, again, did not address the root cause of pest attacks: monocropping, dense planting, poor ventilation, and trees weakened by poor maintenance.

Our two-pronged approach was to first develop a low-cost organic pesticide option for farmers to avoid yield losses by insects. Rob Hardy and Serendipalm's quality control manager Dickson Wenyonu studied the literature, trialed, and produced a neem oil and soap concoction that has been somewhat effective in reducing mirid populations. To promote better pruning, we purchased quality saws, as the Ghanian farmer's beloved machete mutilates trees and branches.

The first three years of converting cocoa farmers were rough. We kept recruiting new farmers, but at least half were afraid of pest-induced losses and ultimately returned to spraying prohibited chemicals; we had to reset the clock on their conversion, or they left the ICS on their own.

Farmers in conversion to organic status also have no economic incentive. The USDA's NOP doesn't recognize "in conversion" status. Even in the EU, which does, virtually all buyers, including Rapunzel, want the organic seal. Organic brands may realize the importance of supporting conversion farmers, but their customers generally don't. Thus, farmers in conversion face all its challenges without financial reward. How motivating is that?

Serendipalm ameliorated the situation by paying for certification expenses and the means of conversion, such as organically approved natural pesticides like pyrethrum and blends of neem oil and soap. Thanks to our field officers' tenacity, we had, by 2016, the first one hundred certified-organic cocoa farmers. And we had interested customers, notably Rapunzel and Theo's, a young US chocolate brand committed to organic and fair production.

When we were first getting started, we hadn't thought much about bean quality. Commodity milk chocolate is sweet, and bean flavor plays a minor role, as long as the beans are not moldy. But how to ensure that beans for the increasingly popular high-cocoa content products have a satisfying and consistent flavor?

As we started bringing more farmers on board, we invited Theo's founder, Joe Whinney, and Stephen Hubbes from Rapunzel's product development for a cocoa quality workshop in Asuom. They opened our team's and farmers' eyes to the complexity of quality and flavor control. Visual assessment of bean quality involves a "guillotine" that cuts batches of fifty beans in half. One then "reads" them to determine the percentages of well-, over-, and under-fermented beans as well as moldy and wormy beans. Very insightful but requires much training.

By late 2017, we had found a local licensed buying company (LBC) we could trust to preserve the identity of our beans and the right importer to verify it upon arrival in Rotterdam. Our first shipment of organic and fair beans to Rapunzel was ready to ship.

By that time, Dr. Bronner's, other US companies, the media, and the public had become excited about the concept of regenerative agriculture and its potential to counteract climate change while improving farmers' livelihoods. With the soil fertility programs in Sri Lanka, India, and Ghana, we already had some regeneration to show off.

OUR JOURNEY TO DYNAMIC AGROFORESTRY— A CONCEPT WITH A FUTURE

As at Serendipol, we realized early on in Ghana that farm productivity was low, and our regenerative work focused on improving field conditions and fresh fruit bunch (FFB) yields of the oil palms. First, we gave farmers hands-on support with training on farm maintenance. We offered zero-interest farm maintenance loans so farmers could hire labor for weeding and mulching. Then we began returning all organic waste from oil production to the fields as mulch or manure, whereas other mills would burn or dump them.

Over some five years, these programs raised average FFB yield from a poor 5 MT per hectare per year to 7.5 MT per hectare per year—still not sensational, but a 50 percent increase in revenue at little extra cost.

Next, we tackled the poor quality of oil palm seedlings and offered farmers high-quality seedlings for replanting, also at zero-interest loans. Dr. Bronner's initially financed these revolving loans; later, KIVA, a US-based microloan NGO, took on the financing. To promote biodiversity and protect these new fields against pesticide drift, all receiving farms had to include, in addition to oil palms, at least forty timber and fruit trees per acre (100 per ha). Newly planted fields had to replace existing old palm fields or be planted into brush on abandoned former orchards. By 2018, we had financed the planting of over one hundred thousand seedlings.

You can tell: we took regenerating oil palm fields seriously. But we hadn't found a way to integrate the regeneration of oil palm with cocoa, which was becoming an important pillar of the project.

Our oil palm replanting campaign had teased us with another insight. When visiting newly planted fields around 2015, I discussed with George Mensah, one of our senior field officers, that farmers had planted bananas, papayas, and cassava in between the young oil palm seedlings. "All farmers intercrop on new fields," he said. "It would be a waste of land not to."

The solution was in our face, though we wouldn't realize that for another year.

In October 2016, Joachim Milz came through Asuom—Barbara Altmann at Rapunzel had introduced us to him. It was, as usual, a warm and humid night, and I sat with my teammates Rob and Phillip on the veranda of our guesthouse, which for six years had been our evening hangout. Traffic noise had died down and the congregation next door was practicing, singing and drumming. The neighbors across the road were burning a small pile of leaves and plastic bags, making for a nice if slightly disturbing smolder.

Yet we were glued to Joachim's laptop screen. It showed photos taken over a three-year period at a 150-acre (60 ha) farm in neighboring Ivory Coast, where his consultancy ECOTOP had been the technical adviser. Planted on a degraded pineapple plantation, the orchard featured regular parallel rows of densely and diversely planted trees and ground crops. Cocoa, oil palm, and rubber were the main crops; fruit, cashew nut, and timber trees were included at a lower density; fast-growing bananas and papayas still dominated the picture during these early years.

What we were witnessing was Joachim's mind-boggling concept he called "dynamic agroforestry" (DAF).

The photos literally took us from the time of ground preparation— the pegging of rows and planting—through the first cassava harvest, to what had now become a young bountiful jungle starting its life cycle. Joachim's barely three-year-old orchard already looked lush and healthy, like designed natural chaos. It modeled, as he explained, natural succession in tropical forests, and supposedly offered numerous benefits compared with conventionally farmed monocultures, large and small. He showed us more examples of such plantings, mostly in tropical countries, and then we bombarded him with questions about his method.

How knowledge- and training-intensive is this concept? What economic and ecological benefits does it provide—and to whom? Will farmers be willing to do the extra work, and what tools will they need? And the biggest question of all:

Was this perhaps the agricultural model we had been looking for in Ghana to integrate oil palm, cocoa, and other crops?

That evening, in Asuom, a discussion emerged that continues today. A German-born agricultural scientist and practitioner, Joachim had emigrated to Bolivia in the early 1980s, initially to work for a German development agency. He fell in love with the country and, in particular, one of its citizens. He and Sandra got married, had five children, and Joachim set up his own farm in the northeastern lowlands of Bolivia, where he gradually implemented organic methods for growing tropical fruits.

He met and learned from the Swiss pioneer of mixed agroforestry, Ernst Götsch, who had named his version of the concept "syntropy" and showcased it through the impressive revitalization of his 500-hectare farm on degraded land in Brazil.

Joachim began practicing, researching, and promoting DAF on his farm and those of his neighbors, including the organic cocoa cooperative El Ceibo. He has since become a leading adviser in mixed agroforestry and been the godfather of many DAF projects, mostly in the tropics.

TO DESIGN A DAF FOREST

How do you design and plan the installation of a new DAF plot? In essence, you determine what main tree species you want to include and design around them. In Ghana it is oil palm and cocoa; in Samoa it is coconut and cocoa. To simplify planting and maintenance, most modern DAF fields are planted in rows and grids. Yet, unlike in gridded tree monocultures, these rows are highly diverse—with a system.

Figure 3 shows the design for a cocoa and oil palm grid we use in Ghana. Note that trees of the same species are spaced quite a bit farther apart than in their respective monoculture. Timber and fruit trees are planted in between palm and cocoa. In West Africa one may, for example, include avocados, oranges, cashews, teak, and mahogany.

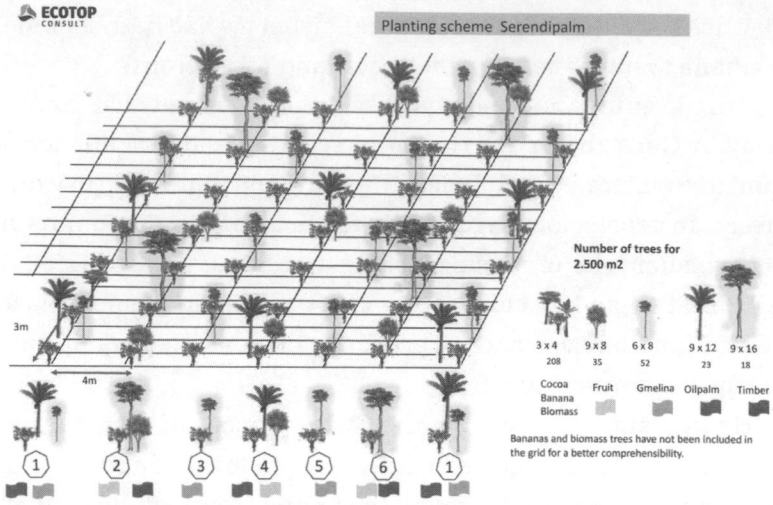

Figure 3. Schematic of the common Dynamic Agroforestry Grid at Serendipalm

You'll also want to include faster-growing, shorter-cycle plants: bananas and papayas, cassava and maize, beans and peas, as I had seen intercropped on newly planted oil palm plots. They create early income and offer synergies. For example, the shade of a fast-growing banana protects a neighboring cocoa seedling.

DAF aims to optimize the output of the entire system, rather than the yield of a single species. Trees aren't machines, and each species has its own growing cycle, ecological niche, and requirements.

Effective DAF designs must give plants the light, nutrients, and protection they need but also consider the principles of natural succession. In the wild, most cereals and vegetables are pioneering plants. They initially occupy spots without trees around but eventually disappear.

Tropical secondary plants, such as bananas and papayas, grow taller and produce for a few years, then are overgrown and replaced by even taller and longer-lasting trees. If a farmer wants to keep growing these tropical fruits, he moves them to newly planted lots or to the edge of an established field. Depending on their natural place in a succession, each tree thus may occupy a stratum in a DAF plot for anywhere from a few years to over a hundred.

Famously, cocoa tolerates shade well and produces plenty of pods, as long as all else is right. Its canopy resides in a lower stratum and can therefore coexist with oil palms that need full sun and whose crowns occupy the top stratum, like coconuts, mahogany, and eucalyptus.

A DAF planting *simulates* a natural forest, but it isn't. Through plant selection and farm maintenance, you design and guide the forest, while letting the trees "do their thing" under favorable conditions. Drone shots of DAF fields will display green, diverse, structured beauty springing up from degraded farmland. From above, mature plots look like natural forests; from below, you discover how designed and productive they are.

DAF fields should include so-called biomass species—fast-growing annuals or perennials. They are trimmed periodically, with the trimmings laid as mulch in the tree rows, where they decay into fertile humus. Once all trees are planted, a DAF mix of cocoa, oil palm, fruit, and timber trees has fewer trees of each species per hectare than in a monoculture but will host a much higher total number of trees—some 2,000 trees per hectare in total, versus 150 for palm or 1,100 for cocoa monocultures.

Don't densely planted trees grow small and thinnish and produce low yields, as we've seen with cocoa monocultures in Ghana? Apparently not. In a well-designed and -maintained DAF plot, tree sizes and product yield per tree are comparable with that in a monoculture. Unlike monocultures, mixed tree assemblies thrive at such high densities because each species occupies its "comfort zone" during a specific time period and at the "right height." There is competition for key resources, such as light and water, but trees also collaborate strongly and build synergistic networks.

In large timber monocultures planted densely to produce tall, fast-growing trees with high yields, competition for sunlight prevails. In comparison, DAF uses a more Montessori-type approach to utility forests. Help each tree develop according to its needs and skills, surround it with many other types of trees, and provide fostering conditions to all. As icing on the cake, the inherent high biodiversity of mixed forests reduces the risk of a catastrophic crop loss caused by pest attacks.

If this isn't a great metaphor for the benefits of symbiotic relationships between humans, what is?

Since 2010, a growing body of research and publications by forest ecologists and practitioners suggests that trees communicate and inform each other of risks, such as insect attacks, and coordinate responses. Trees may develop relationships "for life" and actively protect each other by sharing nutrients and reallocating stored carbon through the vast mycorrhizal network that connects trees in natural forests. This wondrous finding has inspired popular books and films on the subject, like those by the German forester Peter Wohlleben and the Canadian forest ecologist Suzanne Simard.[2] The idea that plants have consciousness, communicate, and support each other naturally speaks to people who think collaboration is a good idea, and sounds esoteric to some hardcore scientists.

But does it relate to the overall higher productivity of DAF systems compared with monocrops? A review of recent scientific studies suggests, on balance, a positive impact of biodiversity on the productivity of mixed forest systems.[3] Studies of mixed tropical agroforestry systems suggest that a higher species diversity combined with proper spacing and compatibility of species can substantially increase productivity. Apparently, the benefits of high species diversity depend on the community of species, its design, and management.

CARBON FARMING

Since DAF plots, by design, promote tree and biomass growth in a favorable environment, they *also* devour atmospheric carbon dioxide (CO_2). This high productivity per area has made DAF and other mixed agroforestry systems the darlings of people promoting tree planting to combat climate change. Such sequestration of the greenhouse gas (GHG) CO_2 in the form of biomass above and below ground—trees and short-lived plants versus roots—is called "carbon farming."

The extent of carbon sequestration by DAF per hectare and its impact on the global carbon balance is becoming a hot topic. As for all agricultural systems, more research is needed on the factors that help optimize CO_2 capture. For now, we know that properly designed and maintained mixed agroforestry sequesters a typical 12 MT of CO_2eq per hectare per year.[4] Whether carbon farming can make a global impact will depend on farmers' willingness and ability to engage in DAF, other knowledge-based practices, and crop diversification at global scale.

How does one motivate farmers of tree crops to renovate unproductive cocoa orchards or replant them using the DAF concept? Very few farmers will make the required management changes simply to counter global climate change. After all, they have much more pressing concerns, namely their economic survival.

Farmers worldwide take reluctantly to a new paradigm, notably one as radical as this: "abandon your convenient monocrops—or at least improve their upkeep—and cut back on agrochemicals." Fortunately, there are signs of a young generation of farmers in Ghana who want to practice novel approaches. They also have plenty of former agricultural land available to lease.

Our experience in Ghana and Samoa shows that several devices are needed to attract cash-poor smallholders to practicing DAF and other forms of carbon farming.

First, someone needs to provide the means (seedlings, tools, financing of land and labor); then the results need to show visible improvements of yields, which may take years. An ongoing financial incentive through a carbon credit mechanism will help—but is difficult and costly to monitor. Finally, one needs to provide hands-on engaging training and demonstration.

If regenerative agriculture and dynamic agroforestry are to make a dent "in the climate," such financial, technical, and training support must be offered to hundreds of millions of smallholder farmers worldwide.

Knowing the inertia of politics, this sounds rather unrealistic. Still, it is well worth trying for many reasons. Helping stabilize global climate is but one—as important is the need to support the productivity, resilience, and profitability of small farms and creation of jobs in rural areas. As already mentioned, smallholders are critical to employing and feeding a large portion of the world. By supporting them you may reach 30 percent of the global population—and give the current global impacts of agriculture and forestry a decidedly positive spin.

In a nutshell, DAF promises to produce things the world needs—fruits, nuts, timber—and provides plenty of other benefits: farmers have more fertile soils and higher yields, trees are less sensitive to drought and pests, the higher biodiversity attracts fewer pests, and more atmospheric carbon is sequestered than in other forms of food production in fields and forests.

Finally, DAF orchards can look very appealing and provide plenty of shade. Not a bad working environment.

BRINGING DAF TO SERENDIPALM

With such a wealth of projected benefits, it's no wonder we swiftly kicked off our mission to demonstrate and implement DAF at Serendipalm. In 2017, the year after Joachim's first visit, Serendipalm established its own DAF training and demonstration farms, a 15-acre (6 ha) farm near Asuom and a 7.5-acre (3 ha) farm near Abaam.

Next, we started trials with some of our farmers and, by late 2019, had helped some twenty-five to install small trial plots on their farms. In parallel, Joachim and his colleague Bastian Pellhammer taught pruning workshops for Serendipalm's staff and farmers in the field. We discovered that many older farmers aren't too motivated to do complex designed plantings or carefully prune their cocoa trees, even after multiple training sessions. Farmer-to-farmer trainings may work in the right setting; they didn't for this knowledge- and labor-intensive concept and this aging crowd.

The Serendipalm field team thus suggested that instead of expecting farmers to practice DAF and cocoa renovation themselves, to offer support in planting and maintenance to farmers as a "for-pay" service. To demonstrate and expand the DAF concept on a commercial scale, Serendipalm and DRB jointly received, in early 2020, a sizeable grant from the German development agency DEG; as usual, we matched it in cash and in-kind.

The project is managed by Serendipalm's team of agricultural field officers and supported by Ute, Rob, and Ryan of the Special Ops team. Over a three-year period, three hundred farmers will plant new DAF fields on overgrown or degraded land. The project finances the seedlings.

Serendipalm also hired and trained some one hundred staff to help farmers in planning, planting, and maintaining their DAF fields and renovating old and unproductive cocoa land. A hundred new jobs is not bad for an area offering little skilled employment. Long term, we hope that this sizeable demonstration project will entice most farmers in our district and beyond to use DAF as a more profitable, manageable, and diverse approach to replanting compared with monocrops.

And while our crews are at it, they will prune and renovate neglected cocoa fields. During their visits, Joachim and Bastian had discovered that a third of cocoa trees produced few to no pods. Taking most of them out reduces tree density and the risk of pest attacks. Over the course of the project our trained farmworkers will renovate some six hundred plots, thus increasing cocoa yields from 350 to over 530 pounds per acre (400 to over 600 kg/ha).

What's in it for the farmer? The higher cocoa yield and overall revenues from a hectare of DAF and the diversification of the product range are a good start. The inclusion of annual and multiyear field crops will translate into income from year one—much sooner than the three to four years needed for palm or cocoa monocrops to produce reasonable yields and income.

Such product diversification sounds great, but many farmers are not set up to market more than one or two primary products. Transportation costs, a lack of fair buyers, and the depressed prices during the peak season all pose challenges. And so Serendipalm has started to engage in the local produce trade. We also naturally look to export, as foreign buyers pay organic and fair trade premiums, whereas local value-added markets are still in their infancy.

Fortunately, Dr. Bronner's regenerative adventures in the tropics are well known in our network of natural products companies, small and large. They now ask whether we can supply "regenerative" peanuts, coconut products, turmeric, ginger, cassava, vanilla. These are crops in high demand but, so far, not available in ROC quality.

DAF tells a multifaceted and rather convincing story that appeals to most people you tell it to. Why wouldn't brands and consumers want to support products with such a story and impact?

With our DAF excitement and programs in Ghana and Samoa, we are riding a global wave. The concept of mixed agroforestry is catching on, promoted by practitioners and scientists and driven by several urgent needs worldwide: to help small farmers make their farms more productive, resilient, and profitable, and to sequester plenty of carbon while feeding a large part of the world's population.

INTO THE CHOCOLATE AISLE

When Serendipalm began its cocoa journey in 2012, we didn't initially target Dr. Bronner's as a potential customer. Mike had occasionally joked about making our own chocolate, but new product development at Dr. Bronner's is slow and deliberate, and we thought it wise to uncouple the growth of organic cocoa production in Ghana from Dr. Bronner's plans for further diversification into foods.

Then, in early 2018, Mike and David first wondered whether we shouldn't develop a line of regenerative chocolate after all. Serendipalm was moving toward dynamic agroforestry and Regenerative Organic Certification. It would be a bold move into yet another aisle, with as strong a story as the move into VCO back in 2011. We would enter a crowded market as new kid on the block. Just having fair and regenerative beans wouldn't do—ingredients and recipes had to appeal to our target audience, too. Should we use cane or coconut sugar? Which novel flavors were promising? And who would produce the chocolate?

In late 2018, Joe Whinney, the founder of Theo Chocolate, became the guide on our chocolate adventure. He helped us develop and taste recipes and steered us toward competent chocolate makers in Switzerland and Italy.

After all, the Swiss are famous for bringing chocolate to perfection. Several Swiss chocolate dynasties—Lindt, Tobler, Suchard—were founded between 1800 and 1850 and majorly contributed to industry development. Lindt, for example, made its name in 1879 with the development of the conching process—a multi-hour kneading and smoothing process that refines the flavor and texture of chocolate.

The production of solid chocolate—a blend of roasted and ground cocoa beans, sugar, other flavors, and, later, milk—took off in Europe in the early 1800s once the grinding of roasted beans into a pourable mass and the production of sugar became commercial.

The Dutch father-and-son team Van Houten developed a critical processing step in the 1820s: separating the ground cocoa mass, or liquor, into cocoa butter and defatted powder. Treating the powder with an alkali then made it water soluble and reduced its bitterness—the birth of chocolate drinks. In the 1870s Nestlé then commercialized milk chocolate from cocoa, condensed milk, and sugar.

The Swiss chocolate factories we visited were awe-inspiring. As you enter the building you're engulfed by an aroma that clearly spells "chocolate." Yet it doesn't just smell like chocolate; one also detects strong acidic aroma notes. Believe it or not, chocolate factories in cities must install odor control, since even the most enthusiastic neighbor will eventually consider the pervasive smell a nuisance.

How do you get from beans to chocolate? Typically, the process is broken into two main steps. Upon their arrival from forest to factory, cocoa beans are removed from bags and cleaned. Next comes roasting, which sterilizes, dries, and develops the flavor of the beans. Roasted beans are cracked, then winnowed to separate the lighter husks from the broken pieces of cocoa, called nibs. Nibs are then milled into a paste called cocoa mass or liquor, the main ingredient in a bar.

Smaller boutique chocolate makers may use the "bean to bar concept." Meaning: all processing steps happen at the factory except for the separation of liquor into butter and powder, as it requires huge machines and is for specialized operators. Larger chocolate factories, such as the ones we visited, usually leave the roasting and milling to others and start with the cocoa mass or liquor.

Depending on the basic type of chocolate—dark, milk, or white—liquor and butter are mixed with sugar, milk powder, and often vanilla. The remaining steps produce the texture and flavor of a fine chocolate: the mix is refined by squeezing it through sets of rollers with a minimal gap to grind sugar and cocoa solids into a smooth paste, giving chocolate its texture and mouthfeel.

Conching follows. It homogenizes the chocolate blend and releases organic compounds with unpleasant flavors: alcohols, aldehydes, and organic acids. Finally comes tempering, a process that determines the crystal structure of a chocolate bar and several of its consumer-facing properties. First, the chocolate mass is melted at 113° F (45° C), which dissolves all fat crystals. Cooling it to 80° F (27° C) while agitating forces the fat to form mostly type 5 crystals—their most desirable structure. Type 5 crystals shrink when the chocolate is cooled, making it easier to remove the bar from the mold. They make the bar's surface glossy and firm, produce the best snap, and raise the melting point to body temperature, just about the best combination of a chocolate's physical properties.

It is not well known—but most of how a piece of chocolate behaves in your mouth is controlled by how long it's kept at the right temperature at the end of production!

What makes visits to large chocolate factories somewhat surreal is the contrast between the large production lines with plenty of stainless steel and conveyor belts, and the finished product, one of humanity's metaphors for desire, romance, and comfort.

As we enter the chocolate aisle in 2021 with our Magic All-One Chocolates, we're optimistic that US consumers will take to our flavors, and Dr. Bronner's brand reputation will carry over into the confectionery aisle. Thus, our line of chocolates will tell consumers that it is possible to grow clean West African cocoa, making improvements to the rather desperate situation of smallholders through farm renovation and DAF planting.

Meanwhile, we have dreams for Serendipalm's cocoa business in Ghana: we will significantly expand acreage and bean output to supply growing demand by committed customers, achieve some scale, and cooperate with other grower groups interested in regenerative cocoa. To leave more value in the country, we may set up the initial cocoa processing steps in Ghana: cleaning, roasting, shelling, and grinding into cocoa liquor. It will surely be bitter, but we can't wait to taste it.

HOPES AND HURDLES

Implementing DAF and renovating cocoa orchards requires training, planting, maintaining. It will cost some money, ultimately paid back to farmers in the form of higher yields and better resilience against the impacts of climate change. Two desirable side effects are the creation of skilled jobs in farming communities and the sequestration of atmospheric CO_2. The real work will be done on the ground—by farmers and companies ready to engage, such as Dr. Bronner's and Serendipalm.

Yet there is a demand side to this issue. What global movements are needed to bring this process about? Who are potential advocates of supporting cocoa farmers in general and of DAF in particular? Our collaboration and trade with committed brands in the north suggests that diversification of tropical agroforestry is a cause worthy to brands who crave tropical raw materials with a beneficial local—and global—impact.

One good example is Chocolats Halba, a Swiss maker of premium chocolates, owned by Coop, the largest retail chain in Switzerland. Since 2015, Halba has started DAF projects at major cocoa bean suppliers in Ghana and Ecuador, with more projects in Latin America and Madagascar under development. Several projects worldwide will partly offset Coop's carbon footprint. With ECOTOP as our common adviser, we informally cooperate with Halba on DAF learning and promotion. Several other progressive and successful chocolate brands, such as Rapunzel and Alter Eco, also see the ecological and economic beauty of DAF and recognize the opportunity to tell a different story. Novel concepts require a push from several directions.

But will this hoped-for shift to more diverse agroforestry revolutionize the global cocoa industries? Not any time soon. West African cocoa and "big palm oil" are structurally in trouble. For palm oil, it's large monocultures; for cocoa, it's the plight of marginally profitable smallholdings in West Africa and its collateral damage, child labor, and destruction of protected forests.

The generally small size of the farms should make the shift to a diversified cocoa production in West Africa more likely than for large oil palm plantations. But this fundamentally requires that motivated farmers can access at least part of the required package of training, financing, seedling supplies, good tools, and professional farm services. That's ultimately the goal of Serendipalm's demonstration project, and also where committed chocolate brands looking for "better beans" can create real impact. Any brand with a bit of heart and knowledge wishing for closer cooperation with its suppliers can use fair and organic cocoa and encourage and support the planting of a new type of agroforest. Even the large global players in cocoa and chocolate know well that consumers prefer chocolate made from "sustainable beans." Accordingly, all large suppliers of chocolate—Barry Callebaut, Mars, Nestlé, Mondelez—have committed to shift to "100% sustainable beans" by 2025.

But what exactly is "sustainable cocoa"? Many large cocoa players use beans certified to the UTZ/Rainforest Alliance (RA) standard and carry its seal. A tough and practical standard in theory—even though it permits the use of some synthetic pesticides—its enforcement by certifying agencies has become so inconsistent that local exporters who have been decertified by strict certifiers simply switch to a "more flexible" certifier. As we know firsthand from Ghana, this problem is pervasive with organic certified cocoa, too. As a result, there will be nowhere near the amount of credibly certified "sustainable beans" that large players plan to process by 2025.

What needs to change? One thing is for certain: farmers need support. Their ultimate customers—chocolate brands and consumers—must be willing to spend more money on beans. Brands, except for real thrifty ones, wouldn't be opposed to that in principle. Even a 20 percent increase in the bean price will have a minor impact on the price of a bar.

Their real problem is transparency. As long as buyers of beans do not know how much of their price premium is passed on to farmers, rather than kept by traders or cooperatives, they will not volunteer to pay such a premium. I cannot blame them. Consequentially, the current review of the Rainforest Alliance standard concentrates on increasing transparency in the system and controlling certifiers, thus plugging current loopholes. If successful, large players may well reengage with a common and, in theory, transparent standard, such as RA—rather than creating and promoting their own in-house sustainability programs, such as Nestlé's "Cocoa Plan." However well-intentioned such in-house initiatives might be, they are less transparent than an independent standard.

Let's assume that Big Chocolate is truly interested in making a change in West African cocoa and is willing to pay for some of it. Effective direct involvement "on the ground" may be tough but is crucial for large international brands. They rarely get involved in agriculture and can't operate in a semi-guerilla style the way Dr. Bronner's does, but cocoa exporters *do* have close contact with farmers and offer agricultural advice and support. But they cannot invest unless their customers—large chocolate makers—are willing to help with financing.

Once again, we the consumers are the ultimate judge on what kind of beans we want. The trouble in West African cocoa is increasingly covered in media in the EU and North America. Yet it is a bit complex and most consumers don't make the connections between farming practices, ecology, farm profitability, and serious transgressions, such as child labor and deforestation.

In this uncertain situation and with the need to appeal to the vague but growing awareness of consumers, most large chocolate brands still just practice damage control by green and fair washing their bean sourcing. Yet a growing number know better. It's our hope that more companies will follow the examples of Halba, Rapunzel, Alter Eco, Equal Exchange, and Dr. Bronner's by creating local partnerships and embracing the conceptual, ecological, and aesthetic appeal of dynamic agroforestry.

It's a long shot, but not impossible.

Sweet and strong—sugar and alcohol from South America

As Dr. Bronner's began to diversify our product line in the 2000s, we also added new raw materials. Cane sugar—and the alcohol derived from it—is one of them. Sugar is the world's largest commodity by volume and one of its most symbolic. It's used in numerous foods and ferments easily into ethanol, the planet's predominant drug. Eighty percent of global production comes from sugar cane—a tall, perennial, grass-like plant with a sweet core.

We use the granulated semi-processed sugar in our sugar soaps and shaving gels and the alcohol as the disinfectant in our increasingly popular hand sanitizers.

Our demand for sugar and alcohol was initially low. Rather than setting up our own project, we decided to look for credentialed partner projects. Ryan Zinn discovered two suppliers at the extreme end of the farming spectrum: for our sugar soaps, we turned to Native Organic Products, pioneer of large-scale regenerative sugar farming and processing in Brazil. For the FTO alcohol in our sanitizers and lotions, our key partner has been CADO, a network of co-ops in Ecuador.

Let's first travel to Native in Brazil, a country that produces some 17 percent of the world's sugar. Not only is Native one of the world's largest sources of organic sugar, it's also a family business, which, as we know, sometimes spawns eccentric leaders who break with a dominant paradigm. For Native, that meant developing alternatives to the practices of large conventional sugar monocultures, such as the setting on fire—or "flaring"—of mature cane before harvesting. Though it's the norm in conventional sugar farming, flaring robs the soil of organic matter, sends it up in smoke, and creates severe local air-quality problems.

Since the 1980s, Leontino Balbo Jr., head of Native, and his team have replaced conventional practices with a method called ecosystem revitalizing agriculture (ERA). The main difference? Instead of flaring off the leaves, a "green harvester" developed by Native separates cane from leaves and blows the latter as a mulch onto the adjacent strip of land. The sugar canes are cut and replanted every six to seven years compared with the normal two or three. Among their other practices, Native grows leguminous cover crops before replanting sugar cane, and they use a system of tillage that increases the soil's moisture-holding capacity.

They've also come up with a unique way to target the "sugar cane borer," a moth whose sweet tooth larvae drill into mature cane, causing significant losses. Native's annual hatching and release of large numbers of wasps that feed on these larvae minimizes cane losses without using pesticides.

As a large and mature project, Native does not need advice or financing from a relatively small customer such as Dr. Bronner's. Of course, we expect that Native, with Ryan's support, will join the club of ROC-certified regenerative organic projects sometime soon.

From Brazil, we'll now turn to a rather different setting in the foothills of the Ecuadorian Andes where CADO—an association of cooperatives with some 160 farmer members working on about 400 hectares of land—operates. During our visit there in 2014, as Ryan and I chewed on pieces of sugar cane—sweet and slightly aromatic—a farmer explained that the smallholders in CADO harvested the cane selectively and by hand, but not all at once. This left a population of cane stratified by age.

This "semi-permaculture" approach ensured the soil on this hillside wouldn't be barren or washed off during the rainy season. The ground between the canes was covered with the leaves the farmers dropped after harvesting. It made for a great mulch that gradually turned into humus. Three miles (5 km) up the road we visited the next step in our supply chain for alcohol: a simple fermentation and distillation plant. A press squeezed the juice out of the cane; it fermented quickly and then was distilled into a 120 proof rum.

From the distillery we could see down into a gorge. Two donkeys carrying bundles of cane on their backs approached a bridge covered by a roof. "That bridge cover is one of the fair trade projects Dr. Bronner's helped finance," explained Carlos Cabrera, CADO's general manager. Remote farmers cross this bridge as they bring their cane on dirt roads to the distilleries for initial processing. The result? A medium-grade rum traded and consumed locally or sold to CADO and then further concentrated at an industrial distillery.

Naturally, the cane productivity on CADO's hilly farms is no match for that on Native's large plantation, which is replanted two to three times as often. On the other hand, since canes produce for some fifteen to twenty years, labor requirements are low, and farmers receive a fair price for their alcohol. Ryan and I are certain that CADO's farming practices will easily pass regenerative organic inspections and certification, thus allowing this traditional production system to gain more global visibility.

Indian farmer in her mint field

CHAPTER 11

Tales of Mint, Deception, and Compost

Uttar Pradesh, India, May 2009

I N MAY 2009, CHRISTEL, MY FUTURE teammate Rob Hardy, and I stood in front of a large shed covered with plastic tarps: a bare-bones greenhouse. Men were setting up new piles of cow dung and vegetable waste next to existing piles filled with an abundance of wiggling earthworms. The worms fed on the digestible portions of the mix—the result, more stable organic matter spiked with worm castings.

A young man named Nihal Singh enthusiastically explained what we were witnessing: the production of "vermicompost." Nihal didn't just know vermicompost, he was familiar with other organic farming practices and clearly had worked on farms before.

He showed an excitement with his work I hadn't seen in anyone else in India involved in our mint oil projects. While chatting he stuck his hands into the compost—he wasn't afraid of getting his hands or his white shirt dirty.

Crossing Nihal's path in 2009 ultimately started Dr. Bronner's drive to introduce regenerative agriculture to the flat plains of Uttar

Pradesh (UP), India's most populous state. Of all our quests for clean ingredients, our Indian trip took the most difficult and opaque road—only to become a pillar in our campaign to demonstrate the benefits of regenerative organic agriculture to smallholder farmers.

When starting our push to fair trade and organic raw materials, finding the right mint source was essential. After all, when creating his liquid magic soap, Emanuel Bronner put his bets on mint—and it remains by far the company's most popular scent. The enigmatic essential oil gives the soap its famous tingle, particularly refreshing when showering on hot summer days. (Caveat: use mint oil with caution on sensitive parts of your body!) Ultimately, mint oil is what turned Dr. Bronner's into the versatile soap for use on almost anything. As with all other Dr. Bronner's organic ingredients, the Bronners had initially purchased mint oil from brokers. They knew it came from India, and that was all. That changed at a trade show, when David met Campbell Walther, cofounder and sales manager of Earthoil Plantations, and learned he was the actual supplier of our organic mint oil. We agreed to work with Earthoil directly and were fair and transparent with our UK broker about our decision to go direct. With the already high volume of mint oils we used at the time, it made all the sense to get closer to the source.

Naturally, we requested that Earthoil also have their project FFL-certified. Campbell was initially skeptical of the merits of FFL certification, but he rose to the challenge. We were his largest customer, after all, and he saw the ethics and value in this move.

And so I made my first visit to Uttar Pradesh in May 2006.

BAREILLY—MINT OIL CENTRAL

I flew from Sri Lanka into Delhi, met Campbell, and then the two of us set out on the 250-km trip to Bareilly, a city of about 1 million people today—and one of the world's capitals of natural mint oil processing.

At the time, the car trip took some seven hours on congested roads through the heart of villages and towns. Before Noida, just

East of Delhi, we passed one of the world's largest trash piles, with crows and seagulls circling. We also spotted many remnants of industrialization, including power plants and cement plants from the 1960s and 1970s.

I had become used to chaotic traffic in Sri Lanka, but India was a notch up. A never-ending orchestra of honking, cars passing on two-lane roads without attention to oncoming traffic, trucks overloaded with produce, some of them tipped over into the ditch.

We crossed the Ganges River with its lively pilgrimage site where devotees and tourists flock to bathe and buy souvenirs. The land of the Ganges' flood plain is level as far as the eye can see. Farmers' fields were small or even tiny compared with those I knew from Germany and the United States. They were dotted with a variety of crops and often lined by fast-growing trees, mostly poplars and eucalyptus.

We stopped at an assembly of skillfully built piles of flat disks made from cow dung, a key natural resource in the area still used as domestic fuel and to fertilize the fields. (The job of collecting dung and beating it into pads is usually that of low-caste women and children.) Then we crossed fields with tall sugar cane, a few large sugar mills, and a large industrial distiller that turned sugar cane into alcohol. In the villages, small sugar cane presses squeezed liquid out of the cane for consumption in juices. Then we saw the first mint fields, in two different shades of green.

As we entered Bareilly, Campbell pointed out several tall towers cladded by sheet metal. These were the distillation columns of commercial processors of mint and other essential oils that supported a large local industry: the distillation, purification, and fractionation of mint oils into a wide range of food and personal care products made worldwide.

Next morning, we set out to the fields in two of the villages that supplied the Earthoil project. We saw a puzzle of small fields, typically less than an acre (0.4 ha) in size. Many fields were bordered by narrow, low bunds to allow for flood irrigation. Motorbikes, tractors, and bullock-pulled carts were the common means of transportation.

Virtually all buildings in the villages were made of red bricks whose origin we soon spotted—the entire area was dotted with shallow open pit clay mines. After mechanical excavation the clay was molded into bricks, then fired in large kilns with tall stacks. Most brick walls were unrendered, creating an ancient look.

Most villages feature small Hindu shrines with the occasional modest-sized mosque towering over the mostly single-story houses. After all, Muslims account for some 20 percent of Uttar Pradesh's population. Cows were lazing in courtyards or bathing in large ponds. Full of nutrients from cow dung and runoff, most of these ponds were overgrown with water hyacinth. Young boys and girls played in villages and fields. Women were reserved and in the background, covered by colorful shawls, with the notable exception of several active women farmers.

In one village with some thirty brick houses, we met a delegation of farmers who sold their mint oil to Earthoil. We walked across a few fields of *Mentha piperita* and *Mentha arvensis*, the two main mint varieties grown in Uttar Pradesh (and whose oil Dr. Bronner's uses significant amounts of). We sat in the courtyard of one farm, had tea, and chatted with farmers about our plans for the fair and organic production of mint oil. As we commonly do at projects, I showed the farmers a bottle of our mint soap and offered them a smell of what had become of their mint oils.

The farmers explained they were in the early days of harvesting and processing of this year's crop of both *piperita* and *arvensis*—both are planted between January and March and are harvested into July. Leaf growth is strongest from April to June, and more than half of the fields were now, in May, under a green carpet, *arvensis* dominating by far.

You can tell the varieties apart by their color. The leaves of *Mentha piperita*, or peppermint, are dark green with purplish veins, while *Mentha arvensis*, also called corn mint or field mint, has smaller leaves of a lighter green. Both have coarse-toothed margins. There were also some corn fields, but much of the land not under mint was fallow.

As we walked through the fields I bent down here and there to squeeze the leaves of both low-growing plants. The essential oil of *piperita* has an aromatic, more balanced flavor, used in peppermint tea, chewing gum, and toothpaste.

The oil of *arvensis* is more pungent, with a strong menthol flavor. It has a much narrower composition and is dominated by one component, menthol, which by weight accounts for over 70 percent of the oil. You know menthol from its use in balms, cough medicines, chest rubs—and, yes, menthol-flavored cigarettes.

One of Emanuel Bronner's strokes of genius was to develop the blend of mint oils that gave the liquid soap its smell and tingle. He blended *arvensis* and *piperita* oils and added a generous 2 percent of that oil blend to the diluted soap. Simplistically, that blend retains the aroma of *piperita*, while the high menthol content adds the punch. We have not changed that recipe much over the decades.

Our next stop that morning was at one of the many preindustrial-looking field distillation units that sprinkle the area. Using a simple steam distillation process, mint leaves and other aromatic herbs are converted into essential oils.

From the distillation unit, placed on a knoll, I now watched the entire mint oil–making process. Separate groups of men and of women in colorful saris harvested the plants with knives, squatting. The cut herb was left in the field to dry. Oxen carts picked up the herb from one field and took it to the field distillation units. Each featured one or two cylindrical tanks, some 2,600 gallons (10,000 liters) by volume. The tanks are filled with water that is boiled to steam by a fire underneath.

As the steam percolates up from the boiling water through the tightly packed dried herb, it volatizes the essential oil and carries it out of the distillation tank. The steam then flows through a water-cooled condenser, reliquefies, and the condensate trickles into a separator, a small drum in which the lighter essential oil floats on top and the water settles at the bottom.

Farmers often watch the distillation of their herb and continuously skim off their very own mint oil into a small field drum. During the harvest season, distillation plants are usually immersed in a cloud of menthol that makes you tear up.

As we learned later, the condensers and separators in most of the hundreds of distillation units just in the Bareilly area are rather inefficient. The condensers may cool the steam down to 158° F (70° C) rather than the target 104° F (40° C), and the hot water discharged from the separators still contains plenty of essential oil. It wouldn't be until 2019 that we were able to tackle this area-wide waste of mint oil and cooling water through redesign of a distillation system.

One wouldn't know from the scattered small fields and small stills, but Uttar Pradesh is the world's largest producer of mint oils, notably *arvensis*. With an annual mint oil production of some 40,000 MT, India accounts for about 80 percent of the global output of natural mint oil and menthol—90 percent of which is grown in UP. As a labor-intensive crop, mint farming and processing gives a livelihood to some 15 million people in rural India. We were, in other words, at the center of global mint oil and menthol production!

The high global demand for and fluctuating price of menthol triggered the production of synthetic menthol, similar to the production of synthetic vanillin. Although 30 percent of the world's menthol production is synthetic, the majority is still made from mint oil.

What makes mint attractive to Indian farmers, and how did it become such an important sector of the local agriculture and processing industry?

Piperita and other herbs, such as holy basil, or tulsi, have been used in Indian traditional medicine and grown in UP for tea for ages. In the early 1970s, agronomists and businesspeople realized that *arvensis* would add an attractive cash crop for farmers. Mint crops fit well into the traditional rotation schemes. They could be grown during the spring, after the winter-grown staple crops wheat and potatoes and before rice planted during the monsoon season in July and August.

Both kinds of mint are grown from suckers planted early in the New Year in the local sandy-loamy soils (they warm up faster than silty or clay soils). *Piperita* is usually planted earlier because it can handle the lower temperatures in January and February. For extra income, farmers usually leave it for a second cut before the monsoon rains start. Another big plus of mint crops: unlike cereal, they are not grazed by cattle or by the nilgai, a wild antelope that causes frequent crop damage. (Nilgai are a protected species, so they can only be chased away onto another farmer's field.)

Aromatic herbs grow well in the alluvial loamy soils of the Ganges plain. Leafy with shallow root systems, both mint species are thirsty and need some forty centimeters per year of irrigation water, usually by flooding of the fields during the relatively dry spring season. To irrigate, farmers in UP rely either on canal water from unpredictable public irrigation districts, or on groundwater they pump up through deep wells.

Mint needs plenty of water but only moderate doses of macronutrients (nitrogen, phosphorus, and potassium). In traditional agriculture, cow dung and mixed farmyard manure were good sources. With the "green revolution" of the 1960s and 1970s, the use of chemical nitrogen fertilizer boomed in India as elsewhere. Fertilizer and irrigation drove up yields per area—important when you grow on small fields.

Yet combined with frequent and deep tillage, the use of synthetic nitrogen gradually destroyed the organic content of the soil, leaving a loamy soil of good texture but almost entirely depleted of humus and other soil organic matter. This in turn had significantly reduced water-holding capacity and increased the need for irrigation water, which swiftly evaporates during the hot spring. In the early years of the project, Earthoil and Dr. Bronner's did not seriously address the soil's low humus content and lack of nutrients.

That failure would come back to haunt us a few years later.

THE ROAD TO OUR OWN MINT OIL PROJECT

Back in May 2006, at the distillation plant, we started attracting much of the village population. Old and young smiled, loved having their photos taken and shown on the display of the digital camera— still a novelty. We went back to the village, sat under a tree on chairs and simple beds, and drank tea with fresh milk while a duo of men performed the most magic music with percussion and some sort of a harmonium.

Campbell and I left India inspired by the potential to develop these villages and fields through commerce. Dr. Bronner's would purchase its entire demand of *arvensis* and *piperita* oils from Earthoil if they made sure it was organic and Fair for Life. As managing director for the project, Earthoil hired a Mr. Lomri, who also ran his own aromatics processing company, purchased the crude oil from farmers in two farm clusters on areas on opposite sides of Bareilly, then sent it through a tall distillation column where water and dirt were removed in a first pass. If needed, the oils would be further *rectified* by selective removal of undesirable components, such as terpenes. Mr. Lomri understood the mint oil business well, but he lacked an understanding of organic practices and a control system—which did not keep him from lecturing about it extensively. He hired two field officers to run the ICS, and we brought IMO India in for their training, as we had done in Sri Lanka.

Realizing the limitations of the local team—and to provide support and transparency—Earthoil UK fatefully hired Rob Hardy, who would ultimately join my team. Living in Bristol, UK, Rob had worked in farming (from small-scale conventional to organic), received a master's in ecological agriculture, then worked for the Soil Association, the UK's largest organic certifier, where he became familiar with the challenges to converting smallholder farmers to organic practices.

At the time, I was preoccupied with Sri Lanka and Ghana and paid less attention to India, even though Earthoil's lack of transparency on project progress and finances was annoying. When Mr. Lomri died in early 2010, his son took over, but was not up to the task of managing such a complex project. Notably, he didn't know how to deal with farmers.

By then, Earthoil had been bought out by Treatt, a large flavor and fragrance company in the UK that wanted to add a "sustainable feather to their cap." Rob became increasingly dissatisfied with Earthoil and Treatt's lack of attention to the needs of the project. He wanted it to be more than a marketing tool to demonstrate Treatt's commitment to "ethical sourcing."

A practitioner at heart who was not interested in green washing, Rob eventually joined Dr. Bronner's and, in September 2011, became my first teammate at Special Operations. Serendipalm lacked oversight, its organic system was at risk, and I was running out of steam. Rob, with his extensive experience in organic agriculture and certification, came just at the right time.

Rob had visited Earthoil's mint oil project frequently, and after joining Special Ops stayed in touch with several field officers and with the owner of the processing company that cleaned and shipped the crude oil to Bronner's. The owner, a smart engineer whom I'll call Ashok, had designed and built his own mint oil processing plant and thought of "going organic" as a way to add value to his production.

Ashok and the field team were also becoming increasingly frustrated with Earthoil's project management and were concerned that the project, at the time including some five hundred farmers, would "go down the drain." Considering all the effort and money invested, we did not like that idea. We evaluated our options, Rob inquired with Ashok and staff on the ground, and, in 2012, we decided that Dr. Bronner's would take over the project and form its own sister company in India.

Somewhat of a coup, this required getting all project farmers to quit the Earthoil project and sign up with the ICS of our newly formed Indian company, Serendimenthe Pvt. Ltd. Earthoil was surprised by our successful move but then swiftly relieved—they knew that their insight into the project had been poor, and they proceeded to buy from Serendimenthe. Rob's standing with farmers and staff was the key; we engaged Ashok as managing director of Serendimenthe, and, for 2013 and 2014, we finally had "our own" organic and fair trade mint oil.

Or so we thought.

Production was going well, and Ashok's operation delivered the quantities Dr. Bronner's needed in a timely manner and of good (and supposedly organic) quality. Our fair trade program grew; we provided farmers with photovoltaic panels and vermicompost at a subsidy and helped build toilets. We organized periodic health camps during which doctors would come to the villages for a few days and provide basic care, basic medicine, and diagnostics at no cost—a huge success. All seemed well, until one evening in late 2013 when Rob and I received a visit in our Bareilly hotel.

It was Nihal Singh, whom we had first met in 2009 at his vermicompost plant. He had joined Serendimenthe as a field officer while also running his family farm.

He told us a chilling story. Ashok, our MD, had conspired with two of the key ICS staff to charge Dr. Bronner's, who bought from Serendimenthe on a cost plus 10 percent basis, "a little above the price paid to farmers for crude oil," and to distribute the difference among staff, with the lion's share going to the instigators.

Furthermore, the distribution of the organic premium to farmers was not transparent, and it was unclear how much of the earned premium farmers actually received. Tracking financial transactions was difficult, since most farmers had no bank account and all payments were in cash. Worst of all, Nihal claimed that our organic farmers produced nowhere near the oil needed by Dr. Bronner's, and that Ashok, in order to meet our demand, had made up the shortfall with conventional *arvensis* and *piperita*.

Nihal had conflicts with Ashok and seemed a little drunk that evening, so we took his accusations with a grain of salt. We did not confront Ashok directly, but installed a comprehensive database to better track farmers and purchases, conducted spot checks among farmers, and convinced ourselves that all was good.

Yet the sluggish communication with field officers did not improve. Serendimenthe hired a general manager who first appeared competent and motivated, then increasingly timid, until he blew the whistle when we visited in late 2014, confirming Nihal's accusations in full detail.

We realized then that fraud was pervasive and irreparable; farmers and distillation unit owners had been involved, and we swiftly decided to close down Serendimenthe. We wouldn't be able to save the project. For better leverage with Ashok, we first had to ship all product out of India and inform Dr. Bronner's and third-party customers that the oil couldn't be considered organic and priced it as conventional and FFL. Then we fired the unsuspecting Ashok during a Skype board meeting.

Afterward, the entire Special Ops team had a terrible "India hangover." We had enjoyed building the project, saw the potential to make a great impact in the area, and knew that not all of our "partners" had sacrificed our vision for some extra cash. But we would now need to regroup and find a new source of organic and fair mint oils.

In retrospect, we saw the signs of corruption. A senior field officer had started drinking—we blamed it on his unhappy marriage. In a village a mob of angry farmers claimed we had cheated them—we didn't take it seriously.

In January 2015, Les Szabo and I went to Bareilly on what we thought would be our final close-out visit to the town. Les had joined Special Ops in 2013 and had been responsible for monitoring project finances and supporting local staff in setting up transparent accounting systems. We confronted Ashok and were amazed by his way of rationalizing his behavior.

"But we gave you what you wanted," he said, meaning: plenty of mint oil with the NOP logo, regardless of origin!

He also claimed he was not really responsible for what his staff did—even though we knew that he had been present and directed the fraudulent behavior.

Such lack of culpability was a new experience for us. Other foreign buyers have had similar experiences, which has eroded the trust in the authenticity of organic products from India. This is especially frustrating knowing that many producers in India are committed to the spirit and substance of a fair and organic project. And organic fraud is no Indian monopoly: there is plenty of organic cheating in both the north and the south.

But during that January visit to cold and gray Bareilly, Les and I also found strong signs of hope. We met with Nihal and his three field officers at Serendimenthe, Rahul Sharma, Subhash Chandra, and Rajiv Sharma, all of whom have been proactive but somehow restrained. In retrospect we understood why.

The four appealed to us to let them build a "real organic and fair mint oil project" in an area not far from the old project, including the village Nihal had grown up in. Intuitively, we had trust in the team. We had nothing to lose, but we insisted on tough conditions: full financial transparency through our old, trusted accountant, who would remain on the project, and a slow ramp-up of project size and output, since excessive growth in demand had been a key reason for comingling on the previous project.

We reserved veto rights on capital expenditures that did not serve the project's purpose. Trying to supply within three years Dr. Bronner's entire demand—by then over 60 MT of mint oils per year—would have incentivized organic cheating and prompted a rerun of the Serendimenthe fiasco. Thus, in 2015, Nihal and team would first recruit some five hundred farmers who had previously farmed conventionally and had to go through a full three-year organic conversion. We would buy mint oil from fields in organic conversion, pay a reduced in conversion premium of 5 percent, and support farmers with subsidized vermicompost. We would pay a floor price that guaranteed a profit.

Nihal and his friends agreed to all our stipulations—notably, financial transparency—and on that gloomy January afternoon we agreed to start Pavitramenthe. It would become, after eight years of trial and error, our first Indian project that shared Dr. Bronner's vision of fair and regenerative agriculture and trade. And it still does.

THE TROUBLE WITH ORGANIC FIELD CROPS

Our Serendimenthe drama illustrates that organic cheating may have reasons other than the greed of businessmen wanting to sell conventional product as organic at a significant premium.

As for many other smallholder projects, the underlying agricultural problem is that farmers who earlier used chemical fertilizer and synthetic pesticides must swear off that use to become organic.

But unless a project operator understands *why* farmers use agro-chemicals and offers alternatives, he shouldn't be surprised that some (or even most) farmers resort to their use clandestinely.

These farmers have been taught by their government's agricul-tural extension services and by sales agents for agrochemicals that chemicals are the low-effort—or maybe even the only—way to con-trol losses and increase yields. And farmers are often not thoroughly aware of the chemical exposure of their workers and themselves and the damage they cause to the environment. Anyone who's tried organic gardening at home knows its challenges all too well! If you lose your squashes or peppers to pests, you might have a slightly less exciting summer meal plan; for these farmers, a much lower crop yield can mean losing significant income.

This simple dynamic explains much of the Serendimenthe case. If smallholders grow an intensive three-crop rotation, which they used to fertilize with urea and diammonium phosphate, they will need an alternative source of nutrients to maintain yields. The ver-micompost Serendimenthe supplies to farmers did not make up for this nutrient shortfall. Furthermore, Serendimenthe paid farmers an organic premium for only one of the three crops in rotation—mint—and none for their potatoes, rice, and lentils. How committed must a farmer be to keep incurring lower yields on *all three* crops with compensation for only one?

Serendimenthe had taught us that farmers who've used agro-chemicals extensively will not be able to abandon them without help. Failing that, they will either drop out of the organic system or cheat and sell products as organic that aren't.

Thus, with Pavitramenthe, we decided to first expand the central production and subsidized distribution of vermicompost and help farmers produce additional vermicompost on their fields. We knew more action was needed to achieve the long-term soil improvement and nutrient supply required to keep farmers "clean and organic." What would we do next?

Before continuing my Indian account, let's talk about what has become another strong motivation for our push on all projects toward regenerative agriculture: its potential to offset emissions of greenhouse gases generated elsewhere in Dr. Bronner's supply chain.

A GOOD CLIMATE—DR. BRONNER'S GOES CLIMATE POSITIVE

We now all know that, for global climate's sake, we better minimize our "personal carbon footprint"—the amount of greenhouse gases we emit to the heavens while we consume, work, drive around, or just sit at home. We can shrink our footprint by using more efficient appliances, building better insulated homes, adjusting the thermostat, driving fuel-efficient or electric cars, eating organic food and much less meat, recycling our waste, and flying less. Yet much of our footprint originates further upstream: in the production of petroleum; the production and use of synthetic nitrogen fertilizer; the burning of tropical forests for cattle grazing and growing animal feed; and farming of the grain, beans, and veggies we eat directly or indirectly as feed for cows, pigs, and chickens.

Agriculture, forestry, and related land use changes, such as burning down forests, are known large contributors to GHG emissions. Yet these sectors could become net carbon sinks, or climate positive, if we allowed regenerative practices to filter back in.

Wouldn't it be nice if providers of consumer goods and services operated in climate-positive fashion—with no release of net GHG emissions on their product? That'll be tough for airlines to achieve within their supply chain. But how about, say, makers of natural food and personal care items that process plenty of agricultural raw materials?

There is a growing family of companies, both small and large, that recognize the power they may have to influence global climate through actions along their supply chain, agricultural or otherwise. An encouraging example is the US-based Climate Collaborative, with now some 700 companies, both small and large, all committed to cutting GHG emissions, sequestering carbon, and reducing waste.

So what is Dr. Bronner's doing to offset our own carbon footprint? How large is it anyway?

Our carbon footprint has a few distinct sources: the use of natural gas and local transportation at our Vista plant, the generation of electric power used in Vista, and from the production and processing of agricultural raw materials, chemicals, packaging, and their transport, staff travel, and outside services. Using models and emission factors, Dr. Bronner's Operational Sustainability and Innovation (OSI) team and a few of our Special Ops team members have estimated Dr. Bronner's total 2019 carbon footprint at about 60,000 MT of CO_2 equivalent (CO_2eq).

How do you offset it—bring it to zero or even below? Most companies or organizers of large public events simply purchase *carbon credits:* voluntary reductions in GHG emissions achieved elsewhere on the planet, usually certified by a third party, and then sold. This is perfectly fine for companies without opportunities to sequester carbon in their supply chains, such as the mentioned airlines.

Yet, as we became devotees of regenerative organic agriculture, Dr. Bronner's saw a great opportunity to become climate positive through action in our own supply chain. Notably, it involved shifting from chemical fertilizers in India to practices that provide nutrients and build soil organic matter and sequester atmospheric carbon in soil—cover cropping, minimal tillage, adding compost, and mulching agricultural waste—and by replanting trees. The latter includes the more than two hundred thousand palms we've planted at Serendipol and Serendipalm since 2007 and the replanting of trees in our DAF programs in Ghana and Samoa, with pruning programs that add biomass to the soil.

On the emissions side, the purchase of electricity from renewable sources, innovation in packaging, the installation of a solar thermal system in Vista to produce process heat, and use of more fuel-efficient transportation will shrink our footprint in the coming years, despite continued growth.

Combining both sides of the balance, we project that Dr. Bronner's will become climate positive around 2025, give or take a few years. (Note that GHG emissions and sequestration figures are based on models. One cannot measure them at reasonable effort—they represent science-based estimates of SOM accumulation, supported by periodic soil testing to confirm the projected gradual SOM increase over time. GHG emissions and sequestration aren't like money. Their metrics aren't suited for scientific experiments. But they show you the way, if you're willing to watch.)

The point we want to make is that by using more renewable energy and implementing regenerative agriculture practices in our supply chain, a medium-size manufacturing company using mostly agricultural raw materials can wipe out its entire carbon footprint through such "insets"—GHG reductions within our supply chain—as opposed to the mentioned "offsets"—reductions achieved elsewhere and purchased to compensate your carbon footprint. Afterward we may even sequester net carbon! If that doesn't create a ray of hope, what does?

REGENERATION HITS INDIA

Bareilly, 2016

Back in 2016, a key objective was to help Indian farmers rebuild the SOM content of soils that had been devastated by decades of deep tillage, the heavy use of synthetic nitrogen fertilizer, the lack of cover crops, and insufficient return of biomass. For that we had to produce something called thermophilic compost—and large amounts of it.

Yet we needed external support to kickstart the process, and it was time to ask for help from the financiers of international development. We designed a hands-on regenerative development project and proposed it to GIZ, Germany's largest development agency, whose develoPPP program had earlier supported us in Ghana and Sri Lanka. We received a $200,000 grant to match the $300,000 that Dr. Bronner's and Pavitramenthe had put up as in-kind contributions. This money allowed Nihal and the Special Ops team to fulfill dreams long held.

One was the production and subsidized distribution of large amounts of compost. Our guru in all matters of compost and soil fertility, Tobias Bandel, and his Hamburg firm Soil & More suggested investing in a robust compost turner from Austria. How do you make compost? Blend raw materials (leaves, branches, manure, crop waste) and set them up in long piles, or windrows. Their easily degradable fractions are eaten up by microorganisms that require oxygen and love heat—they are what's called aerobic and thermophilic. Temperatures inside such a pile may reach 80° C and more, hot enough to burn your hand when you stick it in all the way.

To ensure that thermophilic compost windrows stay aerated and moist, piles are turned and watered every few weeks by our tractor-pulled Austrian Wundermaschine. After two to three months you are left with dark, earthy-smelling, stable humus. To prevent flooding of the windrows during the monsoon rains, we cover them with strong, breathable synthetic fabric.

Another tenet of regenerative agriculture is the use of "conservation tillage"—the less frequent, lighter, and less deep working of the soil to minimize disruptions of the soil biota while still loosening soil and controlling weeds. For that, we needed simple equipment that could be pulled by a light tractor. To alleviate manual weeding and minimize the temptation to use herbicides we introduced more effective hoes from Europe.

Finally, we had to promote the planting of cover crops between main crops by issuing seeds for mustard and for dhaincha, a hemp-like, fast-growing leguminous crop.

Of course, as for any development project, ours included heavy "capacity building." Trainings for all farmers would be held by our field officers and head farmers—those farmers in each "farmer club" of about ten, organized by Nihal, who had shown commitment and leadership.

Changing farmers' practices is as much a challenge in India as it is in Ghana. Training alone rarely changes behavior. Much better to offer a package that also includes credible leadership, hands-on support, and economic incentives to produce and sell higher-value crops.

So far, the largest success in our regenerative program in India has been the production of large volumes of the high-quality thermophilic compost described above. Our initial goal was to produce and distribute some 10,000 MT of compost per year. Quickly, our challenge became finding enough inexpensive organic waste as compost ingredients. Nihal's team roamed the countryside and brought in crop and farmyard waste, water hyacinth that covered local ponds, as well as waste from the processing of sugar cane. We realized that farmers would not be willing to pay the full cost of production, some $20 per metric ton. Thus, the fair trade fund, Pavitramenthe, and Dr. Bronner's subsidized the sale at initially about 50 percent of the cost of production.

Then Nihal and Rob realized that motivating farmers to produce compost on their farms and from their own organic waste would solve part of the raw material and cost problem. Nihal built a close copy of our compost turner and offered on-farm turning service to now some two hundred farmers.

As of 2020, Pavitramenthe produces and distributes some 25,000 MT of compost per year, a huge benefit to farmers and the only way to keep them off chemical fertilizers while helping increase SOM. Meanwhile, the GIZ grant came in very handy for promoting conservation tillage and cover cropping. As of 2020, some 25 percent of farmers have shifted to conservation tillage and grow at least one cover crop—a good start, but we plan to get to 90 percent on both counts.

These practices will all raise SOM content over time. In turn, that will increase soil fertility by improving nutrient supply, soil structure, and water infiltration. Importantly, it reduces water demand by retaining more soil moisture.

The issue of water conservation will soon become critical, as local water supplies are coming under serious strain. Years of heavy pumping from the aquifers under the Ganges flood plain combined with insufficient or poorly timed rain have dropped groundwater levels, in some areas by as much as six to seven meters. Projections are that in the 2030s or 2040s, many farmers in UP will face shortages of groundwater for irrigation due to a further drop in the groundwater table.

Thus, it was heartening to hear from several project farmers how working compost into their soils has dropped the demand for flood irrigation of their mint crops. While they used to flood around twelve times per season, after only two years of heavy compost dosing they can now get by on nine floodings.

No wonder we're planning a follow-up project on water management. Can we drop demand for groundwater irrigation by making soils spongier, less thirsty? Can farmers shift their rotation to less thirsty, value-added crops, at least a little bit?

Possibly, but this move must be market driven. Farmers will grow crops they can sell, not just because they use less water. Finding markets for value-added water-frugal crops, such as many legumes, may well help farmers to spare their groundwater resources. It'll be one of our key projects in the coming years.

I already showed how productive dynamic agroforestry could sequester *a lot* of atmospheric carbon. Could regenerative agriculture in field crops also improve the carbon footprint of our global food production system?

The work we've done to regenerate mint production in India nicely illustrates the two main GHG-relevant benefits of such a shift. By "going organic" and ceasing the use of nitrogen fertilizers, our farmers vastly reduce their emissions of the powerful greenhouse gas nitrous oxide, or N_2O, compared with their former, conventional practices. On the sequestration side, our combined regenerative practices are rebuilding soils and helping to capture CO_2 and convert it into soil organic matter, such as compost, humus, and a larger root and fungal system.

To estimate these two GHG impacts of going generative, we used the Cool Farm Tool—a computer model developed by the Cool Farm Alliance whose membership includes consumer product companies (Unilever, McDonald's, Nestlé, PepsiCo), retailers (Walmart, Tesco), and research and consulting firms, such as our friends at Soil & More.

Our Cool Farm Tool analysis suggested that we were on the right track using regenerative agriculture to turn Indian mint fields from major sources of GHG to significant sinks. We project to eventually cut some 15,000 MT CO_2eq per year of GHG emissions from some 3,500 hectares of farmland, compared with their conventional footprint. At almost 30 percent of Dr. Bronner's company-wide carbon footprint of some 60,000 MT CO_2eq per year, this GHG reduction in India is a key element in our program to become "climate positive" sometime around 2025.

From a global perspective, our shift from conventional to regenerative field crops is just the reverse of what humanity has done over the last two hundred years by shifting to intense and eventually industrial agriculture. It has released vast amounts of organic carbon in the form of topsoil or humus from croplands in essence by plowing and synthetically fertilizing them and chopping and burning down plenty of trees to create new croplands—except we do not have that much time now and require some focused action!

HARD AND SOFT KNOCKS

India was a school of many hard knocks, but there are two key lessons for working with young motivated teams. The first? Establish close cooperation on finances. My teammates Les Szabo and Jennifer Rusu, an experienced accountant and, since 2014, financial manager for Special Ops, have done miracles to establish financial planning routines: generate regular cash flow projections, price transparently, and plan financing needs ahead of time. This requires personal contact: Jenn has visited Pavitramenthe twice, knows the players, often sends loving yet firm encouragement to submit documents on time, and helps build and maintain trust on both sides.

Full transparency of financial transactions with our own companies and with Pavitramenthe is the goal. And it isn't just about trust now, it's about making sure that young companies don't dig themselves a hole by growing too fast and then doing funny things to get back out.

Is this paternalistic? Yes, a little, but as long as one is decent and eventually steps back, I don't see too much wrong with providing such hands-on support. In fact, it's part of our mission.

The other critical area that foreign buyers of organic produce rarely get involved in is "team building and leadership development." Rob Hardy first raised the issue in Ghana, and it spawned campaigns that helped the young and inexperienced management at Pavitramenthe to build its multiple teams—with great benefits for motivation, internal and external communication, and, ultimately, economic success.

GROWING BUSINESS

Just like Dr. Bronner's, Pavitramenthe is a business first and foremost. Unless it makes a profit, it won't contribute effectively to our grand vision of using business to drive social and ecological change.

As a serial small-scale entrepreneur, Nihal Singh swiftly took to heart the principle that a business with a single customer—Dr. Bronner's—and a single product—mint oil—is a bad idea. And so we started our diversification. Most Indians are vegetarians, and farmers in UP grow a range of legumes: lentils, peas, beans, and peanuts. There are vegetables, such as carrots, cauliflower, onions, and okra. Spices include cumin, coriander, chili, and mustard seed. Herbs other than mint include holy basil and chamomile.

With its diverse and effective agricultural and fair trade programs, Pavitramenthe easily achieved ROC silver status in 2019, thus becoming the first supplier of a potentially wide range of ROC-certified products. Rapunzel wondered whether Pavitramenthe could supply peanuts; Gaia Herbs and other makers of herbal teas and supplements searched for a range of regeneratively grown herbs, such as holy basil, or tulsi, and an organic food company is interested in regenerative millet.

Meanwhile, Indian brands and consumers become interested in organic goods. With Pavitramenthe's established credibility, Nihal has great opportunities to diversify locally. Our grand vision for this increasingly complex project? Expand the number of farmers from the current 2,000 to 2,500 on 3,500 hectares of land. Expand our regenerative program such that by 2025 some 90 percent of project farmers apply sufficient compost, practice conservation tillage, and grow cover crops. Each farmer may grow a mint crop every year, and the rest of the land will grow a diversity of crops—food crops for local consumption, as well as value-added organic and fair certified products for the high-end Indian and international markets.

With reduced cost of production, premium prices, improved soil fertility, and increased yields, farmers' margins will increase and offer the next generation of villagers an attractive alternative to moving to the city, or at least a supplementary income. At least that's our dream—and, after fifteen years of pushing, we increasingly think it's realistic.

Crop diversification is not the only way to grow and improve the project. Nihal had always dreamed of building his own central distillation plant, replacing tens of inefficient field distilleries and improving efficiency. Serendipity again intervened and showed us the way to a modern, efficient, and safe central distillation plant at Pavitramenthe. In June 2018, the Special Ops team held its annual retreat in Provence, near Distillerie Bleu Provence, our supplier of lavender and lavandin oils.

The company's founder, Philippe Soguel, showed us his distillation unit for aromatic herbs. It used the same concept and tank size as the field units in in Bareilly but was much more efficient. With Phillip's permission I jotted down all relevant information: temperatures, volumes, energy flow, and took a few photos of the condenser— the cooling system for the mix of steam and essential oil vapor.

From Provence, Rob, Jenn, and I went straight to Bareilly. There, we took temperature profiles of several local distillation units, confirmed that condensate cooling was poor and wasteful, gave Nihal a few basic suggestions, and he listened.

For the 2019 season, he engineered and fabricated six distillation tanks that achieved similar performance to Phillipe's: condensate temperatures of about 40° C, instead of 70° C, thus a 15 percent increase in oil yield by reducing volatilization losses (benefiting the farmers), and much safer working conditions.

This miracle was informal technology transfer at its best. Philippe, who loves sharing his knowledge, was pleased with this "knock off," and he and Nihal laughed hard about it when they first met at the 2020 Biofach.

Many such improvements to processing are rather *physical*. They require understanding of the process, a talented local fabricator, and the drive to test and improve. As a scientist, I like such basic improvements, not just because they lower the cost of production, but because they empower people to think for themselves and to make changes by rather nondigital means. Mastering computers and digital communication is essential to running our projects, but eventually they all grow and process crops—and the rules for that haven't changed enough that you couldn't fix most things with rather basic knowledge-based methods.

That, of course, is one of the biggest lessons of our journey to organic and fair trade ingredients. In a sense we've all created "universities of coconut, palm, or mint oil"—not simply meeting our sourcing needs but helping to train people in building and operating a professional and responsible business.

MINT-FLAVORED FAIR TRADE PROJECTS

The key promise of a fair trade project in smallholder communities is its positive socioeconomic impact. At Pavitramenthe, the fair trade premium, now at some $200,000 per year and still predominantly from Dr. Bronner's, is a key contributor. Our primary clientele are the farmers themselves. They are not poor—at least they own land and simple houses—but they don't make much money, can't show off flashy cars and home appliances, and wonder whether their children can afford to farm. Thus, a good portion of the fair trade premium is still spent on soil improvement programs: setting up vermicompost pits, subsidizing central compost production, issuing tools to farmers.

Dealing with farming communities daily, Nihal and his team developed, over five years, a diverse support program for these communities. Since many villages are short on clean drinking water, the installation of some eighty durable hand pumps was a no-brainer.

Access to affordable health care is a persistent problem in rural India, so the team further expanded the concept of free medical camps. During regular events, doctors from the city serve up to four hundred outpatients per day, treating their acute care needs and infections, diagnosing eye diseases, and providing gynecological care. Since 2015, more than ten thousand people have been treated at these camps.

Then, in 2017 our teammate Julia Edmaier joined forces with Deepika Agarwal, Pavitramenthe's administrative coordinator, to develop projects serving rural women, who face hurdles men don't.

A key problem is the taboo around menstruation and the lack of affordable and socially compatible menstrual products. It causes health problems and is a main reason that girls skip school during their period.

Urban women buy Western products, disposable pads, or, less commonly, tampons. In the village, women can't afford those items. Julia and Deepika evaluated options and eventually discovered in Delhi the producer of highly absorbent, washable sanitary pads.

Ironically, they supply these pads mostly to international aid organizations for distribution in refugee camps in the Middle East. Menstruation being a touchy subject, they had entered the Indian market cautiously and were eager to use our project as guinea pig.

These washable pads seemed well-suited for our local setting: they dry fast (even indoors), women can use them under the radar, and they have a useful life of two to three years. A first trial with fifty initially skeptical women in August 2019 was successful, and virtually all reported that the pads were, in fact, changing their lives. The team scaled the project and, in late 2019, issued four pads each to the first one thousand women family members of farmers, free of charge.

Training women on female health, menstrual hygiene, and product use by an experienced female trainer is a prerequisite for a successful introduction. It requires plain talk between women and a sober assessment of financial, disposal, and cultural issues. Such projects also require men to raise the issue and support a solution. Local schools became a cooperative and effective conduit. Deepika and Julia's goal for mid-2021, COVID-19 permitting, is to supply some seven thousand girls and women in villages and schools with pads, free of charge. In August 2020, India's prime minister, Narendra Modi, gave a nice push when he addressed the problem in a speech and promised support in removing the stigma. Speeches rarely suffice, but they provide a great backing to those doing the work on the ground.

Then, in late 2018, we finally had the kind of drama we welcome. Ryan Fletcher, Dr. Bronner's director of PR and my coconspirator on this very book, came to India to produce the project vignette *Journey to Pavitramenthe,* sequel to the 2015 *Journey to Serendipol.* Ryan and his videographer Steve Jeter collected mind-blowing photos and footage and produced an authentic and inspiring portrait of the entire project—and the motivation behind it. David came along for interviews and his first immersion in India's mintscape.

One evening, Nihal invited the entire team to his home village of Musiya Nagla to a tradition playing out countrywide: a lay performance of India's first poem, the Hindu Ramayana epic, performed during Diwali, the annual festival of light.

The stage was set up in the village's main square, surrounded by farmhouses and covered by a tarp. The Dr. Bronner's team were guests of honor and seated by the side of the stage. The next two hours were my most engaging theater experience ever. The cast was all male, including female roles, and gorgeously dressed. It was all in Hindi, but one could sense the irony, the puns, the playful anachronisms. Meanwhile kids were fighting for chairs, dogs ran across the stage. During the intermission, Nihal, as one of the village's sons, gave a speech and asked David and me to join him on the stage. Finally, being able to see the entire audience, I realized the whole village was there, a thousand people watching the drama. We talked about the Ramayana for days after!

For now, our Indian drama has had a happy ending, even though we rarely stop and look back. I often think of how I first met Nihal Singh at the vermicompost plant, how long it took to bring to bear his unique skills and motivation, translate them into tangible results on fields and in the villages and build a strong team.

Lavender and lavandin: aroma from a place of beauty

Our worldwide second best-selling flavor is lavender. As with peppermint, we use a blend of two essential oils: true lavender, with a delicate sweet aroma, and lavandin, a naturally occurring cross of true lavender and spike lavender, a pungent-smelling Mediterranean native. Worldwide, most lavender and lavandin are grown in Europe by small to medium-size farms. A growing portion is organic. We had bought lavender and lavandin oils, organic and conventional, from brokers; all we knew is they came from Provence.

In 2017, a friend at Weleda suggested I talk to one Philippe Soguel, owner of Distillerie Bleu Provence in Nyons, France. It turned out he had been our indirect supplier for a few years and, not knowing whether requests from brokers were real, struggled to plan oil purchases from farmers. We agreed that buying Dr. Bronner's growing demand directly would eliminate that problem and allow collaboration on getting the "right" blend of lavender and lavandin.

We frequently work with brokers on minor ingredients, conventional and organic. They add value by connecting suppliers and customers, handling logistics and financing, and are rightfully compensated for it. However, in cases like Philippe's, brokers may handicap communication and trade.

Michael Milam and I agreed swiftly to work directly with Distillerie Bleu and began buying from their 2017 crop. We believe in knowing our suppliers, and so I visited Provence with David, Kris, and Maya Lin-Bronner in October 2017. (Christel and I had often camped in France in the 1970s and 1980s, and the prospect of working directly with a project in Provence was personally tempting.) Our meetings with Philippe were cordial and productive; it helped that David knew what our lavender blend was to smell like and gave direct feedback.

But could we also have a gradual impact on farming techniques, and help them to become more "regenerative"?

One afternoon, we stood in a field at the foothills of the French Alps. Lavandin is planted in rows, in between a barren, tilled soil strip some five to seven feet (1.5–2 m) wide. In a low voice David said, "Hmmm, this strip in between doesn't look too regenerative, right? Seems like there'll be erosion when it rains."

We agreed that planting a cover crop in between the lavandin rows could do miracles. Philippe and Jacques, one of his farmers, had overheard our discussion. "We're already talking about it," Philippe explained. "We need to design a new mower that can ride on top of the lavandin rows and mow the ground cover in between."

But first they had to roll out a lavandin harvester that picks only flowers, leaving the sprigs behind for mulch. They were also equipping it with a "bee alarm," a bar mounted in front of the harvester that scoots bees out of the way before the blades approach.

Thus, our first regenerative project in France was born: the joint development of an efficient, bee-friendly mower, funded by modest contributions from the French government and Dr. Bronner's.

Distillerie Bleu is a small but growing firm. It buys oil from around one hundred farmers with field sizes from 2 to 50 ha, much of it distilled at the plant in Nyons. A growing percentage of

Philippe's supply is certified organic, and many farmers experiment with intercropping, such as lavandin with oaks that host truffles. They also grow other aromatic herbs, which Philippe distills: thyme, sage, rosemary, oregano, verbena. Such herbs are an essential resource in a regional economy that emphasizes small-scale and traditional production of tasty and fragrant products—as one would expect in France.

As the distillery's largest customer, Dr. Bronner's has an opportunity to advise strategically on agricultural issues, financially support development of regenerative methods, link Philippe up with other customers, and communicate about trends we see emerging in the United States. Philippe also has a wide network in the global essential oil industry and, as I shared earlier in this chapter, helped Nihal vastly improve his mint distillation system in Bareilly.

As important for me is the personal relationship with a man who is native to this old, modern, and beautiful part of Europe. He advises several smallholder projects in foreign countries, he and his partner Genevieve love California and routinely visit, and I suspect we will scheme plans in aromatic locations elsewhere on the planet.

Samoan coconut farmer

CHAPTER 12

The Quest for an Organic and Fair Global Coconut Oil Trade

COCONUT OIL GOES GLOBAL

Dr. Bronner's quest for fair trade and organic coconut oil began but didn't end in Sri Lanka. After all, Serendipol's successful entrance into the VCO business left us far short of our demand for fair trade coconut oil in our soaps. With our projected growth in soap sales, this gap would only widen. And so our team began to explore locations for a potential new coconut oil project that would engage directly with farmers, as we had done in Sri Lanka and Ghana.

As you may recall, there are essentially two different grades of coconut oil, and Dr. Bronner's needs both: plenty of refined *copra oil* for soaps, tasty *virgin coconut oil* (VCO) for foods. How important are these two in the global coconut oil trade? Global consumption of VCO now stands at some 25,000 MT per year. That is less than 1 percent of the global production of all coconut oil: now typically 3.5 million MT per year.[1] So the heavily hyped VCO accounts just for a fraction of global coconut oil consumption! Where does the balance of coconut oil come from and what is it used for?

Coconuts have long been a staple in the diet of coastal dwellers in parts of the tropics. They entered the international stage through colonial traders. By the 1850s, soap makers, such as the Heilbronners in Laupheim and larger soap empires in the United States, knew that coconut oil wasn't only edible. In conjunction with palm and olive oil, it made nicely lathering soap.

How to get coconut oil to the West? Difficult in liquid form, but there was a genius way of turning whole coconuts into pieces of a dry, compact commodity that can be shipped to ports in Europe and North America. The product was called copra. Commercial copra trade started around 1850 and swiftly became crucial to the emergence of castile soaps and other consumer goods. The copra would be pressed into oil at or near receiving ports.

India and Sri Lanka, then under British rule, and the Pacific Islands, including Samoa, all became major copra exporters. After oil refining techniques were invented in the 1870s,[2] coconut oil also took off as a major food oil in Europe and the United States. While its use in foods declined after WWII, as told in chapter 6, coconut oil continued its rally as the only relevant source of lauric acid, a key raw material in soaps and in many oleochemicals, such as the mentioned synthetic surfactants.

That is, until the already mentioned palm kernel oil (PKO) emerged, in the 1990s, as a low-cost by-product of palm oil with a lauric acid content very similar to that of coconut oil. No wonder that, since 2002–03, annual global coconut oil production has stagnated at around 3 million MT and taken the backseat behind that of PKO, now at more than 8 million MT per year.[3] In a nutshell, the world's demand for lauric oil for technical uses still grows, but copra oil supplies an ever smaller fraction of it, and all growth is supplied by PKO.

Back to copra oil: Drying copra is labor intensive and usually done close to the farm. Since copra may be smoky or moldy, most copra oil is refined, bleached, and deodorized, producing RBD copra oil.

By far the largest exporters of copra oil, crude or refined, are the Philippines and Indonesia. Dr. Bronner's began buying organic RBD copra coil from the Philippines in 2003. We still use it as backup, until all our lauric oils come from sources that are also fair trade and regenerative. This chapter tells the story of that quest.

Mombasa, Kenya, 2011

In 2011, a Dutch friend told me about an existing Fair for Life coconut project with smallholders on the Kenyan coast south of Mombasa—maybe an opportunity to partner?

We visited the project, at the time called Coast Coconut. Set up by the US-based Asante Foundation, it was part of a development project for inland farming communities where tourists, who brought most of the cash into the area, wouldn't normally venture. A simple copra production and oil mill on a small plot of land processed coconuts purchased from several villages around. As in Ghana, much of the work was done by hand—it was a job creation project, after all.

Louis Pope, the founder of Asante, a US businessman turned philanthropist who lived part-time in Kenya, spoke openly about the project's problems. Some farmers had conspired with the mill manager to supply only the smallest nuts to the mill at a steep premium, while selling bigger ones in the local market.

The production of "clean" copra in hot air, rather than smoke, was inefficient, the oil quality mediocre, and Louis could not compete with the high-quality organic food-grade oil that was flooding the US market, including Serendipol's. That his oil was Fair for Life certified did not help, and the project kept losing money.

Louis was open to selling the project to Dr. Bronner's, and so I spent the trip collecting information on seasonal coconut prices, nut size, and market conditions. Kenyans were using coconut milk (but no coconut oil) in home cooking, nut prices were low, and farmers sold their nuts to traders from neighboring Tanzania, who took advantage of their cash situation. Wouldn't this be a worthwhile way to expand our copra oil supply?

Back home, I agreed with the Bronners to convert Coast Coconut into a Serendi project. We invited the project's CFO, a young American, to Escondido, agreed on terms, and in late 2012 purchased the mill and property and aptly named company and project Serendi-Kenya.

While at Earthoil, Rob Hardy had overseen organic programs for tea tree in northern Kenya and suggested we recruit Kigo, that project's manager. By then, Ryan Zinn and Les Szabo had also joined Special Ops—just in time. Rob and Ryan hired key ICS staff for SerendiKenya. I reviewed operations and found opportunities to improve the process while Les set up an accounting system.

Farmer membership swiftly grew to five hundred; farmers who had participated in the earlier swindle were excluded. But because of Coast Coconut's past financial troubles, other farmers were skeptical. We spent much time with them discussing pricing, organic training, and fair trade projects, and we started winning them over; the tone in meetings was lively but respectful.

We all fell in love with a setting full of contrasts, a few kilometers from the Indian Ocean. The area was a key tourist destination where many Europeans spent their cold season. Locals often spoke three to four languages and complained about the slow business after the Kenyan coast had seen violent attacks driven by terrorism or crime. On the beach, young men roamed selling knickknacks and offering diving tours.

Just inland, around the factory and onward, life was rather different. Farms were smallish, growing a mix of food crops, with coconut and other trees included. Few farms had more than two hundred trees, compared with Sri Lanka, where one thousand to three thousand trees were the norm. As in Sri Lanka, coconut trees were old, not very productive, and farmers gave minimal care. The countryside was beautiful—hilly, mostly lush—but roads were poor, often sandy, complicating the transport of nuts from the village to the factory. Houses and villages were simple, and there were very few businesses other than retail stores.

We had taken over Coast Coconut's production staff and built a fifty-strong team of outspoken, generally fun-to-work-with Kenyans, both men and women. Some had worked in hotels on the beach but were laid off when fewer tourists came. Two spoke German, and

I enjoyed chatting with them. They were hopeful about the new direction of the project. Working conditions and compensation were a great alternative to any work they could find in the hinterland, which stimulated loyalty and cooperation. The professional staff, which included field officers, management, and accounting, was largely from up north. No one was older than forty.

Our key bottleneck was nut supplies. Kigo expanded our farmer base, nut deliveries grew, and we added transportation and repaired dryers. Determined to "make it work," our team improved all key steps in production, increased oil yields, and reduced drying times. Color and taste got better, and we often joked with Stephen, the highly motivated production manager, about when it would taste as good as Serendipol's. Yes, it was copra oil, but the copra was dried in hot air, not smoke, thus making the oil palatable. We held workshops with farmers on the production of mulch and compost to improve soil fertility.

By late 2014, nut supplies finally increased, and we processed some twenty thousand nuts per day and shipped some 240 MT of oil per year (one container per month). Yet that was still less than 20 percent of what we hoped for and needed to produce.

In March 2015, Les and I had a heart-to-heart talk. He was spending much of his time overseeing the local accountant, who had trouble submitting documents on time. Our low oil output and high overhead costs made the oil much more expensive than we had projected. "I don't think we should continue the project," he said. "It doesn't nearly meet Dr. Bronner's demand, the oil is expensive, our team spends way too much time and travel on project management. And we can have more development impact elsewhere."

I knew he was right, but by then we counted over 1,100 farmers and some 100 staff we were responsible for. A Danish donor agency had cofunded our work to improve operations, and we saw a chance of becoming a key driver in the sustainable revitalization of the Kenyan coconut industry. Yet none of this made sense if, unlike Serendipol, we couldn't secure enough nuts to meet Dr. Bronner's needs and to make it worthwhile to spend our team's time and resources.

A solution presented itself when we met the new owner of Kentaste, a local brand of coconut milk that had helped us sell some of our oil into local retail: a young American investor named Kyle Denning, who lived in Nairobi and planned to expand. We met and hit it off with Kyle, who had the means to continue our project: local presence and staff, and the goal to tackle the regional market for coconut milk, possibly VCO. By late 2015, Kyle had purchased the entire project, and Dr. Bronner's committed to buying at least twelve containers of oil, provided he maintained FTO attributes and certification.

This was a tough decision: our team had become fond of the project. We loved the setting and felt a mix of sadness and of relief over abolishing a time-consuming struggle. There were employees we liked and had watched grow. Yet we had to focus our limited resources on where we could have the largest impact while producing raw materials for Dr. Bronner's.

As of 2020, Kyle had done what we couldn't: develop domestic distribution for milk and VCO, expand into neighboring countries, invest in new equipment, and add competent new team members versed in the technical aspects of the operation. Rob and Phillip have virtually supported local staff with technical and certification issues, while I periodically share technical and market "intelligence" with Kyle. The first and likely only "Serendi spin-off" thus grows in line with its original mission: to use the making of organic and fair coconut products as a tool for personal, community, and agricultural development. And Kyle tells me that he's attracting other US expats that prefer the relevance of such hands-on rural development over office jobs in Nairobi.

Ultimately, Dr. Bronner's spent some $250,000 in capital on SerendiKenya without seeing a return. Was it worth a try? I think so. We learned lessons we later used on other projects—and planted a few seeds for a meaningful development in rural Kenya. I am particularly thankful to Les for pushing, at the right time, for a solution in line with our original vision. At Serendipol, in 2010, we had found a different solution that allowed us to stay and grow in Sri Lanka:

adding VCO as a new product. In Kenya, transferring the project to a more suitable host was the right thing to do.

No surprise that, by then, we were already on our way to setting up a project alternative in Samoa, an island nation in the South Pacific.

A research trip Les and I had taken to the Philippines in early 2014 had not turned up a likeminded partner; neither had discussions with a friendly US company operating in Indonesia. Then, Gordon told me that a Sri Lankan friend wanted Dr. Bronner's to partner in the production of organic coconuts and oil in Samoa. The project would involve the replanting of several thousand hectares of a neglected coconut plantation owned by the Samoan government.

I was lukewarm on the idea of a multi-stakeholder plantation with government involvement, rather than our preferred smallholder schemes. I couldn't quite see the fair trade aspects of the project, I knew we were not mission aligned with the partners, and I expected friction from the beginning.

Then a fair trade ally from New Zealand told us of an organic NGO project in Samoa already producing VCO and other agricultural products. Their vision was to empower rural villages in Samoa, especially women, through production and trade of organic produce and craft. Women in Business Development Inc. (WIBDI) had built and certified an organic ICS and set up small-scale VCO production on several farms to produce some 20 to 30 MT of VCO per year. On our first visit to Samoa in January 2015, Les and I met with WIBDI and explored a cooperation. Could we build up our own production of VCO or copra oil that would purchase nuts from WIBDI's farmers?

We ultimately could not come to an agreement on who would operate the ICS. Our annual oil and nut demand was about one hundred times what WIBDI had produced. We knew about logistics and staffing challenges from our other projects and would need a strong say in the operation of the ICS. WIBDI didn't see these challenges the same way, and we began looking for other partners.

Luckily, Gordon's friends had also connected us with Kolone

Vaai, a Samoan with extensive experience in government, including as secretary of finance. In his soft and competent style, he advised investors, made sure they understood the lay of the land and local customs, and connected them to prospective Samoan partners. Kolone became a friend and role model as he guided us during our first visits to Samoa and ultimately to the formation of SerendiCoco Samoa.

PEOPLE AND COCONUTS—SETTLING POLYNESIA

Before getting down to coconut business, let's explore the intriguing history of this remote part of the planet and the role it played in one of the great migrations of humanity—that of the Polynesians across the Pacific.

The Samoans are a subgroup of the more than one thousand Polynesian islands scattered over the vast expanse of the tropical central and southern Pacific Ocean. The corners of the Polynesian triangle are Hawaii, New Zealand, and Easter Island, with maximum distances of some 7,500 km across, and Samoa somewhere halfway between Hawaii and New Zealand. Compare this with the 5,000 km between San Diego and Portland, Maine, and picture there's only a few—mostly volcanic—islands in between, and you get a sense of Polynesia.

For a tiny, utterly remote country, Samoa has a rich history—with colonization, the commercial farming of coconuts, and export of copra as more recent acts in the drama. The Samoan islands were first settled by seafaring Austronesians, arriving around 1000 BC from Taiwan and the northern Philippines, with stops along the way. This relatively recent and gradual settlement of Polynesia—in simple canoes without instruments—is one of humanity's most daring adventures.

Archeologists, comparative linguists, and DNA analysts are still arguing over the details of Polynesia's settlement. Yet there's evidence to suggest that for two thousand years after the first settlers arrived, the Samoan population grew slowly, to fewer than five thousand inhabitants living in small scattered settlements, then to around ten thousand, coinciding with increasing agricultural and sociopolitical complexity, but still small compared to the now over two hundred thousand.[4]

A mythology evolved, rich with tales of battles between ruling local families and with neighboring chiefs, notably on closely related Fiji and Tonga. But judging from the friendly and relaxed attitude of Samoans, the overall atmosphere was probably pretty peaceful.

That settlement of Polynesia is closely connected to the history of the coconut. Coconut-like fossils found mostly in New Zealand and west-central India suggest that ancestors of the coconut could have been around for 20 million years, while the coconut's dissemination across the entire tropics is barely four thousand years old.

Recent DNA research found that the world's modern coconuts hailed from only *two* genetically distinct groups of palms. One population traces back its ancestry to palms on the coasts of southern India; the other group descended from palms domesticated in Southeast Asia, the Malay Peninsula, Taiwan, and the Philippines. It is that latter population of coconuts that traveled with the mentioned Austronesians, who eventually settled Polynesia and took coconuts on their long journey for food and as planting material.

Thus, coconuts came to settle the Earth's tropical coasts by prompting humans to take them along instead of relying on ocean currents to carry them, as had been thought.[5]

A smart move by both humans and coconuts! With the varied uses of the coconut tree and nut, who would not take a few nuts along on the trip from Taiwan to Samoa? The coconut was more than just a source of food; it gave you water, fuel, construction materials, ropes, even a bit of harsh clothing. And the nut had a long shelf life as planting seed, provided you kept it dry. No wonder coconuts spread with the seafarers across the Philippines, Indonesia, and Melanesia first, then arrived in Samoa around 1000 BC, and were a key natural resource for the new Samoans. After all, the trees started fruiting after five to eight years.

European explorers showed up in the South Pacific in the 1700s but didn't leave serious marks until British missionaries began their work around 1830. Word of this beautiful place and its unique products got out and, from the 1850s, Germans, Brits, and Americans set up production of "colonial goods": coconuts, cocoa, and rubber. The German trading house Godeffroy & Sohn installed large coconut plantations. As you'd expect from Germans, they were planted in orderly rows; Godeffroy also established the drying of coconut meat into copra. This started the mentioned trade to Europe and the United States of bulk copra, the source of the coveted lauric oils.

Not surprisingly, the presence of three colonial powers caused Samoa more trouble than good. Each of them claimed parts of the kingdom of Samoa, fueling a civil war between Samoan factions. Attempts by the battling colonial powers at treaties with Samoan factions predictably failed, and in 1899 the three parties agreed in the Tripartite Convention to split the Samoan Islands into a German colony, today's independent country of (Western) Samoa, and into American Samoa, still a territory of the United States. The British surrendered all rights in Samoa and received "extensive compensation from Germany elsewhere." Naturally, the Samoans were not asked for their input.

Through the German colonial period (1900–14), the subsequent rule by New Zealand, and despite a 20 percent mortality during the 1918 Spanish flu pandemic imported by New Zealand sailors, Samoa's tropical products industry continued to grow. The Mau independence movement in the 1920s did not achieve its goal, so only in 1962 did Samoa become the first independent nation in Polynesia.

Then, in the 1980s, the cocoa price collapsed, as we heard in chapter 10. Cocoa had been a key Samoan export. Combined with mismanagement of the formerly profitable nationalized plantations, this crash sharply reduced export revenues and jobs. With a very small industrial base and limited tourism, Samoa turned into a country heavily reliant upon international aid and remittances from relatives who had migrated abroad.

Fortunately, Samoa has been a rather stable democracy, and, unlike many developing countries, made good use of foreign support. It strikes a balance between a traditional and a modern lifestyle. It is also on its way to becoming a trading hub, with China emerging as a large strategic benefactor. Yet, to date, it has not been able to attract industrial jobs or regenerate its sizeable smallholder agriculture.

DO WE HAVE THE NUTS?

Les's and my first visit in January 2015 had taught us that the Samoan coconut supply was on shaky ground. With our experience in Kenya, this was naturally a key concern when assessing the viability of a new coconut oil project here. The formerly strong copra and copra oil industry exporting more than 5,000 MT of copra oil per year had been in decline, as it couldn't compete with bigger players and better infrastructures, notably in the Philippines. No wonder nut prices paid to farmers had been a pittance of some USD 0.07 per nut, and farmers had no incentive to replant their aging trees.

Questionable government surveys suggested that Samoa still produced over 100 million nuts per year, yet yields from the increasingly senile palm trees would certainly decline. We hoped to produce eventually up to 10,000 MT of copra oil per acre in Samoa. This would require 110 million nuts, and we knew we'd be physically short on nuts sooner or later.

Kolone introduced us to government ministries in charge of agriculture and trade; everyone agreed on the need to replant. Yet the drive and funds to take replanting action seemed scant.

It took Les and me three trips to figure out how to produce fair and organic coconut oil in Samoa, but we adored the country from our first trip in January 2015. The drive from the airport to the capital, Apia, was in stark contrast to the foggy and cold trip from Bareilly to Delhi we had made just the day before, after the memorable restart of the mint oil project. The Samoan ocean was blue, but the real eye-catcher was the architecture. There were some fifteen Christian churches along the road, most relatively new but in a style reminiscent of those in old European towns.

More unique were the occasional beach huts, oval-shaped with wooden posts holding up a domed thatched roof and without walls. As we got closer to Apia, we saw, on huge lawns in front of single-story houses, larger, posher versions of these wall-less huts. They were oblong with numerous columned posts holding larger domed roofs, usually made from corrugated sheet metal.

"What are these houses?" we asked the driver.

He identified them as fales (pronounced FAH-lays), the Samoan universal word for "house." Unlike the smaller oval beach fales used by fishermen and tourists, these serve for gatherings with your extended family on evenings or weekends. Evening get-togethers in fales, with perhaps fifty people in attendance, is a common sight. In the countryside, though, an open fale is often the actual family residence, with entire farmer families occupying one or two of them and hung blankets providing privacy. We've since had quite a few cups of Samoan chocolate or of kava in such fales, most on Savai'i, the larger, less-populated, and more traditional of the two main islands.

Gordon de Silva, our Sri Lankan friend and partner, joined Les and me on this first visit. After all, it was his friend who had made the initial suggestion to check out Samoa. We also knew his keen observation would be helpful in discussions with potential partners and officials.

We lodged at Lynn's, a hotel in a huge private house with a couple of additions. A very comfortable place, and many guests from all over the world were interns at the nearby general hospital, making for a lively atmosphere at the communal dinners. Traditional Samoan food isn't spicy, but if the ingredients are ripe and have flavor, it is very tasty. Lynn's chef treated us to oka (raw fish in coconut milk), roasted or boiled roots or fruits (taro, yams, breadfruit), and palusami (taro leaves cooked in coconut milk). There may be fresh fruit salads, and roasted pork from truly free-roaming pigs.

Alas, America's fast and processed food influence can be seen everywhere, and obesity has become a major public health concern. Many hotels rely on supplies of fresh food from abroad, understandable for logistics and supply security but somewhat odd in a country where everything grows. Fortunately, that trend is slowly reversing as at least some farmers realize that selling organic produce to the local market may be an augmentation of or alternative to remittances.

On our first Samoan trip we had spent two days with WIBDI to visit family farms on Savai'i, and we have been back many times since. Savai'i is the largest island in the neighborhood and sixth in size in Polynesia, including all islands of Hawaii and New Zealand. Savai'i island consists of one large volcano peppered with over one hundred small craters.

Its soil hails from volcanic rock, often black basalt. Large lava fields from the most recent eruptions (between 1905 and 1911) cover some 40 square miles (100 square km)—and in some places are up to 300 feet (100 m) deep—but you can see vegetation making its gradual return.

Savai'i has some forty thousand permanent residents. From space, it looks all green, except for a few villages and crater ridges.[6] On the ground: hedges, meadows, and lawns, expanses of coconut palms and natural forests, some reaching inland for several miles. A larger family coconut farm is typically planted with tall to very tall coconut palms in loose arrays, not the regular plantings seen in most of Sri Lanka. On some farms, herds of cattle roam under coconut trees, mostly for domestic consumption.

One Sunday, Les and I dropped Gordon off at a Catholic church, then took a drive once around Savai'i's coastal road; on a bright morning with big white clouds, it couldn't be called anything but psychedelic. The two-lane road is in good shape, the grass neatly trimmed by teams of workers roaming the whole country, with little trash and a constant variation of green: coconut farms, taro fields, cocoa orchards, dense jungle, a range of decorative plants in villages: hibiscus, jasmine, ginger, some with colored leaves, some groves overgrown with kudzu on the outside.

Small villages feature fales with surreal roof constructions—usually in corrugated sheet metal and resembling helmets—and the constantly changing views of an ocean and only few medium-size beach hotels.

Then there are uncountable churches and families of parishioners of various Christian faiths walking to service. Women are mostly in dresses, while men wear black lava-lava, the traditional men's skirt, often combined with a nice shirt. Few ties and always flip-flops. In Apia, we had already made this out as the standard office outfit with government officials, all the way up to the prime minister. For comfortable formal clothing for men, nothing beats Samoa.

We drove through smaller villages with people preparing the large open fales for Sunday lunch, a traditional family feast. Clouds of appetizing smoke rose from each settlement. We knew these Sunday lunches from Lynn's guesthouse—the only meal we received and needed on that day! On future trips we often readied ourselves for that lunch with an early hike to the tomb of Robert Louis Stevenson on Mount Vaea, an almost 1,600-foot-high (500 m) summit with a spectacular view of downtown Apia, just 4 km to the north. Kolone had taken us there on our first trip on a slippery and steep trail through dense diverse forest.

The Robert Louis Stevenson museum below offered a great snapshot of Samoa's recent history. The great Scottish storyteller, author of *Treasure Island* and *Dr. Jekyll and Mr. Hyde,* spent his final years (1890–94) with his family on his 160-hectare estate above Apia. He became involved in local politics and wrote about the conflicts between local indigenous factions trying to maintain their traditional system, and the colonial powers of Great Britain, the United States, and Germany, each trying to wrest control. His quote "I used to think meanly of the plumber; but how he shines beside the politician!" suggests he was disgusted with the performance of colonial administrators.[7]

As Les and I explored this Pacific treasure, we heard the concerns among politicians, local businesses, and foreign diplomats about how Samoa needed to become more competitive, develop new industries, and create jobs in rural areas. By 2015, the obsolescence of the copra infrastructure, lack of new investment, and the distance from emerging value-added markets had all but eliminated exports of coconut oil, and the hopes of creating value-added exports of VCO by groups such as WIBDI had not materialized. There was just too much competition from better-positioned VCO producers and not enough committed customers. Our proposal to government officials to help revitalize the coconut industry generated front-page coverage in the *Samoan Observer*, but ministries in charge offered no tangible support to tackling our key concern, the eventual lack of coconuts.

By our third visit to Samoa in August 2015, Les and I were not sure where to go. We had evaluated leasing a dilapidated DC mill in Vaitele near Apia, as we had done in Sri Lanka, and converting it into a VCO production mill. This would produce a versatile oil for food and for soap, but we hadn't found the right partner who knew how to expand and operate such an integrated project.

Then we remembered that on our first visit we had briefly stopped at a large copra oil mill run by a company called Pacific Oil—and Kolone told us he knew one of its owners, Charlie Westerlund.

One intriguing aspect of a small island country is that everybody knows everyone, almost. Connections through families, churches, or former businesses make the country rather familiar in a short period, even for outsiders. It makes you feel like a local to be able to understand key issues and actors on the ground and how your business may relate to them. I think that this closeness and the unavoidable gossip also reduce the risk of corruption—whatever you do, it will likely come out at some point. One thing you learn quickly: do not speak badly about a Samoan in absentia. The person sitting across from you may be their brother-in-law!

We met with Charlie and his partner Etuale Sefo. Pacific Oil was the only remaining producer of copra oil in Samoa and had successfully exported up to 5,000 MT per year until cyclones in 2011 and 2012 dropped most coconuts from the trees, seriously cutting supplies. In parallel, the global copra oil price had declined to levels at which Pacific Oil could not compete. Yet they obviously had years of experience collecting copra from the over one hundred small copra dryers in Samoa, most of them also farmers. This was a partner who knew the entire supply chain for coconut oil production and the local context.

We soon learned that Charlie and Etuale were among the most respected and successful people in Samoa. Yet both were low key and adamant about the need to offer livelihood options to farmers on both Samoan islands. Our suggestion to join forces, convert and certify farmers, produce organic and fair copra oil, and engage with replanting and improving farmers' livelihood was well received. It would return Pacific's idling high-capacity mill into production, generate income for remote farmers who now couldn't sell their nuts, and allow us to produce all the FTO coconut oil needed to satisfy Dr. Bronner's growing demand in this most unique and beautiful setting.

Dr. Bronner's wouldn't have to build or buy much of anything. Infrastructure and equipment were in place; Etuale had already planned the installation of a small refinery to turn the crude oil into food-grade oil for the local market. It would come in handy for refining oil before shipping it to Vista, too.

Etuale and Les finalized the JV agreement in record time and with very few arguments. In early 2016, we formed SerendiCoco Samoa (SCS) as a fifty-fifty joint venture between Pacific Oil and Dr. Bronner's. Pacific brought in its assets, Dr. Bronner's matched them in cash. As on other projects, pricing would be on a cost plus basis with some caps, guaranteeing the JV profitability and protecting Dr. Bronner's from excessive prices.

We knew the routine: before we could start oil production we had to set up an organic ICS, recruit farmers, have them certified organic, and set up a fair trade system. We hired Tusitina Nu'uvali as ICS manager. She had formerly run the Samoan Special Olympics, was authentic and skilled at building and motivating teams, and wanted to translate the love for her country into capacity building.

Tina is a great example of educated, younger generation Samoans who respect rather hierarchical traditions, but are not stifled by them, and combine goal orientation with a sense of humor that causes bursts of laughter. Our teammate Ryan Zinn had joined Les and me on our third trip to Samoa, took on the management of the organic recruitment and certification aspects of the project, and then became our "Special Ops man on the ground." Ryan's multiyear on-the-ground experience with development projects in Latin America came in very handy.

By May 2017, we had more than one thousand farms certified organic, and the entire project was FFL certified. This included the backbone of Samoa's copra industry: over one hundred mostly smallish, family-owned copra dryers who'd buy the nuts from farms, dry them to copra, and supply to SCS.

Once we started buying in May 2017, copra supply grew swiftly to some 170 MT per month. Still only 60 percent of what Dr. Bronner's needed, it was nevertheless an indication that the prices we paid for copra and coconuts, some 50 percent over previous levels, did motivate both farmers and dryer operators.

Yet, unexpectedly, copra intake gradually leveled off, and by 2018, average monthly intake was only around 100 MT. We raised copra prices twice more and helped dryer operators hauling nuts from the farms. All in vain, and copra intakes kept shrinking through mid-2019, with occasional bursts around the holidays when people needed extra cash.

What was going on?

REGENERATING SAMOAN AGRICULTURE

We realized that we were in the middle of a systemic change of coconut farming and marketing in Samoa. The older generation of farmers had not minded lugging nuts from remote fields to their houses and then to the dryers, whereas their children did. Many dryers were smallish and run by elderly people and their family members. Our extra requirements for fair payment and safe working conditions made small-scale copra production increasingly unattractive. The few larger commercial dryers did not have the trucks to collect nuts from remote farms and thus couldn't increase nut intake, no matter what we paid for copra.

Even worse, surging demand for fresh coconuts in Australia and New Zealand had driven up nut prices. Good for farmers, except nut exporters would collect only the bigger fresh nuts, pay on the spot, and leave the small nuts. Why bother carrying nuts from a remote field if you can have some of them picked up at a good price? And for the balance, one would rely on remittances from family members who had emigrated to New Zealand or from the annual pilgrimages there by younger family members to pick apples for a few months.

Would our project go under—not for physical lack of nuts but from a complete change in industry structure? From field visits by our staff, we knew there were many nuts that went uncollected— how could we get them from the field to drying and expelling at our factory? After all, we had by mid-2018 finally started up the small refinery we had purchased from an Indian supplier and were now able to ship RBD copra oil to Vista.

After a year of trial and error, Etuale's team finally found the solution. We built our own dryer at the factory, bought two large off-road military trucks in Australia, and began weekly pickup routes to farmers in Upolu and Savai'i. Whereas we had first bought copra from dryers—not coconuts from farmers—we now finally could directly take the pulse of farmers, who became comfortable with the regularity of our service and the extra income. Unlike fresh nut buyers, who take only large nuts, we would buy the entire crop because, for copra, the nut size does not matter as much. That way we increased our competitiveness, even though peak prices for fresh nuts paid by traders were some 50 percent higher than the 13 US cents we now paid for nuts across the board.

Our move to get close to the farms worked. By early 2020, copra intake more than doubled to over 200 MT per month. We built a second dryer at the factory in Upolu and began trucking nuts collected on remote farms in Savai'i to the few larger dryers on that island. In combination, these measures had again changed the coconut economy of the whole country.

And while as of this writing the coronavirus has not made it into Samoa in 2020, it initially reduced remittances from family members in New Zealand and further motivated farmers to use coconuts for supplemental income. SerendiCoco is on course to produce some 2,000 MT of copra oil in 2021, more than double our previous record in 2018. This turn of events got us closer to our original economic goal of producing the majority of Dr. Bronner's demand for FTO copra oil, but not only that. After all, we had started the project with the vague vision of regenerating smallholder agriculture in this island nation by rejuvenating the coconut tree stock, improving soil health, and developing value-added markets for organic and fair by-products.

Until 2018, we had made no progress on the urgently needed re-planting of Samoa's aging coconut palm population. We could not agree on a replanting strategy with the Ministry of Agriculture and Fisheries (MAF), and their funding channels were opaque. Yet by then we had planted our first DAF plots in Ghana, and it struck Ryan and me to use the same approach to replanting coconut trees in Samoa: designed mixed plantings of coconuts (instead of oil palm), cocoa, fruit, timber, and biomass trees.

We invited our DAF guru Joachim Milz for an initial visit and for a talk to farmers and staff at MAF. And suddenly things started happening. Unlike in Ghana, where farmers had become used to planting palm trees in monoculture, many Samoan farmers still used the traditional way of mixed cropping. A DAF plot appealed to their aesthetics, and creating excitement was easier. Then Kolone alerted us to an opportunity to receive a grant for a larger DAF demonstration program from the World Bank, and an EU program offered funds for developing seedlings production—we ultimately received both.

In May 2018 we planted—with broad participation by farmers, MAF staff, and the press—our first quarter-hectare DAF demo plot. By mid-2020, we had planted some 630 small DAF plots and demonstrated cocoa pruning to some 650 farmer families all over Samoa, since many of our coconut farmers also grow cocoa. Some of the plantings were on volcanic rock—amazing to see how cocoa seedlings would germinate and grow in such settings, but they do.

By now we do have sufficient experience to engage in the next wave of plantings, both mixed plots and replanting of coconut orchards, some of them grazed by cattle. We project regenerative organic certification for SerendiCoco by 2021. Marketable high-value intercrops for export to the United States include turmeric and vanilla. Their processing is relatively simple and can be done at SerendiCoco's factory; shipping to the United States is very straightforward, as there is nonstop service from Apia to LA. Of course, we plan to include some Samoan cocoa beans in our chocolates, too.

Dr. Bronner's and many of our regenerative allies in the EU and United States have demand for the products of Samoa—and for its story: an exemplary turnaround of a multi-decade trend toward unproductive conventional agriculture. We see signs that many Samoans who would like to stay in their motherland and need a livelihood are reconsidering farming. New industrial jobs are most unlikely to arrive, and the potential for tourism is limited, especially on beautiful but rocky Savai'i.

I remember discussions with Etuale and Tina about our vision of helping Savai'i to become more prosperous through knowledge-intensive regenerative agriculture and forestry and to revitalize smallholder farming as a livelihood. It may only require improved transportation, tools, and support in value-added marketing to get a younger generation of Samoans interested in producing diversified, higher-value regenerative products.

After five years of debottlenecking the coconut industry in Samoa, we are now ramping up production, gradually replanting the palm stock, increasing nut supplies to feed a growing demand for coconut products—and diversifying while we're at it. There's no more rewarding excuse to travel back to Samoa and enjoy the goal-driven yet relaxed cooperation with our partners at SerendiCoco.

In the fifteen years since we started Serendipol in Sri Lanka, we've now seen coconut production and processing close up in three tropical countries. What started out as the production of just VCO now includes all other relevant coconut products—all driven by the concept of an organic and fair production. We've learned firsthand about all aspects of coconut agriculture, processing, and marketing—and now think there are more regenerative ways to plant new coconut palms and to improve soil and productivity. With the crucial importance of coconut oil for Dr. Bronner's, we'll likely be busy regenerating coconuts for decades to come.

Jojoba oil from the Mexican desert

In 2010, Denny Finneran, a long-time hempster and friend of David's, told him of an amazing desert area in Mexico's state of Sonora on the shores of the Gulf of California. It is home to the only two remaining families of Comcaac Indians (commonly known as Seri)—a total of one thousand people with a language distinct from all others in the region, an "isolated language."[8]

The area was rich with jojoba bushes that had been wild-harvested in the past by the Seri and sold to traders. (Jojoba oil is the liquid extracted from the seeds of the shrub, which is native to the arid areas of Arizona, southern California, and northwest Mexico.)

Since Dr. Bronner's uses growing amounts of jojoba oil in our balms and liquid soaps, could we set up our first FTO project in Latin America and support sustainable development with Native Americans?

David was all for it. He reached out to Ryan Zinn, an activist friend from the Organic Consumers Association who had lived and worked in agricultural development in Latin America for years. (It was the beginning of a great friendship; as you've read in earlier chapters, Ryan later joined Special Ops and proved his hands-on and world-wise approach when setting up SerendiCoco in Samoa.)

In November 2010, several of our team met in Sonora's capital, Hermosillo, with Elizabeth Caballero and Efrain Soto, a young development-minded Mexican couple who wanted to coordinate the project for us. We drove through an increasingly dry terrain to the beach town Bahia de Kino, where we met a delegation of Seris from the village of Punta Chueca, 20 km up the coast. We explained to the tribe our plans for using jojoba to make oil and create employment. The atmosphere was welcoming, with an attitude of "Show us what you do, and we'll see."

Back in Hermosillo, we met lawyers and accountants, agreed with the tribe to allow us to collect seeds, property of the tribe, in return for employment and a fair price for the seed. As with other projects, we incorporated a local sister company, Serendipity Jojoba. The project promised positive impact in a unique and engaging setting, and we got started on the details.

And yet, just under three years later, in July 2013, we had experienced about all the agricultural problems one can have with a nonirrigated, organic, wild collection project in a desert. First, a late frost in April 2011 killed most jojoba flowers across the area and into Arizona—and we had but a few kilos of seeds to collect during the July harvest. Ryan continued his visits, trained ICS staff and collectors, and we hoped for a better harvest in 2012.

That year, with below-average rainfall, we collected a hundred kilograms, just about 0.3 percent of the 30 MT of seeds we needed. A low turnout by villagers for the harvest contributed. Ryan and I had visited during harvest and come to appreciate that collecting seeds in a midsummer desert, with collectors covered to avoid sunburns, was uninviting work. Low turnout was further aggravated by a cooler alternative: fishing on the Sea of Cortez, a beautiful stretch of water with a rugged desert shore, few boats, dark blue water, and flocks of pelicans overhead.

We engaged David Palzkill, an expert on jojoba from Arizona, and toured the area in March 2013. His assessment was sobering.

The plant density was low, with a high percentage of male plants—good only for pollination. The results of the earlier survey indicating plentiful supplies now looked shaky. David also noticed signs of foraging by wild sheep and cows. He told us that annual jojoba yields in this setting would vary hugely with frost and rainfall, and we never would have a predictable annual crop.

We recruited and trained collectors and prepared for the harvest in July 2013 and prayed. Due to competition from fishing, only twenty-five of the sixty registered collectors showed up, delivered some 200 kg of seeds, double the 2012 amount but not even 1 percent of what we needed.

With a heavy heart we agreed with the Bronners to terminate the project. We conducted two more of the medical camps we'd begun to set up, donated the two purchasing centers to local women's projects, and kept Elizabeth and Efrain on until the end of the year to close things down. Unlike at SerendiKenya, there was no one to take over this project.

Dr. Bronner's will not start another wild collection project in the desert—however exciting the physical and social setting. Instead, we're looking to Nasser Abufarha, who has started a project to intercrop olive trees with jojoba in the West Bank—a tried and tested practice. At the same time, our friends at LUSH North America, another pioneering personal care company, and fellow activists in DIY regenerative supply chains, have set up a jojoba project with existing farms in Arizona. We will become a supportive buyer and may help turn it into a Fair for Life project.

Special Operations team in Zoomland

CHAPTER 13

Soap Making and Special Operations in the Time of Corona

I N MID-FEBRUARY 2020 MOST OF THE Special Ops team attended the world's largest organic trade fair—Biofach in Nuremberg, Germany—to catch up with fellow Bronnerites and friends in the organic products industry. The ascent of corona in China still was faint. The first rumbles were the absence of the Chinese attendees and a steep rise in recent US orders for our hand sanitizers. Americans began worrying about sanitation.

But there were more exciting things to talk about at Biofach. Four of our team then continued on to Serendipalm. As we were in Ghana in late February, the world started slipping into a crisis like it hadn't seen since the fear of nuclear war in the early 1960s—the global spread of a rather infectious and dangerous virus of the corona type, to be joined in June by nationwide protests and civil unrest over racial injustice in the United States.

I returned home to California in late February, just before our beloved mammoth annual Natural Products Expo in Anaheim collapsed.

A traditional gathering point of the US Bronners tribe, it became one of the first corona victims among large public events.

Since 2005, I had spent half of my time on the road. Now I stayed at home for six months straight, no trip farther than to the beach 30 km away—and I enjoyed the much quieter life. Christel and I saw just a few friends, hardly used our car, and we hiked and biked on streets with little traffic. I finished writing this book, and our team started and advanced numerous projects remotely. I virtually spoke to, and reflected with, many more people than I had done in a while: colleagues, friends, and family in the United States and Germany. We sure were very fortunate to have meaningful and creative professions, a secure job, and no school-aged kids.

By mid-March we became concerned: How would the looming lockdown in California affect Dr. Bronner's operations in Vista? How would our projects worldwide be affected? Would their harvests, processing, and shipping be blocked? Would the Bronners have to make some of the hard decisions of other businesses: deal with a drop in revenues, furlough staff, cut back on philanthropy and activism?

Ultimately, none of this came to pass in a major way. Quite the opposite, as you will see! For Dr. Bronner's operations in Vista, the course was clear. Business had to go on if at all possible: because we manufacture products for sanitation, we were swiftly classified as essential and kept our doors open without interruption. A rational and practical corona protocol and precaution program was speedily put in place and fine-tuned where needed. HR kept current with the emerging understanding of "how corona works" and applied it in their rules for staff; officers engaged and supported, including citations of noncomplying staff. No room for lengthy arguments about the merits of covering your face when close to your colleagues.

More important: How to support families with kids, notably single parents? Decisions to subsidize childcare and give paid time off were made in management meetings instantly with an impressive mix of rationality and compassion. It illustrated that you'll be more compassionate if you personally know those affected by your decision, more likely the case if you are small or medium-sized.

The pandemic also affected the work of our Special Ops team—in many ways.

Zoomland, April 2020

It's session two of twelve of the Special Operations team's 2020 annual retreat. This year, we're meeting in Zoomland, at 8 a.m. on the West Coast, 4 p.m. in the UK, and 5 p.m. in Spain and Germany. By special invitation, Les Szabo, honorary team member who now runs Dr. Bronner's Constructive Capital department, briefs us on the company's activist and philanthropic agenda. I look at the faces of eight dear people and marvel at the balance of lightness and substance in our communication. It creates unique vibes—definitely positive.

No, it's not like meeting at a regenerative farm in Portugal, our original destination—but we know each other well, connect effectively and warmly along the agenda Julia and Ryan have built. It would be nice to have dinner afterward. Next year. For now, we enjoy how effective and cordial virtual team meetings can be. For us, this will be a main corona lesson. We were well prepared for it.

How did our main projects around the globe fare during the pandemic? As of October 2020, each has faced serious challenges, but none suffered disastrous corona impacts.

Early and strict lockdowns in Sri Lanka interrupted production at Serendipol for four weeks. Workers were furloughed but with guaranteed wages. Professional staff continued their work—at a distance. Nut stocks ran low, prices were volatile. Yet the loyalty of farmers and the fact that Serendipol purchases all nuts, not just "the big ones," kept supplies up and at reasonable prices. In the end, Serendipol's highest priority became continued employment and protection of the livelihood of workers and farmers. Production resumed by late April, and shipping was never interrupted.

Samoa has stayed corona-free through late 2020 due to an early closing of its borders. No more visits by our team but more frequent Zoom meetings. The closedown cut revenues from tourism, and remittances from furloughed relatives in New Zealand shrank. No one goes homeless or hungry in Samoa with its strong family networks, but the loss of other income made sales of coconuts to SerendiCoco even more attractive. After struggling for two years with low nut supplies, we now benefited from our weekly reliable nut collection system for remote farms, prompt payment, and engagement with farmers. This predictable purchase of nuts from over one thousand farmers and the continued employment of factory staff and workers at copra dryers in Savai'i was SerendiCoco's contribution to the well-being of the country during a serious economic downturn, while the virus was kept off the islands.

As for Ghana, we knew things were getting serious when Gero Carus, a German student and son of my friend Michael Carus, who interned at Serendipalm in early March, was greeted at a local pharmacy not by the usual "Hello white person, how are you?" but by "Oh no, corona," and people averting their faces. As case numbers grew in Europe, Ghana promptly closed its borders and imposed early partial lockdowns.

For Serendipalm, it was the middle of peak harvest and processing season, and a shutdown would have spelled disaster; for Dr. Bronner's, it would have meant the loss of an essential supplier. We couldn't possibly turn off production and the direct livelihood for some four thousand locals and had to employ a multi-pronged strategy to confront the challenge head on. Gero's partner and fellow intern Milena, a medical doctor from Germany, rose to the occasion and trained staff in hygiene and sanitation.

We already had plans to start a local soap production to diversify Serendipalm's production and make better use of the second-grade palm oil. With advice from Vista, Safianu's team accelerated the project and cranked out cold-poured bar soap from our palm oil and some palm kernel oil within a week. Serendipalm distributed bars to staff and needy Asuomers for free, a great opportunity to preach and demonstrate the blessings of washing your hands.

We also needed masks. Christel designed and sewed masks from colorful Togolese and Sri Lankan fabric, we broadcast cutting patterns and photos, and Safianu's team organized a mask production in Asuom. There, sewing dresses, pants, and shirts is still a widely practiced art. We finished the 2020 peak season in good style and didn't miss a container of oil.

Yet, by late July 2020, case numbers were on the rise, including the first ones in Asuom. Serendipalm immediately started an area-wide program to educate locals, distributing some ten thousand masks and face shields plus soaps. Its goal: keep corona small. It took me five minutes to obtain the needed $20,000 of matching funding from Dr. Bronner's in the usual non-bureaucratic and open-hearted style. Rapunzel and Root Capital also pitched in.

India became a worrisome scene as the federal government imposed a poorly planned countrywide lockdown on March 24 that forced thousands of now unemployed migrant workers in Delhi to return to their home village on foot. Pavitramenthe's production was not affected—mint harvesting, distillation, and purchasing would not start until mid-May.

The real problem was the situation of four thousand landless, often low-caste, casual farmworkers who normally helped our farmers with planting, weeding, and harvesting. Now, only the farmer and one family member were allowed to work in the field; thus, they could not hire labor. This left some twenty-four thousand people—workers and their families—without income and access to food.

Hunger doesn't wait, and government programs were noneffective—the situation required immediate response. With a $25,000 seed grant from Dr. Bronner's and matching money from the fair trade fund, Nihal, a master of direct action, organized three deliveries of essential foods to all four thousand families. During the first distribution many recipients were emotional, as they had not had enough food for days.

By May all farmworkers were allowed back to the field, but we knew this wouldn't be the end of corona. The number of cases and deaths kept rising. Fortunately, the German GIZ again helped out. They had been impressed by the performance of Pavitramenthe and Special Ops on the "soil regeneration" project and trusted we'd be able to implement a COVID-19 relief project under tight conditions. They committed $200,000 for additional emergency food supplies, a large number of village-made face masks, a home-gardening program to boost food security, medical camps, expansion of the menstrual pads program, and ongoing support to farmers to deal with the administrative chaos sure to emerge. All the while Nihal and team preached social distancing—tough in crowded India—and avoided any cases at Pavitramenthe as of late September.

All in all, Dr. Bronner's and German taxpayers spent some $350,000 in cash and in-kind in India on short- and long-term COVID-19 support for some twenty-four thousand farmworkers and family members. That money also helped another twelve thousand people—farmers and their families—to stay in business for the next year while strengthening their base. This project well demonstrated the power wielded by a business committed to getting things done in a generous and open-hearted manner. Its guerilla-style approach reminded us of how Serendipol had started in the first place—a privately organized relief project to support coastal Sri Lankans devastated by the 2004 tsunami. Very different setting, similar approach: inventory what's needed, go shopping, and distribute the goods efficiently.

This likely won't be the end of corona for our projects, but our experience from the first round in 2020 suggests that watchfulness, effective communication, generosity, decisive action, and, notably, continued commercial operation are very effective in avoiding calamity.

CUSTOMARY SPECIAL OPERATIONS

How does our Special Operations team operate in non-corona times? Throughout the book you have seen examples of how we collaborate with the teams at our supply projects—in moments of relative calm and crisis alike. Since our model may interest other companies who plan to engage with their suppliers of agricultural ingredients, here are a few more reflections on how we work.

What distinguishes Special Ops fundamentally from the strategic raw materials departments in other companies are our tangible stakes in, and operational responsibilities to, both the supplier—say, Serendipalm—and the customer—such as Dr. Bronner's or Rapunzel—of our ingredients. In effect, Special Operations mediates between two production systems and must understand and reconcile the needs of both sides. We're not just buying raw materials; we're also producing them

Our ultimate mandate is to help produce raw materials in the tropics, take them into the production of soaps in Vista or elsewhere, and, in the process, improve local and global conditions just a little bit. Our team cannot shrug when equipment breaks down in Ghana, raw material supplies are low, a supplier is short on cash, or the pandemic strands farmworkers in India without income.

We must find solutions, sometimes real fast, lest we cause damage to the project or to Dr. Bronner's. Being sandwiched between supply and demand will occasionally cause stress. We literally feel the responsibility for hundreds of staff, for thousands of farmers, and for Dr. Bronner's. Fortunately, not all the time!

Each of our four main supply projects requires a different level of support. In Sri Lanka, Sonali and Gordon run Serendipol's operations autonomously. Special Ops mainly supports customer development, marketing, and certification. A recent example: when Serendipol became the first worldwide ROC-certified coconut project, our team first supported the certification pilot audit and then connected them with US brands looking for ROC-certified ingredients.

To Etuale's team in Samoa we offer mostly support on agriculture, including DAF projects, certification, project expansion, and financials. In Ghana and India, Safianu and Nihal are building teams that appreciate more operational involvement: from designing new processes and facility construction to completing applications for donor-funded grants and planning financing of crude oil purchases. Another more mundane Special Ops service: Phillip and Rob have shipped numerous good-quality secondhand pickup trucks, agricultural vehicles, and equipment from Europe to Ghana, where you simply cannot find them. It's helped us solve several operations problems in Asuom—and saved more than a hundred thousand dollars!

As all projects mature, the issue of teambuilding gradually takes center stage. The same happened in Vista, where, in 2017, Dr. Bronner's executive team began its quest for a more structured, explicit, and inspired collaboration across the company.

Our coach and guru Eric Kaufmann and his team at SAGATICA taught us teambuilding and leadership development. What can this elevate in a company that's already on a mission? A competent team of coaches may help team leaders to be more open, listening to what their team members think, say, and feel—thus improving communication, conflict resolution, planning, and goalsetting. This experience, still ongoing, had an enormous impact on spirit, atmosphere, and efficiency at Dr. Bronner's—and it sure helped us maneuver corona as well as we did.

In Ghana, we had started this teambuilding process even earlier. We first sent Safianu Moro to leadership trainings at WYSE in Italy; his teammates Samah and Chris came next. All complimented the remarkable benefits to their challenging teamwork. When I asked Safianu what the WYSE training did for him, he just said, "It made me much more open." It shows. Nihal at Pavitramenthe had a similar experience when joining a WYSE program in Brazil. In 2019, Sonali and I conspired to bring Eric Kaufman to Serendipol for a first round of teambuilding and leadership training. Just in time to help Serendipol's management team grow in a trying situation.

Special Ops also supports local teams with the hiring of key staff—a demanding job anywhere on the planet. We help clarify the attitudes and skills needed for a job. Interviewing candidates, gauging what they're good at, and helping to make the ultimate selection may all be part of our role.

One eternal challenge is to keep motivating young professionals to pursue technical, commercial, and developmental goals that inspire them—as a team in a commercial company. With all projects, whether we have an ownership stake or not, we gradually step back from operations and focus on strategic orientation, teambuilding, and networking.

I'll illustrate Special Ops' involvement with examples from our February 2020 trip to Serendipalm. A frequent venue: Safianu's office at our cramer in Asuom, Ghana, hosting varying groups of Serendipalm and Special Ops staff. The fan keeps things cool; the adjacent fruit-cleaning section with some 150 workers during the peak season, tractor traffic, and crowing roosters make for a great soundtrack.

Our main topic on this trip: the pending approval of a sizeable matching grant by the German development agency DEG. It will accelerate the scale-up of our pilot DAF planting and cocoa-pruning campaign. The project will train, in classroom and field, some one hundred agricultural workers so they can later provide paid-for services to farmers.

Contract completion has taken DEG a bit longer; the April to July rains, which we'll need for planting, are upon us, and we need to start spending money. Should we gamble and start the fieldwork before contract signing lest we lose this rainy season?

If so, how best to hire and train some sixty people? Where will we house the extra staff? Should we add second stories to the existing offices or build elsewhere on the increasingly crowded cramer site? Lawrence and his accounting team join to discuss DEG's requirements on accounting, reporting, and auditing. We ultimately decide to go ahead, and DEG finally approves two weeks later.

Another key topic is palm oil production: 2020 demand is leaping, and we urgently need to expand the capacity of the fruit-cleaning section—so far, an entirely manual process. The key challenge: How to maintain some 150 manual jobs while mechanically boosting fruit-cleaning capacity during the peak season? After a lengthy review, Phillip, Safianu, production manager Bempah, and I had ultimately decided to buy two low-cost, proven mechanical fruit strippers from China. Now we need to install and test them.

Phillip and team install the strippers in two days, then start trials. Within a week they find that three- to five-day-old fruit bunch runs best—virtually all fruits are stripped off unsquashed. We also assure the workers that the strippers would not eliminate their jobs—just make them less stressful during peak season.

These are just two of many examples of how Special Ops gets involved, helping to plan, design, finance, coordinate—always with an eye on transferring responsibility and support from behind. How do we keep things moving without suffocating local ownership and enthusiasm? How do we engage with mid-level managers on practical decisions while keeping their supervisors in the loop? A challenge if staff you work with lobby for their preferred course of action without sharing their boss's well-reasoned objections—and you go along.

There is no silver bullet; we found openness to the situation and one's counterparts' concerns, showing personal appreciation where due, ego checking, all while sticking to our values, work rather well. After all, we can't really derive genuine authority from our coownership of the project or just because we're its main customer. Ownership gives leverage, plenty of it. But authority needs to be earned and justified to be effective. It's much more enjoyable, too!

FROM ASUOM TO VISTA

Our team's main mandate is to help Dr. Bronner's source raw materials and represent their interest as customer vis-à-vis the suppliers—on quality, price, certification, timeliness of delivery, you name it.

Thus, I visit Vista periodically from my home office in Berkeley to meet members of the operations, quality control, finance, and marketing teams. Their offices have air-conditioning and no roosters, but the approach is the same as in Asuom—moving from meeting to meeting helps build and grow relationships while choosing strategy and tactics on this end of the supply chain.

Here's an assortment of issues we dealt with on recent visits:

When and how fast will we start rerouting Serendipalm's palm oil shipments to Vista, where our refinery is ready to scale up operation? How do we fit Special Ops into this year's marketing and staff training calendar?

How can we help Pavitramenthe finance this year's purchases of mint oil, since their local bank still won't lend the entire amount? How do the peppermint oils from the 2019 crop smell after the installation of the more efficient distillation system? Do we have backup sources in case our demand escalates or shipments from Pavitramenthe are delayed?

Young projects, such as Pavitramenthe, face multiple obstacles when they build direct links with customers in the north. Language is one. Few speak perfect English, and India is 13.5 hours ahead of California. This makes exhaustive discussions of technical and quality issues by telecom an unforgettable experience. My familiarity with local conditions on both sides usually helps us to get on the same page.

A company can't shift to a regenerative supply chain unless management is committed, and operations, finance, and HR departments are on board. This requires collaborative spirit. The open culture at Dr. Bronner's has allowed me to work with colleagues across departments without concern about my position; after all, no one in Vista reports to me.

This integration of Special Ops into the larger organization faced challenges at first. We needed to earn departments' trust and support and consider their preexisting mode of supply and current constraints with openness. Ryan and I sure stepped on multiple toes but learned fast. It's much more productive and fun if you are part of the machine, even if you usually operate far outside of it.

Talking about our work in Vista helped integration. In addition to regular Serendi updates to the Bronners, early on, I began telling Serendi stories to staff in sales, marketing, production, and quality control. The occasional "lunch and learn" talk to our annual batch of Fair Trade interns has also become an institution. This visual communication has made colleagues in Vista who wouldn't know about our work otherwise go the extra mile when needed.

My personal hobby in Vista has become to conspire in the conceptual planning of special projects involving processing, engineering, or the use of renewable energy. Imagine installing a full-fledged vegetable oil refinery at our plant. It has given us full operational flexibility with regard to the quality of the oils we're using in soap making.

Or how about putting a sizeable solar thermal system on the roof to preheat process water for our new soap reactor? Combined with internal process heat recovery, that system will reduce Vista's combustion of natural gas by some 60 percent. It would be a dream for any eco-minded physics student to help conceptualize these apparatuses. Even better: knowing well that Edwin Gomez's operations team would lay out and connect them to the existing and growing Vista organism and deal with the contractors. These projects make me realize that studying physics wasn't a poor use of my time, after all.

I believe company and colleagues in Vista benefit from this special cooperation in two ways. For one, cooperative problem-solving furthered an already open structure. Permeability and cooperation between departments enriches a company's culture and efficiency— you can feel it. Second, Special Ops inspires colleagues—at least some—because it visualizes the world-changing concepts their employer pursues in unusual settings, often involving coconuts and with a sense that "this is for real."

Not every company needs a Special Ops team to regenerate its supply chain. Yet the idea of a team that works across department lines and engages staff on their core issues with an outside perspective intrigues not just me. It cross-pollinates and stimulates ideas for cooperation that may not arise otherwise. Any such team better also have a real job to do!

Our type of work couldn't tolerate the "us versus them" attitude that often embodies relationships between buyer and seller, at least not for long. Instead we take a mercilessly constructive—while skeptical—approach to conflicts over quality, payment terms, and the like. Both sides must be transparent and open so we can understand each other's needs—a solid foundation for constructive solutions. And while this may all sound trite, it still took us some ten years to get to such attitudes and relationships.

HIERARCHY AND COMMUNICATION

How about structure and hierarchy? Special Ops has a flat hierarchy without internal departments. Each member has a focus area, such as finances, technology, agriculture, regeneration, fair trade, HR. Most have several areas of interest, allowing for cooperation and role switching on almost any project.

This may not work for large manufacturing operations; in a small professional team, however, it fosters collaboration and avoids unneeded conflicts over authority. Interestingly, after its leadership and teambuilding exercise, Serendipol is now also exploring the concept of having a team of leaders (predominantly younger and driven) instead of a classical hierarchy with senior people at the top. I'm optimistic.

Complex international projects require effective communication. Here's a salute to the internet. Our network of smallish projects with constant need for exchange could not have flourished without it. Email is a blessing and a curse; it helps us address diverse audiences at minimal cost across projects, continents, and time zones. It requires that people know how to write and read emails. Email has been a source of misunderstandings in many teams—some hilarious, some not funny. Our rule: if an email thread gets sticky and argumentative: better talk. Playing argument ping-pong by email is a frustrating waste of time.

Special Ops lost "physical contact" with projects in March 2020— no more visits for the entire year, just as we carried out and kicked off several major projects. We had been well prepared, having had international Skype calls with up to five people since 2013.

We've learned to set agendas and define expected outcomes—implicitly and explicitly—a good idea when scheduling between fifty and eighty calls per week team-wide. Sharing a common spirit, keeping your ego on a leash, avoiding animosity in the face of frustration, and being sensitive to the other parties' needs are good guidelines. With several teammates, I've intentionally worked on addressing idiosyncrasies in our mutual communication styles, without much coaching and rather successfully. Openness again was key—be willing to understand how a partner perceives your communication style, adjust if you can, be patient.

SALES, MARKETING, AND NETWORKS

Our team realized early that our projects should diversify: produce and sell products other than the one we built them for; say, palm oil at Serendipalm. Yet they first needed to become stable operations. Then, as other brands became interested in fair and regenerative agriculture, we saw market opportunities that would help our projects grow and diversify and develop their management, staff, and farming communities.

By now, several of our team members have gotten involved in product development and marketing of agriproducts from our projects: palm oil, coconut oil, milk and chips, cocoa, peanuts, herbs, turmeric, cassava flour. Most customers are mission-aligned, natural products companies who appreciate our values and our no-nonsense approach to real challenges. This can turn hands-on product sales into an enjoyable and world-saving learning experience.

Our close engagement with suppliers has spawned a cluster of companies serious about using their supply chains as vehicles for tackling social and ecological problems in farming communities. A campaign launched by Ryan Zinn and colleagues at our ally LUSH is gathering companies interested in "regenerative ingredients." The working group shares opportunities and challenges and is developing a "good list" of ingredients from suppliers with positive impact.

This will generate ideas for products, inspire joint public education campaigns on the power of regeneration, and who knows what else.

Another Special Ops domain is public education. It would be a waste not to use our firsthand experience of life and agriculture "in the jungle." We present to staff in Vista, contribute to blogs, develop websites, participate in the production of short films and videos about our work, generate media contacts for interviews, work closely with the PR department on strategic communication generally, train the team of Dr. Bronner's Europe in "clean supply chains" for use in their campaigns, and give talks in a wide range of venues in the United States and Europe.

It mostly comes easy—we just need to talk about whatever aspect of our work the audience is interested in, enthusiastically yet realistically. Our talks document we're "on the ground" in a way that photos of smiling farmers cannot. Talking about real problems and joys gives our presentations and articles authenticity and credibility. We don't need to exaggerate to leave an impression, and the closest we get to propaganda is if we spin the impact of our actions just a little to make a point.

WHAT DRIVES US?

What keeps our team going under highly variable, often adverse working conditions, long working hours, and often too many responsibilities?

A key driver is having a credible employer who radiates vision that people can relate to. We know that our work serves a purpose beyond profits (i.e., to support development of disadvantaged small farmers and their communities and improve dire ecological conditions worldwide). Meaning and purpose are essential concepts in life and business; they've become buzzwords. I've tried using them sparingly, lest I make them as meaningless as, say, "sustainable." Yet, as Nasser convinced me early in our relationship, these concepts make the world go round. He's right: for some, nothing is more rewarding than earning a living by improving the planet with inspired teams and talking about it!

On a personal note: I cannot remotely imagine more motivating and enjoyable work than what I've done at Dr. Bronner's with our ingredient suppliers and the many other projects I fell into. It's what drives me, gives a frame to Christel's and my life, and inspires friends. I think that's similar for my teammates—and I suspect my retirement is still quite a ways off.

Dr. Bronner's supply chain integration has become notorious and respected in the natural products industry. It speaks to the yearning of brands and their customers to know the source of their products, to understand the story, and to have a positive impact. Special Ops and its style has been essential to that process, by helping to develop projects and building a network of relationships with likeminded firms, institutions, and people.

CORONA IN VISTA

And our work has passed the corona stress test—as did Dr. Bronner's operations back in Vista.

There, Michael Milam's operations team had responded fast to skyrocketing demand for soaps and sanitizers. By early March, open orders had jumped from the usual $7 million to $11.5 million, then peaked at $20 million. Production had to double its output within two weeks—that had never been tried.

The Operations department achieved that goal by chasing one bottleneck after another in a calm fashion, using trial and error, rule of thumb, and intuition. First they added a second bottling shift, ran out of soap bottles, found new supplies, and added a second shift at the soap reactor. That shift was operated in part by members of Dr. Bronner's Magic Foam Experience (MFE) team, an example of yet another unconventional team at Dr. Bronner's that works across department boundaries. With some ten members, MFE is a unique tribute to Jim Bronner's work inventing and using firefighting and special effects foam for fighting fires, entertainment, and bringing joy to kids and adults alike.

During non-pandemic times, MFE drives its converted, beautifully painted fire truck to schools, festivals, and other events and foams up the place using a lightly scented foam with a simple recipe: our liquid soap (any flavor), water, and pressure. People marvel as their world is covered and transformed by foam, dancing and jumping around with glee, foaming each other up. Jim would smile at the enthusiasm with which MFE engages with schoolkids and mud runners requiring cleaning. MFE members often play welcoming committee at events in Vista, such as the symposia of our international distributors, and create a warm, slightly surreal atmosphere. They routinely participate in disaster relief projects countrywide and produced a recent "All-Love Kitchen" to support protests for racial justice in Washington, DC. As their "regular work" disappeared during the pandemic, many MFEers brought their spirit to the late soap making shift.

Motivation ruled. Officers closely engaged in planning, praising, and commenting on output and performance in emails sent to all staff and during the regular virtual COVID-19 meetings. I hadn't seen such spirit of practical camaraderie before—and I wasn't even there!

Media had conjured up the specter of supply chain disruptions—notably for firms relying on imported ingredients. Yet none of the deliveries of our main ingredients were interrupted, and if they had been, backup suppliers and Michael's habit of keeping copious but calculated safety stock (up to five months' worth of inventory) would have prevented production standstills. Some of the disruptions Dr. Bronner's experienced were for lack of packaging (notably the small plastic bottles for our hand sanitizer) to meet skyrocketing demand. More important, due to continued high demand, the operations team had to further debottleneck all product lines or find bottling alternatives, and even established three shifts in some lines.

In California, too, corona affirmed our commitment to community support. Practical needs emerged immediately. NGOs around the country that offer shelter, services, and other support to low-income and unhoused communities, homebound seniors, and other at-risk populations contacted us with urgent requests for donations of hygiene products, specifically hand sanitizer, which was in scarce supply and unaffordable to many due to surges in demand and related price gouging. By March, we were donating 2 percent, then 4 percent of our hand sanitizer production to NGOs supporting vulnerable populations such as the Navajo Nation, which was facing a high per-capita COVID-19 incidence and death rate.

NGOs feeding people via soup kitchens and meal delivery services also received liquid soap and Sal Suds, our all-purpose cleaner. A grant by the Dr. Bronner's Family Foundation supported projects serving immigrants. Several partner NGOs saw their funding dry up, not uncommon after disasters. With our cash flow in good shape, we advanced our already committed annual donation to keep priority NGOs from going under—like one would do with a valued business partner.

Nothing better illustrates the authenticity, commitment, and generosity of Dr. Bronner's than a late July meeting of our executive council. The officers tallied up the windfall earned from the sales spike in the spring and then committed a significant portion of that profit, some $2.5 million, to key ballot initiatives in the November elections that supported, almost all successfully, some of our key themes: responsible integration of psychedelic therapy, reform to the criminal justice system and drug policy, plus more support to local COVID-19 relief initiatives. This commitment came in addition to a pledge in June of $1 million over ten years to the Movement for Black Lives and to boost the support to the cash-strapped NGO partners mentioned above. Another $ 1.5 million was added in October when it became clear that global revenues in 2020 would be about 40 percent above 2019 levels, with a corresponding growth in profits.

Please imagine that scene in a video call and you'll understand that I smiled for the rest of the day. An employer who takes much of the windfall they just earned "cleanly" during a pandemic and immediately and generously reinvests it in causes you care about? Never mind the generous and practical support to its staff struggling with the domestic fallout of the lockdown. I suppose that's "putting people first." Such behavior gives me as much hope as the public debate and emerging action on causes of and remedies for racism and the abuse of police power.

I won't speculate about the long-term societal fallout from the pandemic, except for one. I've been utterly impressed by the speed at which people with vision managed to regroup and organize meaningful virtual events aimed at networking global movements targeting climate change, racial injustice, social disparity, and other issues in practical ways. This trend nicely correlates with the experience of the Special Ops team: virtual communication during our no-fly period strengthened existing working relationships across the globe and, if anything, made exchanges more targeted—without losing passion. A trend to be watched!

Last, but not least, our experiences in Samoa and India suggest that smallholders worldwide may revisit the benefit of growing at least some of your own food and some cash crops during shaky times like this—a more reliable source of nutrition than money from abroad or from jobs in the city. To be sure, this is not just for the Global South. Similar considerations and movements sprang up in the United States, too.

This somewhat optimistic view of a global catastrophe takes us to the conclusion of our trip—for an insight into the climate and workings of Dr. Bronner's—and on whether our style of business may yet become a world-changing trend.

Good Business Is the Engine That Makes It All Possible

HONOR THY LABEL HAS TOLD THE story of Dr. Bronner's long journey toward a clean, green, and ethical agricultural supply chain. Now, looking far beyond our own chain, we're impatient to motivate and collaborate with others intent on turning their companies into "engines of regeneration." It's part of our mission and a good bet. Does the concept of regeneration have that potential, and could it spread fast enough to help get planet Earth out of currently tight straits? What role can privately owned businesses play in it?

Scaling regenerative agriculture is one of a few "plant-based" options for stabilizing atmospheric CO_2 levels. I'm optimistic it will catch on because it offers many non-atmospheric benefits, too. As you've read, it does the planet's soils good, and farmers worldwide need more fertile and resilient soils to withstand increasingly wobbly weather patterns. I also believe that, in combination with other biological sequestering techniques, such as marine permaculture,[1] regenerative agriculture, and agroforestry at global scale, will, within two to three decades, help stabilize atmospheric CO_2 at current levels, as long as we concurrently manage to shift global energy supplies to renewable sources. This will require that environmental movements become noisier, that governments with vision come to ambitious agreements with teeth, and that more committed companies engage in their supply chains and become climate-positive.

This scenario is realistic, and many who watch businesses, drivers, and trends in the economy agree.

First, there is no need for a full revolution of our economic system for great shifts to occur. Our story illustrates this. After all, Dr. Bronner's is just making soap while operating under the rules of a capitalist economy; of course as you've read, we do break all kinds of capitalist conventions, and this *is* necessary.

Yet could it be that Dr. Bronner's—with its visionary founder and current leadership, secret recipe, and family tradition—is too unique for its practices to be replicated by others? Not really.

Yes, our roots are in Dr. Bronner's credo of a goal-oriented business with the well-being of planet and people at heart. Emanuel Bronner practiced what his son Ralph dubbed "constructive capitalism" and left it for his children and grandchildren to implement and scale. Its key trick: businesses must treat desired societal improvements as if they were real business objectives and handle them accordingly, meaning: internalize them.

Fortunately, having a visionary grandfather or eccentric leader isn't a prerequisite: all history starts somewhere. In fact, there are more and more committed companies developing their own brand of constructive capitalism. No one size fits all, and most details will emerge along the way.

So if you, your team, or company don't agree with Milton Friedman that "corporations have no higher purpose than maximizing profits for their shareholders,"[2] where to start with the good work?

TWO KINDS OF GOOD

For simplicity, activist companies can do good in two main areas: first, *inward facing*—that is, in their own sphere of economic influence.

That entails being generous and supportive to employees, to suppliers of agricultural ingredients and other raw materials, to providers of services, and, critically important, to the environment. This generosity generates benefits all around, but will also raise your cost of production, at least short-term. The second area is *outward facing*—by donating profits to philanthropy or charity, supporting the disadvantaged, tackling causes of societal problems. Dr. Bronner's acts extensively in both areas, with activist philanthropy as outlined in chapter 1.

Naturally, a genuine activist firm will prioritize *inward-facing* action. Dr. Bronner's has spelled out its approach to uniting Spaceship Earth in six "cosmic principles." They've developed organically out of our practice, were eventually codified, and have, in recent years, become an institution. They expand on customary vision and mission statements—but are more authentic and filled with life.

My favorite inward-facing cosmic principles are "Treat employees like family," "Be fair to suppliers," and "Treat the Earth like home."[3] Taking care of your employees is humane and good business. Dr. Bronner's high productivity is testament to that. Michael Milam suggests "there is a behavioral element to our productivity, part attitude and part organization. . . . Most of our staff feels purpose, because they are treated well from a deep place in management." That purpose better be genuine and visibly guide decisions made by management and its interaction with staff. Anything short of that generates lingering cynicism instead of higher productivity.[4]

Special Ops' job is to ensure that we are also fair to suppliers. This connects Dr. Bronner's and our customers to the farms and people that grow and process our ingredients. It helps them build more resilient soils, more profitable farms, and hopefully stronger communities.

And then there's the ecology, a wide field that offers companies excellent opportunities for inward-facing green action (energy consumption, packaging, transportation, waste streams, and, of course—most importantly—the use of regenerative raw materials) with positive impacts, locally and globally. At Dr. Bronner's, that responsibility lies with several teams, Special Ops included.

Yes, a company must be profitable to do good, a serious hurdle—notably for underfunded start-up companies. My experience at Dr. Bronner's offers comfort: being good will cost you money, but in the long run, it will raise profitability through improved motivation and efficiency, increase sales without expensive advertising, lower the cost of energy, and more. And it makes you more attractive as a reliable partner, for grant-funded projects and for collaboration with likeminded companies.

COSMIC PRINCIPLES IN ACTION— FACING INWARD

Advice on business matters is often trite, but I hope this book's accounts spawned ideas for action. Here are a few examples of how our cosmic principles may translate into inward-facing action, allowing companies to leave a beneficial trace inside and outside of their operation.

- Listen to your employees' needs and concerns, ponder how to accommodate them generously, but keep an eye out for abusive behavior. Act consistently. Occasionally remind people of these benefits without overdoing it. Be open and genuine.
- Occasionally check in with your fellow shareholders on the purpose of your company: your mission beyond just making money. Project that rationale to your staff, and show that you're serious about it. See that your mid-level management supports your agenda and knows how to get the message across to their teams in a credible way.
- When buying agricultural ingredients specifically or just sourcing materials generally, develop relationships of mutual respect and trust as much as possible. We've cherished going "all the way to the field." Prioritize ingredients that come from smallholders in the Global South. Break down your ingredients by category and origin. Ponder where a shift would be most feasible, impactful, and rewarding.

- Also consider whether your raw materials and finished products should be certified (regenerative) organic or fair trade as a way of documenting your seriousness about change making to consumers. If you buy from smaller individual suppliers you work with directly, understanding what they do may be more important than a certificate, provided there is trust. Yet remember that certification isn't just for the consumer. It also gives the brand independent assurance of "decent conditions" on the ground.

- When building a regenerative supply chain, integrate your suppliers into your domestic operations in a meaningful way. Horizontal mobility, permeability of department boundaries, and cooperation between departments are all very helpful to that goal. As important: a spirit of openness and inclusiveness, preferably on both sides. Steadfast support by officers is a sine qua non.

- Genuine relationships with your suppliers of raw materials are worth talking about, to your staff, customers, and the media. Do not oversell what you do; mention challenges, too. It makes you so much more credible.

THE CASE FOR CORPORATE PHILANTHROPY

How about *outward-facing* generosity? Philanthropy is what countless successful people, companies, and their foundations practice to benefit people and the planet. I'm sure you can name at least ten such foundations in no time.

I find nothing fundamentally wrong if people with disposable income support good causes using the money they earned—provided that money was earned "the right way." One critique of corporate philanthropy is that elites attempt to offset the problems their business behavior has created or sustained in the first place with donations.[5] How one makes their money and how they donate it is crucial. Ethical consistency is key. Producing a *clean soap* to fund generous donations to causes one espouses sounds like a consistent approach. Don't you think it's backward to focus on where to donate your profits without first making sure you run a clean shop?

What's clean? That's for shareholders, management, and other stakeholders to decide. To enthuse customers and the public at large, a company should strive for transparency and most of all be accountable. Only that way can a company compare what it says with what it does. Yes, public education and marketing needs stories, but there's much room for factual narration that avoids the misrepresentations of green washing and fair washing.

Critics of corporate philanthropy also suggest that governments should instead raise tax rates on profits and high incomes, strengthen their tax base, and do good with the money. I am all in favor of taxation to maintain our societal systems: infrastructure, education, health care, some reasonable defense, pandemic relief—too many to number.

Yet there are many societal problems that governments are just not good at tackling; at least, not at first.

Most societal progress in the United States and Europe after WWII was initiated by civil society, by NGOs, activists, and sometimes corporate charity. A case in point: in the United States, most environmental progress was privately initiated, very often in battle with established interests—large manufacturing industry, its lobbies, and government agencies who at first didn't "get it."

Effective governments eventually pick up on such leads—but will rarely lead, let alone initiate. The hard work of uncovering intolerable environmental conditions and finding solutions is often left to public interest groups and their sponsors. That's what philanthropy and activism are good for, after all.

There is no shortage of outward-facing philanthropy or change making in other areas to spend corporate profits on. An example on Dr. Bronner's list of causes is the therapeutic use of psychedelics. Evidence exists that the use of psychedelics combined with psychotherapy has great potential to relieve or permanently heal the mental suffering of many—depressions, trauma, drug addiction, end of life anxiety—and help them regain their lives. But virtually no government in its right mind would touch such a hot potato and initiate action without serious nudging. Again, that's what private, science-based initiatives, some of which Dr. Bronner's supports strategically, have done—with mind and heart. And governments start listening—they are interested in cures, too—and I'm rather optimistic about the outcome.

RETHINKING YOUR CASH FLOW

How does a company pay for such inward- and outward-facing generosity? There is no free lunch. A vision-driven small or medium-sized enterprise that seriously wants to advance planet and people must likely consider a decisive reallocation of the company's money.

That's what Dr. Bronner's started doing in the 1990s, by explicitly capping executive salaries and not paying owners dividends for personal use. Such steps are effective tools but require determination—and are still rarely taken in such a radical way. This is at the core of a global discussion about economic equality and fairness: companies that limit the salaries of their top executives and the distribution of profits to owners simply have more money available to be generous to other internal and external stakeholders: employees, farmers, and workers in the Global South, the "community at large."

Sounds like a socialist slogan? Well, Dr. Bronner's took this step voluntarily, and it sure works for what we want to accomplish; it hasn't impoverished owners and executives or bankrupted the company. Quite the opposite. This long-term approach has been critical to making us as successful as we are.

A CRITICAL MASS OF ACTIVIST ORGANIZATIONS?

One cannot build national economies on companies such as Dr. Bronner's—not in developed regions such as North America and the EU, and not anytime soon. We don't cover nearly all sectors of the economy, nor is there enough spirit, yet. But there is plenty of room for such companies—whether in manufacturing, agriculture, trading, or information services—to grow in numbers and infiltrate economies.

Could they eventually form a critical mass, driven by a credible vision that offers its staff meaning and purpose, and ruthlessly applies the "triple bottom line": profit, people, and planet? Will there be enough drive among company owners and managers?

Several trends in the Global North point in that direction. Research by the Dutch Rabobank suggests that companies are "making their own climate commitments and acting on them . . . especially when policy falls short." Why? They speculate that "thinking beyond direct self-interest, corporations may well be motivated by genuine concern for the environment and by a long term view on the going concern for their company."[6]

Numeric indicators include the worldwide growing number of Certified B Corporations, the rise in the number of Benefit Corporations in many US states, and the emergence of networks of activist companies and sustainable businesses, such as OSC[2] or the Climate Collaborative.[7] A European example of coordinated corporate activism is the fledgling Economy for a Common Good movement. It pursues goals similar to a B Corp, but a bit more holistically, and targeting changes to political rules, too.[8]

What's the difference between Certified B Corps and Benefit Corporations? Companies will incorporate as a *Benefit Corporation* if they want their charter to include nonfinancial goals—say, a positive impact on society and environment. The status of a Benefit Corporation will protect them from future attempts by shareholders to return to a single bottom line that considers only financial goals. Apparently, owners are increasingly willing to self-impose such rules.

One step further, *Certified B Corps* often are Benefit Corporations but are also certified by the nonprofit B Lab as meeting ambitious standards of social and environmental performance, accountability, and transparency.

Mike Bronner puts it well: "Being a Benefit Corporation gives Dr.

Bronner's legal protection to do good things with our profits. Being a B Corp proves to the public that we are actually doing those good things."[9]

In 2015, Dr. Bronner's joined the growing movement of Certified B Corp companies, now numbering some 3,500 from over 70 countries and 150 industries. Once every three years, they are rated rigorously on performance according to social, environmental, and financial indicators. Most Certified B Corps are privately owned SMEs; some are larger, such as our regenerative ally Patagonia. A few B Corps are subsidiaries of public companies, such as Seventh Generation, Danone North America, and Ben & Jerry's, a company with a serious activist history.

Unfortunately, publicly traded companies themselves have a hard time qualifying for B Corp certification. Their shareholders will invariably block some of B Corp's basic requirements on transparency and balancing social and environmental benefits with profits. Shareholders in most private companies will object to that, too. Yet they have the freedom to decide not to, as Dr. Bronner's did, or even transfer company ownership to a foundation, a young but growing trend—for example, in Germany.

Some shareholders may also take to heart the wisdom by Harvard Business School professors Joseph Bower and Lynn Paine that maximizing shareholder value as the ultimate measure of a company's success is "flawed in its assumptions, confused as a matter of law, and damaging in practice." Jack Welch, former CEO of GE and uber-hero of maximizing shareholder value, at age seventy-four famously declared that this approach is "the dumbest idea in the world. . . . Shareholder value is a result, not a strategy."[10]

How does Dr. Bronner's do on its B Corp score? After first becoming certified in 2015, we have, since 2018, consistently earned the third highest, and now have the second highest, B Corp score worldwide. We also are the highest-scoring consumer products company in the world. From our perspective, B Corp certification uses meaningful metrics to assess its members' benefits to the planet!

What external factors may be driving the rise of the responsible economy? One growing trend among consumers is to buy from companies that stand for an idea or at least a moral principle—say, fairness. That trend is particularly strong and obvious in the natural products industry and still a domain of a relatively well-educated segment of the population. Many companies respond by green washing and fair washing without substance, but that often catches up.

One other indicator that companies small and large respond to consumers' growing interest in ethical companies is their annual reports. Today, these must include chapters on sustainability and social responsibility. Responsible corporate behavior is increasingly rewarded by investors. All else being equal, companies public and private with good ratings on ESG (environmental, social, governance) factors perform better as an investment.[11]

Banks and insurance companies now realize that climate change creates risks like shortages of raw materials caused by catastrophic weather events and declining soil fertility, and increasingly consider it when appraising applications for loans and insurance coverage. This rethinking is prompting larger companies across Europe to reevaluate their sourcing strategies for agricultural products.[12]

An example of this shift is the Capitals Coalition, launched in January 2020 with a growing membership of some four hundred organizations, ranging from small to large corporations, to NGOs, to government and research organizations. Its goal is to help change the way companies include natural, social, and human capital in their decisions and account for their *true cost* by providing information and tools to decision makers. Again: no need to overthrow capitalism. Instead, include externalities in a company's accounting and decision-making. It's becoming quite a trend, even in large public companies![13]

WHY WE'RE NOT ALL-ONE—YET

I hope I gave an inspiring if not convincing account of the mounting internal and external forces that motivate companies "to be good." Responding to external pressure is like being a good kid just because you are afraid of punishment. Some such social stress won't hurt per se. Yet isn't it more satisfying to operate responsibly because you enjoy doing business according to your values and with a positive outcome? My colleagues at Dr. Bronner's, our many allies and friends, and I know that our work serves a purpose beyond profits, making for plenty of All-One spirit.

Yet there's one key area where cloning that spirit hits a major barrier: the established financial privileges of ownership in privately held companies, notably those with external investors. Making purely values-based decisions such as those inspired by our cosmic principles costs money that shareholders could use for personal purposes.

At Dr. Bronner's, our compensation policy takes that issue off the table. In companies without such policy, the desire to do good will clash with the bedrock concept that ownership entitles one to financial rewards. Unless owners accept limitations to that entitlement, little will change.

Personally, from speaking with owners, employees, and customers of small and medium-sized companies in the United States and the EU, I believe that many yearn for seeing companies as agents of the public good. Of course, that's self-selected, as I rarely speak to people who have no interest in "our kind" of change-making. But when members of our Special Ops team attend and speak at trade shows, conferences, and industry gatherings, the optimism of the audience, many of them millennials and members of Gen Z, and their eagerness to be "part of the solution" is striking. And maybe enough to generate critical mass.

I find the same optimism in routine conversations with competent and motivated university students looking for a job where they can use their skills to collaborate on improving the planet. No wonder studies show that millennials, more than preceding generations, actively seek out purpose in their employment.[14] They hope there will be enough companies to offer them such jobs—or a market to sustain their own business. Will there?

For many business owners, including the Bronners, following a vision, acting on their values, and enjoying the rewards has paid off. After all, many, if not most, shareholders close to the people and operations of their company would prefer meaning and the power to do good over extra discretionary income. Could this corporate altruism grow beyond the still small number of committed beneficial companies? How would such a shift benefit a company?

And what change of mind will this require—among owners and employees? Maybe less than we think.

Our guts may tell us that most people enjoy collaborating on projects with a positive triple bottom line, with meaningful work added as a bonus. Now, beyond our intuition, there's a growing body of scientific evidence that humans are in fact hardwired to be nice to each other and enjoy companionship and cooperation. Whether they follow that program seems to depend on whether they have the right environment and a meaningful vision.

Several reports have summarized the findings from an impressive array of studies—in psychology, neuroscience, economics. More enjoyable reads are the well narrated treatises on "altruism and openness" in the seminal books *Humankind* by Rutger Bregman and *How to Change Your Mind* by Michael Pollan.[15] Their success reflects a longing for openness, for "meaning and purpose"—something innate to humans but in business too often condemned to the backseat by established and unimaginative practices.

So what has science discovered about human nature? First, in real economic life—doing business, shopping—most humans do not decide and act solely to maximize their economic benefit. This model of *homo economicus* had driven economics, social science, and public perception for decades. Yet, since the 1990s, Nobel Prize research in behavioral economics shows that people don't constantly calculate and optimize their welfare. They use heuristics, trial and error; herd behavior, where people follow the examples of others, is common. The well-known manipulation through nonfactual advertising is a great example of not-quite-rational behavior. People consider many factors when making economic decisions, and we're not even aware of most of them.[16]

And how do people behave toward fellow humans? How do we make moral decisions? It turns out that with few exceptions, such as those generally called sociopaths, humans do not constantly and consciously try to screw over others to maximize their own profit when meeting on a level playing field. We enjoy when others benefit, too. Most would have guessed that. Studies in fact found that people generally follow the concept of *egoistically biased altruism*. It means: when given a choice, most people tend to act to benefit others. Even if that diminishes your own take—and as long as it doesn't cause you pain. Apparently, this research suggests that the beloved concept of a win-win deal is very compatible with human nature. Yet actual behavior will be rather context specific.[17] Bregman suggests two factors may corrupt our inclinations to be nice: the opportunity to gain power over others, and loyalty to a peer group performing undesirable acts. War crimes by soldiers, conspiracies within a company to commit fraud, or just the usual beating up on your competition and suppliers as hard as you can. It would be naive to ignore these obvious facts of life. Yet the above suggests that such common behavior in business may be much more driven by external factors than by our natural leanings.

Finally, there's a proliferation of the idea that openness improves life and business. Researchers call it *intellectual humility*. Its components include respect for other perspectives and the willingness to revise one's own viewpoint. People who score high on openness enjoy overall higher life satisfaction, a desirable goal even outside of business.[18]

Shouldn't companies offer a workplace that speaks to this human precondition? Promote collaboration and openness, be good and authentic examples, be generous, and support good causes? I suspect so, and my impression from the companies I worked with closely across the planet since 2005 is: it pays off in many ways, not just financially. If you need to double your production of soap or other products on short notice, if you have a serious product quality problem, a spirit of cooperation and openness will come in very handy!

Creating conditions that let your employees follow their human tendencies is not an uphill battle if you have your heart in it. Our imaginative model of a private sector pulling its weight in saving the planet will just require ever more companies to become such hands-on and inspiring training grounds. I'm ultimately optimistic that many will go that direction—after all, science suggests it's human nature! The precondition: to create the right environment in the office and on the production floor, compatible with the country and culture you operate in.

So if you run your own business, are starting up a new one, or just work with people you value, how would *you* promote and practice openness and stimulate collaboration?

How will you wear your values on your sleeve and put them into action, as we at Dr. Bronner's do in striving to Honor our Label?

Acknowledgments

THE CREATION OF THIS BOOK AND the multistranded story it tells relied critically on a few people; many others were irreplaceable. Here is my heartfelt credit to them. First, on the book.

In 2016, I conspired with Ryan Fletcher, Dr. Bronner's director of public relations, a good friend and ally, for me to write a book about "our supply chain work." Ryan had extensively publicized our Serendi work, including the video "Journey to Serendipol." A book would be another opportunity for us to collaborate on spreading the All-One message.

I didn't know where to begin; Ryan did. Without his resourcefulness, persistence, and continued engagement this book wouldn't even have started. He brought on board Jud Laghi, a literary agent. Jud knew there was an interest in books on Dr. Bronner's. He also knew the process of writing a proposal, shopping it around to publishers, and creating a book in his sleep. He suggested we engage a cowriter for the proposal and introduced us to Sarah Rainone, who joined the journey in late 2018. After several interview sessions in Manhattan, she turned my draft proposal into something presentable, and taught me about structure and flow and how to find my narrative voice. In short, Jud then successfully offered the proposal to Penguin's Portfolio imprint and expertly guided us through the contractual work and the entire production process, always available to tackle emerging "issues." He also taught me much about the publishing business in the United States. Our counterpart, Penguin's senior editor Trish Daly, made producing a readable and comprehensible manuscript most inspiring and congenial. She also taught me "to kill my darling," i.e., cut a section that just doesn't fit, even though you consider it great poetry.

Naturally, Sarah continued on as cowriter for the book. I did most of the writing in spells when the spirit spoke to me. We then jointly restructured, cut, and fixed language. Her two visits to Dr. Bronner's headquarters immersed her in the reality of soap production and team work Bronner's style. Sarah swears this made the story much more real than just my accounts.

As I approached completion of the manuscript, I asked my teammate Ute Eisenlohr to use her uncanny skills in detecting slow or jumpy flow in text. Ute also knows the technical substance and many of the characters of the story firsthand and researched critical topics, notably on cocoa, an area of her expertise. Integrating her input into the revisions I concurrently completed with Sarah was a remarkably smooth process.

And there was Christel, who knows the entire story and all of its characters, and gave critical guidance and practical suggestions, from properly and fairly representing actors and subjects to the capture of local atmosphere.

I found the eighteen-month process of writing and editing a book with a completely new team congenial, efficient, and, over long stretches, enjoyable. It gave me a great excuse to relive and reflect on the journey and on my life and key relationships.

The story itself involved many more people. It owes everything to my parents, not just for the obvious reason. They raised me to become a curious, adventurous, mostly responsible kid with a sense of social justice and a perspective on history.

Two of my university teachers were critical to the emergence of this story. Dieter Wohlleben, my physics adviser at the University of Cologne, suggested in 1985 that I switch continents. I did, and it changed our lives, but sadly Dieter didn't stay around to see the fruits of the seed he planted. Arthur Winer, my doctoral adviser at UCLA taught me to write technical English and coauthored my first peer-reviewed publication in the US. His openness and wisdom helped me through dire straits. Mark Gold, my first friend at UCLA, and I were on the same trip: environmental activism and science are very compatible. He gave me no-nonsense versions of the goings-on in the US and keeps me posted on exciting new developments in California, be it in plastics or in the ocean.

In the US, six friends in particular had a large impact on Christel's and my life. Dagmar and John Gunderson helped us understand the country and its culture. Barbara Smith and Cort Cooper offered me professional opportunities at two critical junctures in our lives with vast implications later on. Silvia Bercovici taught us the compatibility of Tibetan Buddhism and psychotherapy during difficult times. I don't know where we would have landed without her. Frank Riccio taught me much about the business of natural fibers, notably hemp, with open-mindedness and great stories as key ingredients. Jutta Millich and Thomas Giesen were German friends who lived in Berkeley for two years and prompted us to move there from LA in 1996. We never left.

Other German friends joined the story of this book at some point. Petra Pless oversaw the hemp food and drug testing study that became key evidence in the trial against the US DEA and got David interested in our work. Franjo Grotenhermen helped design and review this study. Without Michael Carus and Bernd Frank, I would not have fallen into hemp in the first place and would never have met David Bronner. Bernd, with his tendency to practical and humane approaches to life became my multi-purpose coach in Serendipol and Serendipalm. He had introduced me to Markus Gröber, who designed and built the first version of Serendipol's press section. Ulli and Norbert Wansleben architectured the first buildings at Serendipol and gave the project a frame that integrated functionality and esthetics. More projects to come. My sister Monika Leson and my preschool friend Christoph Eschweiler critically supported the website launch and fundraising for SecondAid, our tsunami relief project without which Serendipol wouldn't have happened.

Once our projects produced oil, several German companies who were committed to organic and fair production became customers and friends. Josef Wilhelm and Barbara Altmann of Rapunzel, Werner and Gudrun Baensch at Ölmuehle Solling, and Stephan Beck at GEPA taught me about the organic and fair oil business and its requirements in the most cooperative and enjoyable way. They also were proof of a vibrant scene of German SMEs that are serious about wanting to change the world.

The path to real organic and fair trade certification was arduous. Several of IMO's staff and inspectors made it almost enjoyable: Murugiah Rajasingham (Raj), Florentine Meinshausen, and Malika Mathew were key among them.

Of those who taught us a few tricks in regenerative agriculture, Joachim Milz and Bastian Pellhammer of Ecotop and Tobias Bandel of Soil & More stood out—with their combination of hands-on-ness, technical expertise, and open-mindedness. Other important technical advisers were Luis Spitz, who knows everything about soap, and Laurence Eyres, who taught me and our Vista team much about refining vegetable oils.

Yet it's the Dr. Bronner's executive team—Trudy, Mike, and David Bronner, and Michael Milam—and Kris Lin-Bronner who ultimately made things happen. Their confidence and trust in our Special Ops team's commitment, honesty, and competence were rather beyond belief. Needless to say, David was the initial driver, but over time all became engaged and supportive. I'll never work for anyone else. There are too many dear colleagues at Dr. Bronner's to mention who gradually helped our Serendi ship come in. I hope to work with them for years to come. The spirit of comradery, constructive resolutions to minor conflicts, joint fun—this is how planet changing work should be done—with all its minor and major troubles.

As for the local project teams, I can only name a few of the tens of people I worked with closely. Critically responsible for making our crazy idea of a green and fair supply chain a reality were Sonali Pandithasekera and Gordon de Silva and several of their Serendipol team. In Ghana, without Safianu Moro, Lawrence Acquaye, Christian Boahen, Samah Arkaifie, Dickson Wenyonu, and Andrews Bempah, Serendipalm may have never ended the special period and grown into an exemplary project. In India, Nihal Singh and his friends Rahul Sharma, Subhash Chandra, and Rajiv Sharma and Deepika Agarwal got a stranded ship back into the water under a new name, Pavitramenthe—but not without critical support from Nitish Tandon and Shiv Singh. In Samoa, the calm and considerate style of Etuale Sefo, combined with a vision for his country and the versatility of Tusitina Nu'uvali, lead SerendiCoco Samoa through its rough first years. Yet without our wise mentor Kolone Vaai we wouldn't even have come to Samoa or started the project. And there are no better guides to the Holy Land than Nasser and Karmel Abufarha and Shai Friedman—who through business and friendship helped us grasp this magnificently unholy part of the planet.

With Special Ops I had a dream team to build and develop our projects and to tell the story. I'm still not clear how we manage to cover such a wide range of tasks without too much friction or chaos, and to always be on the lookout for new opportunities to grow and develop. My deep gratitude and friendship to Rob Hardy, Ryan Zinn, Les Szabo, Jennifer Rusu, Phillip Eschweiler, Julia Edmaier, Ute Eisenlohr, and Anke Buhl.

Christel Dillbohner has been my inspiration for the story and the book. Without her often close involvement in planning, construction, and team management, and a keen visual perception, our projects and overall campaign would have been much for the worse or not even come about. She had suggested in the mid-2010s I start writing some of our stories down—for therapy and so they don't get lost. Narrating our meandering past and lessons learned to each other has made the struggle of writing all worth it. Should our souls rematerialize in another life, I hope Christel and I will get to collaborate on other planet-saving and mind-boggling projects.

Notes

Chapter 2: Hemp and Hysteria

1. Moises Velasquez-Manoff, "Can CBD Really Do All That?," *New York Times Magazine*, May 14, 2019; Alex Berenson, *Tell Your Children: The Truth About Marijuana, Mental Illness, and Violence* (New York: Free Press, 2019).
2. Eric Limer, "Back When We Thought Hemp Would Be a Billion-Dollar Crop," *Popular Mechanics*, April 20, 2018, https://www.popu larmechanics.com/science/environment/a19876318/popular-me chanics-billion-dollar-hemp.
3. Jack Herer, Mathias Bröckers, Katalyse Institut, *Die Wiederentdeckung der Nutzpflanze Hanf Cannabis Marihuana* (Frankfurt: Zweitausendeins, 1993).

Chapter 3: The Dirt on Soap

1. Luis Spitz, *Soap Manufacturing Technology*, 2nd Edition (Urbana, IL: AOCS Press, 2016); Luis Spitz, Personal communication.
2. For a good visualization of how soap works, see Ferris Jabr, "Why Soap Works," *New York Times*, March 13, 2020.

Chapter 4: How to Make Clean Soap

1. S. K. Lowder et al., "The Number, Size, and Distribution of Farms, Smallholder Farms, and Family Farms Worldwide," *World Development* 87 (November 2016): 16–29.

Chapter 6: Riding the VCO Wave

1. Stephen Cunnane et al., "Can Ketones Compensate for Deteriorating Brain Glucose Uptake During Aging?" *Annals of the New York Academy of Sciences* (March 2016): 1367.

Chapter 7: German Roots, German Connections

1. *Die jüdische Gemeinde Laupheim und ihre Zerstörung.* Gesellschaft für Geschichte und Gedenken e.V. (Laupheim, Germany: 2013).
2. Images from this first trip to Heilbronn and Laupheim are covered in the YouTube video "Dr. Bronner's: 150 Years of Soapmaking," https://www.youtube.com/watch?v=eFbTo4ucAug.

Chapter 9: Palm Oil—Redeeming an "Evil Crop"

1. For a more detailed overview by F. I. Obahiagbon, "A Review: Aspects of the African Oil Palm (*Elaeis guineesis* jacq.) and the Implications of its Bioactives in Human Health," *American Journal of Biochemistry and Molecular Biology* 2, vol. 3, (2012): 106–19, https://scialert.net/fulltext/?doi=ajbmb.2012.106.119.
2. "Report on Global Market Supply 2018/19," UFOP, accessed December 2, 2020, https://www.ufop.de/files/4815/4695/8891/WEB_UFOP_Report_on_Global_Market_Supply_18-19.pdf. Re: acreage under oil palm, see "Transforming the palm oil industry," Unilever, accessed December 2, 2020, https://www.unilever.com/sustainable-living/reducing-environmental-impact/sustainable-sourcing/transforming-the-palm-oil-industry/.
3. Re: percentage of palm oil produced and sold as RSPO certified, see "Impact Update 2019," RSPO, accessed December 2, 2020, https://www.rspo.org/library/lib_files/download/976; A. Ananthalakshmi and Emily Chow, "Palm Oil Body to Wield Stick to Get Consumer Goods Giants to Go Green," Reuters, October 16, 2019, https://www.reuters.com/article/us-palmoil-sustainability/palm-oil-body-to-wield-stick-to-get-consumer-goods-giants-to-go-green-idUSKBN1WV0RT.
4. Norimitsu Onishi, "Left Behind; As Oil Riches Flow, Poor Village Cries Out," *New York Times*, December 22, 2002, https://www.nytimes.com/2002/12/22/world/left-behind-as-oil-riches-flow-poor-village-cries-out.html.
5. An indicator of continued struggle between Chevron and local militants: Hilary Uguru, "Militants Shut Down Chevron's Escravos, Onshore in Nigeria," *Seattle Times*, May 26, 2016, https://www.seattle

times.com/business/militants-shut-down-chevrons-escravos
-onshore-in-nigeria/.

Chapter 10: Cocoa—The Path to Regenerative Chocolate

1. "Bitter Sweets: Prevalence of Forced Labour & Child Labour in the Cocoa Sectors of Cote d'Ivoire & Ghana," Walk Free Foundation and Tulane University, September 2018, https://cocoainitiative.org/wp-content/uploads/2018/10/Cocoa-Report_181004_V15-FNL_digital.pdf.

2. Peter Wohlleben, *The Hidden Life of Trees* (Vancouver, BC: Greystone Books, 2016); Suzanne Simard, "How Trees Talk to Each Other," TED Talk, June 2016, https://www.ted.com/talks/suzanne_simard_how_trees_talk_to_each_other.

3. H. Jactel et al., "Positive Biodiversity–Productivity Relationships in Forests: Climate Matters." *Biology Letters* 14, vol. 4: 20170747, http://doi.org/10.1098/rsbl.2017.0747.

4. Own calculations adapted from literature data, e.g., Eduardo Somarriba et al., "Carbon Stocks and Cocoa Yields in Agroforestry Systems of Central America," *Agriculture, Ecosystems and Environment* 173 (2013): 46–57. Reported sequestration rates are highly variable depending on setting and tree species.

Chapter 12: The Quest for an Organic and Fair Global Coconut Oil Trade

1. No reliable data on annual global VCO production are publicly available. The estimated 25,000 MT per year is based on discussions with industry insiders. USDA appears to offer the most consistent figures on copra oil production, Oil Crops Yearbook, USDA, accessed December 7, 2020, https://www.ers.usda.gov/data-products/oil-crops-yearbook/oil-crops-yearbook/#Vegetable%20Oils%20and%20Animal%20Fats.

2. "Today in History: Inventor Alexander Ashbourne, Refiner of Coconut Oil," *Atlanta Blackstar,* August 21, 2014, https://blerds.atlantablackstar.com/2014/08/21/today-history-inventor-alexander-ashbourne-refiner-coconut-oil/.

3. Statistics of Oilseeds, Fats, and Oils, National Agriculture Statistics Service, USDA, accessed December 2, 2020, https://www.nass.usda.gov/Publications/Ag_Statistics/2007/CHAP03.PDF; Oil Crops Data: Yearbook Tables, Economic Research Service, USDA, accessed December 2, 2020, https://www.ers.usda.gov/webdocs/DataFiles/52218/WorldSuppyUseOilseedandProducts.xlsx?v=9497; Oil Crops Year-

book, Economic Research Service, USDA, accessed December 2, 2020, https://www.ers.usda.gov/data-products/oil-crops-yearbook/oil -crops-yearbook/#Vegetable%20Oils%20and%20Animal%20Fats.

4. "Genomics Used to Estimate Samoan Population Dynamics Over 3,000 Years," *Science Daily*, April 17, 2020. Source: Brown University.

5. A fascinating story suggesting that the spread of coconuts to coastal areas in the tropics was almost entirely due to humans, not, as had been suspected, transport via oceans. Anecdotally, Florida's coconut population owes its existence to a shipwreck that spilled a cargo of 20,000 coconuts from Trinidad in 1878 near Palm Beach, supposedly baptizing the area. Bee Gunn et al., "Independent Origins of Cultivated Coconut in the Old World Tropics," *PLOS One*, June 22, 2011, https://www.ncbi.nlm.nih.gov/pmc/articles/PMC3120816/; Lucas Brouwers, "Coconuts: Not Indigenous, but Quite at Home Nevertheless," *Scientific American*, August 1, 2011, https://blogs.scientificamer ican.com/thoughtomics/httpblogsscientificamericancomthough tomics20110801coconuts-not-indigenous-but-quite-at-home -nevertheless/.

6. Aerial photo of Savaii, NASA Earth Observatory, accessed December 2, 2020, https://earthobservatory.nasa.gov/images/44746/savaii -samoa.

7. Robert Louis Stevenson, *A Footnote to History: Eight Years of Trouble in Samoa* (New York: Charles Scribner's Sons, 1895).

8. Russ Rymer, "Vanishing Voices," *National Geographic*, July 2012.

Conclusion: Good Business Is the Engine That Makes It All Possible

1. An emerging technique to improve marine ecosystems while sequestering carbon dioxide. See, for example, B. von Herzen et al., "Marine Permaculture to Regenerative Ocean Productivity," American Geophysical Union, Fall Meeting 2018, https://ui.adsabs.har vard.edu/abs/2018AGUFMGC23G1278V/abstract.

2. Milton Friedman, "A Friedman Doctrine: The Social Responsibility of Business Is to Increase Its Profits," *New York Times Magazine*, September 13, 1970.

3. Visualized and contextualized at https://www.drbronner.com/about/.

4. Robert Quinn and Anjan V. Thakor, "Creating a Purpose-driven Organization," *Harvard Business Review*, July–August 2018, https:// hbr.org/2018/07/creating-a-purpose-driven-organization.

5. Anand Giridharadas, *Winners Take All: The Elite Charade of Changing the World* (New York: Alfred A. Knopf, 2018).

6. Alexandra Dumitru, et al., "The Future of Carbon Investment after the Paris Agreement," RaboResearch, 2017, https://economics.rabo bank.com/publications/2017/november/future-of-carbon-invest ment-after-paris-agreement/.

7. OSC_2, founded in 2012, is a growing Northern California (and increasingly national) association of sustainable businesses intent on driving positive social and ecological impact: https://www.osc2.org/. Founded in 2016, the Climate Collaborative is a group of now about seven hundred mostly US-based companies committed to taking action to combat climate change: https://www.climatecollaborative .com/about.

8. Economy for the Common Good, accessed December 2, 2020, https:// www.ecogood.org.

9. Steve Banker, "A Progressive Manufacturer Thrives Despite Coronavirus," *Forbes*, August 1, 2020, https://www.forbes.com/sites/stevebanker /2020/08/01/a-progressive-manufacturer-thrives-despite-corona virus/#198c14bc1457.

10. Steve Denning, "Making Sense of Shareholder Value: 'The World's Dumbest Idea'," *Forbes*, July 17, 2017, https://www.forbes.com/sites/ste vedenning/2017/07/17/making-sense-of-shareholder-value-the -worlds-dumbest-idea/#16cd04682a7e.

11. For an overview of research, see, for example, John Rotonti and Alyce Lomax, "Does ESG Investing Produce Better Stock Returns?," *Motley Fool*, May 22, 2019, https://www.fool.com/investing/2019/05/22/does esg-investing-produce-better-stock-returns.aspx.

12. For example, "Climate Change Strategy of Allianz Group," Allianz, September 2019, https://www.allianz.com/content/dam/onemarket ing/azcom/Allianz_com/responsibility/documents/201909_Allianz _Climate_Change_Strategy.pdf; "Triodos Bank Calls for Complete Change of Food and Agriculture Systems," Triodos Bank, press release, June 13, 2019, https://www.triodos.com/press-releases/2019/trio dos-bank-calls-for-complete-change-of-food-and-agriculture -systems.

13. Capitals Coalition, https://capitalscoalition.org/.

14. For example, Louis Efron, "Why Millenials Don't Want to Work for You," *Forbes*, December 13, 2015, https://www.forbes.com/sites/lou isefron/2015/12/13/why-millennials-dont-want-to-work-for-you /#244c3b111bef. More recently, re: loyalty and meaning in the workplace, Nathan Peart, "What Does Millenial Loyalty Look Like in Today's Workplace?," *Forbes*, October 30, 2019, https://www.forbes

.com/sites/nathanpeart/2019/10/30/what-does-millennial-loyalty
-look-like-today-in-the-workplace/#479dd17b28f4.

15. Rutger Bregman, *Humankind: A Hopeful History* (New York: Little, Brown and Company, 2019); Michael Pollan, *How to Change Your Mind* (New York: Penguin Press, 2018).

16. OECD, "Beyond Growth: Towards a New Economic Approach," Report of the Secretary General's Advisory Group on a New Growth Narrative, 2019, https://www.oecd.org/naec/averting-systemic-col lapse/SG-NAEC(2019)3_Beyond%20Growth.pdf.

17. Lukas Volz et al., "Harm to Self Outweighs Benefit to Others in Moral Decision Making," *PNAS*, July 2017, https://www.pnas.org /content/114/30/7963; James Sonne and Don Gash, "Psychopathy to Altruism: Neurobiology of the Selfish-Selfless Spectrum," *Frontiers in Psychology* 9 (April 2018): 575, https://www.ncbi.nlm.nih.gov /pmc/articles/PMC5917043/.

18. For example: Luke Smillie, "Openness to Experience: The Gates of the Mind," *Scientific American*, August 15, 2017, https://www .scientificamerican.com/article/openness-to-experience-the -gates-of-the-mind/.

Index

Page numbers in *italics* refer to photographs and illustrations.